# CONNIE

# CONNIE

### *A MEMOIR*

# *CONNIE CHUNG*

**GRAND CENTRAL**

NEW YORK  BOSTON

Grand Central Publishing
Hachette Book Group
1290 Avenue of the Americas, New York, NY 10104
grandcentralpublishing.com
@grandcentralpub

First Edition: September 2024

Grand Central Publishing is a division of Hachette Book Group, Inc. The Grand Central Publishing name and logo is a registered trademark of Hachette Book Group, Inc.

The publisher is not responsible for websites (or their content) that are not owned by the publisher.

The Hachette Speakers Bureau provides a wide range of authors for speaking events. To find out more, go to hachettespeakersbureau.com or email HachetteSpeakers@hbgusa.com.

Grand Central Publishing books may be purchased in bulk for business, educational, or promotional use. For information, please contact your local bookseller or the Hachette Book Group Special Markets Department at special.markets@hbgusa.com.

Print book interior design by Marie Mundaca

Library of Congress Cataloging-in-Publication Data

Names: Chung, Connie, author.
Title: Connie : a memoir / Connie Chung.
Description: First edition. | New York : GCP, 2024.
Identifiers: LCCN 2024014004 | ISBN 9781538766989 (hardcover) | ISBN 9781538767009 (ebook)
Subjects: LCSH: Chung, Connie, 1946– | Women television journalists—United States—Biography. | Asian American women—Biography. | Television broadcasting of news—United States—History.
Classification: LCC PN4874.C518 A3 2024 | DDC 070.1/95092 [B]—dc23/eng/20240603
LC record available at https://lccn.loc.gov/2024014004

ISBN: 9781538766989 (hardcover), 9781538772034 (signed edition), 9781538772027 (special signed edition), 9781538772010 (special signed edition), 9781538767009 (ebook)

Printed in the United States of America

LSC

Printing 1, 2024

*To the two men I could not live without, my dearest Maury
and my precious Matthew, who give me unimaginable love.
And to my dear daughters, Susan and Amy.
With all my love forever.*

# CONTENTS

# Contents

# CONNIE

# CHAPTER 1

# Male Envy

I didn't start out wanting to be a guy. But in the late 1960s, when I broke into the overwhelmingly male-dominated television news business, all I saw around me was a sea of white men. Bosses, colleagues in the newsroom, competing reporters, and even interview subjects were all the opposite sex. They were tall, wore identical staid suits and ties and wing-tipped shoes, and had deep, stentorian voices. I envied their bravado, their swagger, the way they could walk into a room and command it. When they spoke, it was with confidence and authority. They were entitled to respect because they were men.

I didn't have close to their level of experience. I was twenty-three, wearing polyester, bell-bottoms, miniskirts, and shoulder-length hair, which I teased and sprayed into a flip. Since I stood only five feet, three and a half inches (don't forget the half), I compensated by wearing stilettos. I wanted to be as close as I could be, eye to eye with the men. I did not want to look *up* at them. I wanted to be their equal. I tried to lower my voice to mimic theirs and copied their on-air cadence.

I knew they could easily bully me, and I was powerless to fight them, so I joined them. I knew I could never *be* one of the boys, but surely, I could adopt pages from their playbook. It was easy to imagine myself as just another white guy.

I became aggressive, tough, bawdy, and extremely competitive. Yes, I looked like a lotus blossom, but I talked like a sailor with a raw sense of humor.

Even though I had always been quiet and demure at home, I could not survive in the news business without being assertive, a fierce go-getter. The men were cocksure, so I mustered all the confidence I could to be the same. The guys thought they were made of the right stuff. By golly, I was too.

In fact, I had so thoroughly convinced myself that I was one of the white guys that when I walked past a mirror or a storefront window, I'd be startled to see a young Chinese woman staring back at me!

My four older sisters were shocked when I pursued a profession that required speaking before millions of viewers. "Our little Connie, who would not speak up, even when we asked her what she wanted to order at the drugstore lunch counter." Growing up, those sisters were my own personal squad of helicopter moms—bossy and hormonal—who thought they knew better, always telling me what to do and what to say. The relentless cacophony of chattering voices was deafening. I never made a sound because I couldn't get a word in edgewise.

But when we were all doing our chores, I would take the hose of a vacuum cleaner and "interview" people—anyone. The truth is, being a reporter fit perfectly with my personality. I preferred to observe, watching what unfolded before me, never expressing my opinion.

I morphed from the youngest of five sisters who had no voice at home, never uttered a peep at school, never raised a hand to answer a teacher's question, into someone who was fearless, ambitious, driven, full of chutzpah and moxie, who spoke up to get what she wanted.

The problem was: men simply did not understand that I was one of them. They just didn't get it. Many men in television news, especially those who became anchormen, contracted a disease: *bigshot-itis*. It was characterized by a swelling of the head, an inability to stop talking, self-aggrandizing behavior, narcissistic tendencies, unrelenting hubris, delusions of grandeur, and fantasies of sexual prowess. Very few women got the bug. If they did, they got milder cases. The disease created hurdles I had to either jump over or find a way around.

The desire to be a man came from a seed my father planted early in my career. He often typed letters to me on his manual typewriter, each beginning the same way: "My Darling Daughter, Connie." It was his way of confiding in me while documenting his roots and ancestral history. I was in my early thirties, already in the news business, when I first read one of his letters in particular. He made a request of me, saying *he* had "wanted to be prominent and important, not only in the Chung family but in society, work and government." But he never achieved that dream, so he assigned me an unusual mission: "Maybe you may like to carry on the name of *Chung* both in Chinese and English and tell how this Chinese family came to the USA."

The reason this was such a strange assignment was that in China, as in many cultures, women were never expected to carry on their family names. In fact, we were expected to give up our last names when we married. Only males would automatically carry on the family name through generations. My parents had ten children, of which three were boys. But all three sons died as infants. I was the tenth child, the very last and the only one born in the US.

With no surviving males in the Chung family, I realized I could be the son my parents desperately wanted. I would find a way to carry on the family name Chung, to make our name memorable, a part of history. Wouldn't it be the ultimate act of *filial piety* to honor my traditional Chinese parents and give them a son in me? It became my dream too, not just for them, but for myself.

Eventually my decision to be such an obedient, dutiful, and humble good girl to my parents and my bosses became a debilitating nightmare that I would not have been able to endure without my dear husband, Maury. More about that later.

Then a surprising twist. In 2019, a reporter named Connie Wang contacted me to tell me she'd discovered that an extraordinary number of Asian parents in the 1970s, '80s, and '90s had named their baby daughters Connie, after me! What? I'd had no idea my *first* name would be carried forward—to spawn a sisterhood of Connies. It may be difficult to believe, but I didn't know I'd had such a profound impact on Asians. I was flabbergasted. And my head is still spinning.

It was a gigantic cherry on top of my cake. Here's why. I could never declare success for myself. That's probably a woman thing combined with a Chinese thing. I have always been proud to be Chinese, but at the same time, I knew we Asians were perceived by some as different, as foreigners, as second-class citizens. I was shocked that those Asian parents had seen me as someone who had broken the race barrier. Someone who was accepted. Someone whose name they wanted to carry on.

Throughout my career, I had striven for acceptance and equality and to be taken seriously, but I'd never assumed I had achieved *any* of those goals. Suddenly the Connie Generation declared success *for* me.

What a journey. I was bold, yet humble. I think that dichotomy was a Chinese thing. What a festival for shrinks!

As we say in television news, all that's coming up. My family. My glorious highs and deep lows in the news business. My beloved husband, Maury. Our precious son, Matthew. The Connie Generation and so much more. Don't go away.

# CHAPTER 2

# Tradition

To understand how I became the person I did, let's roll back the videotape to pre-Communist China, where my parents were born and raised with antiquated mindsets and ancient traditions that shaped my life.

My father was the oldest son of six children, born in Suzhou in 1909. His parents named him Chung Ling Jai-pao (in Chinese the family name, Chung, comes first). Suzhou was an ancient cultural city built in 514 BC, considered the "Venice of the East" because so much of the city was covered with lakes, streams, and canals. Artistic, elaborately carved bridges arched gracefully over the canals. It was a spot so spectacular, Chinese emperors vacationed there.

Daddy took his status as number one son seriously even though his older sister was the true firstborn. But she was a girl. In chauvinist Chinese society daughters were considered expendable. They weren't quite stuffed in bags with rocks and tossed in the river, but you get the point.

My grandfather owned a jewelry business that sold to foreign buyers, and he needed someone to interpret for him. He sent his number one son to school not only to learn English but also for a broader education. In 1915, at age six, my father began learning with a tutor. At nine, he was enrolled for third grade at the Atkinson Academy, a private Methodist school that required tuition. He thrived, skipping grades and becoming managing editor of the yearbook.

Attending Atkinson changed the course of my father's life. Headmaster Dr. Tsiang, a graduate of the University of Minnesota, ignited a spark in Daddy when he spoke on graduation day. Dr. Tsiang told the students he hoped they would go abroad and see the world. Travel, he said, would not only broaden their minds but also help their wider understanding of humanity. Daddy vowed right then that if he ever had a chance to venture out in the world, he'd grab it. Fresh out of high school and equipped with his proficiency in English, my father set his sights on America.

Mommy was born Mah Pih-liang in 1911 in the ancient metropolis of Nanjing, one of four great capitals of China during dynastic rule and one of the most important cities in the world, a center of tourism, culture, education, arts, and history.

Mommy's father owned and operated a paper factory. Her mother was the manager of the employees, all of whom lived at the factory. It was common for the working class to eat and sleep at their workplaces. My maternal grandmother had live-in maids, cooks, and nannies at home. Since paper was an essential commodity and controlled by local strongmen, Mommy's father was powerful in

Nanjing. So much so, according to family lore, he was like a Mafia boss.

Mommy's parents, the Mahs, had been childless for a decade. So when she came along, she was spoiled and coddled, especially by her father. Her grandmother insisted my mother's feet be bound in gauze, an ancient Chinese custom that dates back to the tenth century. Tiny feet, as small as three to five inches, were inexplicably desirable, like the tiny waists imposed on women in Victorian England. Bound feet were seen as essential for a marriageable daughter in the upper echelons of society. But my mother, at five years old, bitterly complained, "It hurts!" Despite her grandmother's fears that "no one will marry her because she has big feet!" her father insisted he'd support his daughter if no man would have her. End of binding.

Much as she didn't want her feet bound, Mommy did not want to go to school either. Her father relented on that too. Middle- and upper-class Chinese girls typically didn't get much education anyway. Their role in society was to bear children, sew, knit, crochet, do needlepoint, enjoy mah-jong, and never lift a finger. She could not read or write Chinese, and in later years, my mother hid the fact as best she could. She was embarrassed and suffered great self-loathing for her illiteracy.

Mommy was pretty, with a round face, a small nose, a perfect heart-shaped mouth, lips painted with raspberry lipstick by Elizabeth Arden, and the most amazing soft, supple, flawless skin with no lines or wrinkles even into her nineties. She wore her hair pulled back in a classic bun at the nape of her neck.

She loved jewelry—earrings, rings, brooches, hairpins for her bun. Wherever she went, she always wore lovely earrings. They were clip-ons, not pierced, because of a horrible incident in China. One day when she was walking on a street in Shanghai, a thief came up from behind her and yanked her earring off—splitting one of her earlobes. None of her daughters, including me, ever had her ears pierced. The story spooked us.

Mommy's deep voice belied her five-foot frame. Her hands, arms, and body were strong too, matching her personality. There was never any doubt where she stood on any issue because she was definitive and unwavering. When she told me to do anything, all I needed was the look on her face to know she meant business.

These two forces of nature didn't come together by chance in a love marriage. Mommy was only twelve and Daddy only fourteen when they were forced by their parents to become engaged. It was a classic arranged marriage, common in China at the time. They had never set eyes on each other and did not even *meet* for the first time until five years later, on the day they were married.

Both sets of their parents were Moslem and needed to be certain their children would carry on the family heritage with a suitable partner. China's relationship with Islam dates back as early as the seventh century, when Silk Road traders from the Middle East intermarried with the Chinese. In those blended families, the Moslem religion often melded with Confucian practices. Whatever my Moslem ancestors in China were practicing was different from the practices of the rest of the Islamic world. Our parents never knelt on prayer rugs. My mother never wore a veil. They never knew any Chinese men who had more than one wife. There were no religious traditions practiced in my family besides good old basic values: honesty, respect for elders, humility, and obedience to parents.

While that obedience to *their* parents was paramount, neither of my parents was happy with their arranged union. Tradition forced them to obey their parents' wishes. My father even dared to strongly object, but he was summarily overruled. As the number one son in the family, he knew he could not rebel; as he put it, "I surrendered." My mother never discussed the matter with me.

As an engagement gift, her future father-in-law, a jeweler, gave her a special ring made of deep-green jade, a rare stone because of its intense, rich color. Expert jeweler that he was, he'd fashioned it into a graceful oval held by prongs set on a thin, classic gold band. My mother cherished it.

The moment of truth arrived on October 4, 1928, when my parents wed in Nanjing. My mother, seventeen, wore a traditional Chinese embroidered jacket (which I still have) and a satin culotte skirt. My father, nineteen, also wore traditional Chinese attire. His father had saved a piece of 24-karat dark gold for her wedding ring. The gold was so thick and soft, I could see where the ring was joined together. My father did not wear a wedding band.

After the ceremony, the newlyweds boarded a carriage for the bumpy 120-mile journey from Nanjing to Suzhou, where my mother joined her new family of strangers. Chinese women were expected to spend the rest of their lives with their husbands' families, living with their in-laws.

My mother, a sheltered teenager, left the warm security of her adoring parents, brother, and sister, forced into a relationship with a fellow who wanted nothing to do with her. I can only imagine how sad and terrified she was. Her parents sent along a dowry of jewelry, silks, and more. And even though there was a staff of maids, servants, and cooks at her new husband's home, her father also sent along Mommy's favorite maid to wait on her in case the new family did not take proper care of his beloved daughter.

My father's childhood home now became hers—a big house with a front gate, a walled-in courtyard, and a grand front door opening to a large living room. All six Chung children and their growing families were under one roof. Maids and cooks lived in rooms beyond the dining room and kitchen.

Mommy was lonely and feeling the sting of her mother-in-law's resentment. She'd sensed it from the moment she stepped into the house. My sisters told me they'd had the impression that our paternal grandmother did not want to share her son with this new young woman. Also, it did not sit well with her mother-in-law that Mommy had arrived with her own personal handmaiden to a household filled with servants. Even my father admitted his own mother was domineering and not particularly nice. When I look at my grandmother's photo, it astonishes me how much a picture can convey. I can see the mean in her face.

Another key matter that fueled my grandmother's animosity was that she blamed my mother for not producing a grandson.

My parents' first baby, born in 1931, was a girl, Yu-hsiu, my oldest sister.

Three years later came my second-oldest sister, Yu-jen. My grandmother was already muttering, "Where's my grandson?" Clearly two girls in a row was unacceptable.

Baby number three was a girl who died of strep throat at the age of one. Infant mortality was common in those days.

Baby number four was again a girl, Yu-chien, my third-oldest sister. Oh no! The news was met with great distress. As far as my grandparents were concerned, it was all my mother's fault. (They did not know, as many don't, that it's the sperm that determines the gender of a baby.)

When my mother was pregnant with baby number five, she had to rush home to Nanjing because her mother had suffered a stroke, but she did not make it before my grandmother passed. My grandfather urged Mommy to stay in Nanjing to have her baby, but Mommy was adamant that she return to Suzhou. If her baby was a boy, her mother-in-law could see for herself that her grandson was not switched at birth. Sure enough, it *was* a boy. Tragically, he died as an infant. I don't know what illness he had. That loss, on the heels of the death of her mother, caused Mommy unbearable pain.

In a year, my mother was pregnant again with baby number six. My father, who was working in Shanghai at the time, had a ghostly dream that baby number six was wrapped in a white shroud. It turned out to be prophetic. The new baby, a coveted boy, died as an infant too. I don't know what caused his death either.

The loss of those two baby boys prompted my traditional Chinese family to take a dramatic step. Someone, I don't know who, decided that my third-oldest sister would be dressed as a boy. We have photos of her standing in front of a desk, with a boy's buzz cut, a shirt, and boys' shorts. She looks exactly like a boy. It was an experience she never wanted. As the story goes, when she went to school, she came home crying, upset that she could not go to the girls' lavatory. The family relented and dressed her as a girl. Nobody talked about it, but it had a profound effect on her the rest of her life.

While my mother was spending the first decade of her marriage making babies, my father was commuting between their home in Suzhou and Shanghai, seventy-five miles away, working for his father's jewelry company. I don't know how or why he left his father's business, but at some point, he attended a special training institute for intelligence to become a spy. A spook! For his cover job, he packed a pistol and held the rank of lieutenant colonel in the Military Police. But in reality, he served as an intelligence officer for the Nationalist Chinese (pre-Communist) government of Generalissimo Chiang Kai-shek. The Chinese equivalents of the

Central Intelligence Agency, the Federal Bureau of Investigation, the Defense Intelligence Agency, and the Military Police all fell under one umbrella intelligence agency. Daddy kept the nitty-gritty of his work a secret from everyone, including my mother. My mother hated that he would never tell her where he was or what he was doing. That spurred her distrust of him, which was amplified when she discovered he was a philanderer.

While she was home in Suzhou, he spent months at a time in Shanghai, a big, bustling, cosmopolitan port city, much like New York City, with all the attendant vices. It had been taken over by foreigners hundreds of years earlier, after the two Opium Wars, which China lost to the British and the French. British and French enclaves lured my father into a fast life. With his wife and three children home in Suzhou, my dashing and debonair father, the spy, was enjoying liquor, unfiltered British cigarettes, and lots of women.

I have a favorite photo of him from those days, dressed like a Brit in a starched dress shirt, tightly knotted tie, and fur-collared coat. He had thick black hair, clear-framed glasses, a strong, prominent nose, and a mustache.

Once my mother traveled to Shanghai to see him for a few days, leaving the children home with nannies. She was to meet him at a restaurant for lunch. When she got there, she told the maître d', "I'm Mrs. Chung. Please seat me at Mr. Chung's table." The maître d' looked at her, perplexed. "But Mrs. Chung is already sitting at the table." My mother was livid. A girlfriend!

At another point, my father landed in the hospital for a long stretch. Mommy went to visit him during his recovery. What was his illness? Two of my sisters speculated that it was a venereal disease. I don't know. China had a long history of concubines, of philandering males who faced no consequences. Male dominance, female subservience. My mother felt there was little she could say or do. She was married to this man, and there was no way she could change that. Her choices were zero. But those incidents fueled a seething anger. She begrudged the fact that she *had* to stay married to him forever, which she did.

Daddy had ideas for their future she could not have imagined. He hit a turning point when he was accompanying the Polish chargé d'affaires to a hotel in Chongqing, China. Daddy was waiting in a hotel lobby for the Polish official when he spotted two Chinese teenagers speaking fluent English. Their mother, a beautiful Chinese woman wearing American clothes, got off the elevator. She spoke Chinese to her husband, who was wearing a Western-style suit. The couple spoke English to their children. That did it. Then and there, my father told me, he plotted out a way to bring his family to the USA to learn to speak English and, as he put it, "live happy lives."

# CHAPTER 3

# The Exodus

The story of the Chung family exodus from China is etched in my mind, but not because I experienced it myself. From my earliest moments of awareness, I gleaned bits and pieces of the daring escape that had led my family to their new lives in America. And I was acutely conscious of the capstone of that terrifying journey—that because of their migration, I became the lucky one, the only one to be born a US citizen.

But it wasn't until I read the detailed memoir that my father meticulously typed out on his manual typewriter that I fully grasped the enormity and complexity of their journey—much less his and my mother's unwavering bravery throughout their harrowing odyssey. Daddy must have understood that it was only as I grew older that I could fully understand what they had endured. What shocks me each time I revisit those delicate onionskin pages is that at every step of the way, any one of a thousand different outcomes could have ensued. And if any of them had, it is quite possible I might not even exist.

The migration of the Chungs began in 1937, spurred by the Second Sino-Japanese War, as Japanese forces encroached on Suzhou. A declaration of martial law meant all movement in the city had ceased. Luckily, Daddy's work as an undercover agent for the Chinese military gave him special status. His connections allowed him to finagle rickshaws to spirit away my parents and sisters, along with my paternal grandparents and several other members of my father's family—a dozen people in all. All along the way, bombs exploded around them.

Next they boarded two boats—one to carry the Chung family, the other to transport their cargo, fifteen suitcases packed with their important stocks and documents and their precious lifetime possessions, including a green jade stone that weighed twenty pounds. As they traveled along the canals, a bomb blasted the cargo boat, obliterating it and everything they owned in an instant. Luckily, the Chung family escaped unharmed.

As they made their way over the next twenty-six miles to Wuxi City, bulletins from the front lines revealed that Suzhou had been lost to the Japanese. The Chungs had escaped just in the nick of time.

My father's "sources," as he called them, arranged for a special bus to take the family to Nanjing. Air raids and bombs hastened the buses' departure before the family arrived. Thinking fast, Daddy dispatched two Military Police officers in a jeep, ordering them to seize the bus and force it to return. When it did, the Chung family boarded and off the bus sped again, dodging aerial attacks by Japanese planes and arriving safely in Nanjing in the middle of the night.

With martial law in force there, too, all shops were closed, adding to the precariousness of daily life. How would they access provisions, the basics necessary to survive? My father learned that the Chiang Kai-shek government would be clearing out of Nanjing and that the Chungs could soon evacuate too.

Military Police officers helped the family board rickshaws with what few belongings they had left. It was a quiet night—no air raids. They traveled easily and quickly onto main highways, transferring to two carriages, riding two hours to the harbor. Next they boarded a cargo ship. There were no rooms, so the dozen of them spread out in a corner of the deck as the ship quietly sped out of Nanjing at dawn.

Mercifully, they had escaped Nanjing just before Japanese forces invaded the city in a devastating six-week campaign of horror known to history as the Rape of Nanjing. Japanese imperial soldiers savaged as many as three hundred thousand Chinese, many by decapitation, mutilation, and burning alive. Thousands of Chinese women and girls were sexually attacked and gang-raped.

As my family steamed toward Hankou, the captain turned off the lights to avoid detection. But when he stopped the ship to help a sister vessel with engine trouble, the Japanese spotted them idling in the middle of the river, and the bombing began.

Still, they managed to arrive safely in Hankou, where they settled into a cramped rental apartment. Two or three times a day, air attacks sent them all running. My father was determined to relocate to a safer part of the city, a little colony known as the French settlement. Despite an edict from the French consulate that only white people could live there, my father managed to persuade officials to let the family move in.

Nine months ticked away in Hankou as China withered under the protracted war. Soon it became obvious to Daddy how important it was to evacuate farther inland. What did everyone want to do? He explained his plans to his parents and extended family: he would take my mother and three sisters to his next assignment in Chongqing, the wartime capital of Chiang Kai-shek's government. Did the others wish to join them?

Their answer was no. They decided instead to return to an unknown future in their hometown of Suzhou, even though it was now fully under Japanese control. Daddy dutifully arranged for his parents and relatives to travel on circuitous routes to avoid running into violence and provided money and tickets for each leg of their journey. This was no easy feat, given all the security clearances and exit permits that would be necessary.

Neither was it easy for my parents and sisters as they left Hankou. Their journey to Chongqing was rife with miserable obstacles, from the blistering heat in a ship that ran aground to a listing ship they feared would capsize. When they arrived, they were able to breathe a sigh of relief. They'd moved thirteen times over the past year. Perhaps now they could rest easy for a bit.

But not for too long. My father recommitted to bringing his family to the United States. Until he could accomplish that, he set about Americanizing his wife and daughters as best he could while still on Chinese soil. He commissioned a tailor to sew American-style dresses for my sisters, and to complete the outfits, he bought lace-up leather shoes in the style of the 1940s. He took the family to Western-style restaurants so they could learn how to use knives and forks. And they went to a movie theater to see the animated Disney classic, the quintessential American movie, *Snow White and the Seven Dwarfs*.

In the meantime, Mommy became pregnant with baby number seven. When she went into labor, a doctor could not get to her side in time, leaving my father to deliver the girl. Tragically, the baby died not long after from an illness unrelated to her birth.

My father's work made him privy to intelligence that the Nationalist government of Chiang Kai-shek found valuable. Communiques he intercepted showed that some American diplomats favored Communist Chinese forces led by Mao Tse-tung, who were vying for control of China. Officially, the US was encouraging Chiang Kai-shek to partner with the Communist Chinese. Neither side trusted the other. The fragile alliance between the two ideologies did not last long. The Chinese Communists were making inroads with the Chinese peasantry, gaining their confidence as Communist forces overpowered the Japanese in guerilla skirmishes. Which side would win?

My father was not about to wait around to find out. He intensified his search for a way out of the country. While he did, my mother gave birth in 1942 to baby number eight—Yu-yen, my fourth-oldest sister.

The war situation was increasingly dire. Generalissimo Chiang refused to negotiate with the Japanese or to surrender. By 1944, my father had fortuitously shifted to the Passport Division of the Ministry of Foreign Affairs, which enabled him to obtain the necessary papers for my mother and sisters to travel. Then he learned that Chinese cadets would be sent to the United States, where they'd be trained to fly by US Air Force pilots. He did not know how to fly a plane, but he cleverly figured that he could be their administrator. He managed to have himself immediately commissioned as a captain in the Chinese Air Force. Here was his golden opportunity to travel to the US on official business. There was only one key question: Could he bring along his family?

He requested special permission from Generalissimo Chiang, even though he knew it was a long shot. Somehow my father defied the odds. The word came down: yes. That opened up a new host of challenges. Now Daddy had to obtain a matrix of exit permits for the family from Chinese officials, as well as visitor visas from the US government. His years of dealing with Chinese bureaucracy and official applications greased the way to success.

With the help of Chinese aviation officials, the Chung family got seats on a commercial flight from Chongqing to Calcutta, India, the only route by air to the outside world. Unthinkably, four passengers were yanked off the plane to make room for them. It was Christmas Eve, December 24, 1944.

Days later, they boarded a train to Bombay, where my father met the seven hundred Chinese Air Force officers and cadets he would oversee as an executive officer in the US. With the help of American authorities, he arranged for the family to join him on the USS *General William Mitchell*, a transport ship that was traveling to the US. A perfect exit strategy! Well, almost. This plan was scuttled with one edict from the captain, who refused to allow my youngest sister to board the ship because she was a toddler.

The only path seemed to be for my father to proceed to the US alone. He made arrangements for my mother and the girls to stay in Bombay until he could find a way to get them to the US. During those war days, Chinese men were notorious for abandoning their families, promising to send for them later and then vanishing forever. Would my father be one of those selfish men?

No, Daddy was devoted to his family, as evidenced by letters he left for my mother, in Chinese and English, detailing his US contact information for whenever they managed to arrive. He knew my mother was a strong woman and could handle the difficult road ahead.

So while Daddy made his way to America, Mommy found herself trapped in a Bombay hotel with four girls, ages two to thirteen. Here she was, only thirty-three, never having been outside China and unable to speak any other language than Chinese. She rationed the money she had, much of it gathered by selling her own jewelry. She needed about $700 a month for expenses. How long could she make it last?

The challenge of budgeting for daily existence paled in comparison to what happened next. Mommy found out she was pregnant. She discovered that ships to America would not allow children under the age of two to board. She faced an excruciating dilemma.

One day she told my older sisters that she was going to the hospital. The ten-year-old was to take care of the two younger girls at the hotel—and the oldest, thirteen, was to accompany Mommy. She had no idea how long she'd be gone. It turned out to be two days. When she returned, she announced that she was no longer having a baby.

Over the years, I recall my sisters giving me conflicting answers to my burning question: Did Mommy have a miscarriage or an abortion? For this book, I interviewed my second-oldest sister, Charlotte, who was the ten-year-old my mother assigned to babysit. I pressed Charlotte for the answer. Dear Charlotte, who always was uncomfortable with uttering a word like "divorce" or "cancer," finally whispered, "Mommy had an abortion."

It pains me greatly, knowing my mother had to make this decision entirely on her own, with no one to talk to. She proceeded so that she could raise her family in the US. How she arranged the procedure we have no idea. She couldn't speak English or Hindi—only Chinese.

What might have happened to the Chungs had she not made that unilateral decision? I shudder to think about the magnitude of her actions.

The added tragedy was that the baby was a boy, that coveted boy. My sisters don't remember my parents ever talking about that baby boy. They said Daddy just *knew* what had happened.

\* \* \*

Days turned to six long months of limbo in Bombay. On May 8, 1945, my mother and sisters watched the celebrations of victory in Europe when World War II's Allies formally accepted Nazi Germany's unconditional surrender. Finally my father sent my mother and sisters a Western Union telegram and wired them tickets through American Express to board a luxury ocean liner, the MS *Gripsholm*, a repatriation ship chartered by the US State Department to carry American and Chinese diplomats, officials, international missionaries, professionals, and their families to the United States and Canada.

The words "Gripsholm" and "Diplomat" were painted on the port and starboard of the ship, which was operated by a Swedish captain and crew. Fearing Japanese submarine attacks and floating mines, the captain took a longer but safer route, through the Arabian Sea, the Red Sea, the Suez Canal, and the Mediterranean. He avoided traveling in the Pacific, where the war was raging.

My sisters enjoyed the luxuries of the ocean liner—to a point. As nonwhite passengers, they were permitted to eat their meals only during a second, segregated seating. Their encounter with racism didn't trouble them—it was just something they noticed.

In August 1945, my mother and sisters and fifteen hundred other passengers on visitors' visas arrived at Jersey City Pier in New Jersey—not Ellis Island, where immigrants and refugees usually docked. Everyone on board the ship, including the Americans, was immediately examined by a doctor, a standard procedure at the time.

Despite their age difference, Charlotte, eleven, and June, eight, were dressed alike and looked like twins. Charlotte's eyes happened to be a little red, perhaps from an eye infection or conjunctivitis, which could have blocked the family from entering the United States. But the doctor didn't notice it because he accidentally examined June twice. Ha ha! The family passed through with no issues.

When they finally disembarked, greeting them at the pier was the American secretary of my mother's cousin, the owner of a New York antique store. The secretary immediately chose American names for my four sisters. Family legend has it that a princess from some foreign country named Joséphine-Charlotte was visiting. And so my oldest sister became Josephine and the next oldest Charlotte. The third was given the name June because that was her birth month. And my fourth sister became Maimie because "mei-mei" means little sister in Chinese. My parents also had American names, Margaret and William, but the secretary had nothing to do with that. I don't know how my mother became Margaret because no one in my family called her anything but Mommy. My father had named himself William in Shanghai after the popular American actor William Powell.

Next the secretary took the girls shopping. I love the adorable photo of Charlotte and June in the aftermath of the spree, beaming broad smiles in their brand-new matching red gingham checked dresses and white Mary Jane shoes with ankle socks trimmed in lace, clutching matching little purses—the quintessential American girls. Unfortunately, I can't find the picture to show you.

Four days after their arrival, the United States dropped the atomic bomb on Hiroshima. On August 14 and August 15, 1945, my mother and sisters watched the celebrations of victory over Japan from their New York hotel window. Finally World War II was over.

Not long after, my father sent tickets for the three-day train ride to join him at the US Air Force base in Montgomery, Alabama, where American pilots were training his cadets. There he had rented a three-bedroom rambler on a friendly tree-lined street where all the houses looked alike.

My father was proud to wear a Chinese Air Force captain's uniform. He enjoyed being in charge. His life was good. Meanwhile, my mother became a traditional, hardworking housewife, one who spent her days cooking, cleaning, and washing clothes—the exact opposite of her privileged life back in China. Josephine and Charlotte helped out by walking a mile each day to shop for the food she prepared. People would trail after them, curious because they'd never laid eyes on a Chinese person before.

Since my father was the only person among all the Chinese Air Force men who had a family with him, my mother generously opened her home to the Chinese cadets for home-cooked dinners. Thankfully, she had watched the cooks back home and was able to replicate their traditional dishes.

Josephine, Charlotte, and June were enrolled in public school. However, because they could not speak English, they were placed in grades well below their ages—Josephine, at fourteen, was assigned to second grade. They were mortified and offended. After three days of humiliation, toughies that they were, the girls went on strike, refusing to go to class. The following week the principal and teachers paid a visit to the Chung family home. Ever the diplomat, my father suggested that the girls be placed in the correct grades and paired with student volunteers who could help them learn English. It worked. In six months, they were fluent.

Around then, my father was transferred to a US Air Force base in San Antonio, Texas. He knew it would not be long before that gig would end. Daddy requested a transfer to the Chinese embassy in Washington, DC, as a Chinese Air Force attaché.

And so, in the spring of 1946, my parents and sisters moved to Washington. That's when I, entirely because of their bravery and fortitude across thousands of miles, got to be the beneficiary of that journey: the lucky child born on US soil.

# CHAPTER 4

# Another Girl

B aby number ten was the last hope. Would the Chung family at long last get that coveted boy?

You know the answer. My arrival at Georgetown Hospital in Washington, DC, on August 20, 1946, quashed that dream.

My father called home to break the news to my sisters, who were anxiously waiting by the phone. He gave them an assignment: find their baby sister a name. With just a year in the United States under their belts, the girls were already fans of American celebrity movie magazines like *Photoplay*, *Motion Picture*, and *Screen Stars*, the precursors of *People*. Giggling and excited, they fished through their stack of magazines and selected a special year-end issue, one that featured a single photo of a different movie star (male or female) on each page. They made a pact to choose a page at random, and whatever movie star appeared on that page would be their sister's namesake! One of them stuck her thumb in the middle of the closed magazine.

Ready? OK. Flip!

Hello, Constance Moore, a B-list actress/singer with long brown hair whose career mostly consisted of wartime musicals. She also had the distinction of having played the lone female character in a 1939 movie serial, *Buck Rogers*.

And so, with the addition of a Chinese middle name, I was officially welcomed to the world as Constance Yu-hwa Chung. No one ever called me Constance. From the start, I was Connie. My father affectionately called me Con-Con, often with a smile and a single clap. My mother (who called me "Dahling") told me I was the only baby of all ten whom my father played with.

When people asked me to translate my middle name, Yu-hwa, I would tell them with a straight face, "It means the melodious ivory keys of a grand piano playing, as a babbling brook weaves its way through a serene garden of gorgeous flowers...soft petals blowing in the wind"—or something like that. Some people actually fell for it.

As a kid, I was terribly timid. When I enrolled at West Elementary for kindergarten, I was terrified to leave home and meet other children. I'd hide behind my mother outside the classroom, crying, begging her to take me home. Eventually I would let go of my mother's skirts, although some days, I'd start to cry again.

Luckily for me and not so much for her, my sister Maimie attended the same public school. She was four years older and a superb student. The teachers loved her and expected me to follow in her footsteps, but there was no way I could live up to her sterling reputation. Maimie was often yanked out of her third-grade class and told, "Connie is crying again. She wants to go home." Maimie had every right to disown her wimpy, annoying little sister. But each time, she patiently coaxed me back to class.

My elementary school teachers intimidated me. I was tiny, and from my point of view they were as imposing as the prison matrons in those old black-and-white movies. If I could have burrowed into the inkwell hole in my desk, I would have gladly disappeared. A few years ago, I discovered my report cards from back then. One teacher had written three words that succinctly described my biggest problem, "Speaks too softly."

Despite my painful shyness, I fantasized about becoming a prima ballerina and performing before audiences around the world, a dream that grew out of my favorite book, *Kiki Dances* by Charlotte Steiner. I envisioned myself in a tiny tutu and ballet slippers pirouetting across the stage, or wearing tights and leg warmers, practicing at the ballet bar. Every day, following the tutorial pictured in *The First Book of Ballet*, I stood before a full-length mirror and diligently practiced the five positions. I begged my parents, "Please let me take ballet lessons." Their answer was swift: "We don't have the money." Their definitive no devastated me and I cried a lot. Each sister tried to comfort me, promising, "Someday you will take ballet lessons." It never happened. I survived.

My four sisters didn't seem to be dreamers like me. Like the four March sisters in *Little Women*, each one had a distinctive personality. My oldest sister, Josephine, was sixteen years older than me. Blunt and direct, she'd often remind me she was like my second mother: "I changed your diapers." During her high school years, she held a part-time job after school and on weekends at Liberty Mutual Insurance Company. Jo never had her head in the clouds, never tried to achieve social status, was always realistic and down to earth. She referred to us as "the bookends"—the strong, stalwart, dependable daughters. Without the two of us holding up the three sisters in the middle, she declared, "they would keel over."

My second-oldest sister, Charlotte, was sweet and serious but also very stubborn, trying to prove she was as good as number one. I always abided by Charlotte's rules—there was no arguing with her. She, too, got a part-time job during high school, at Hecht's Department Store. She scored so impressively on the math portion of an aptitude test that the store waived its rules against hiring Asians and brought her on, in the accounts department. Both Josephine and Charlotte turned their paychecks over to my father to help with the family finances. Years later when I began working, I did the same.

Third in line was my rebellious sister, June. As a teenager, she was always trying to sneak off to the movies. June was the only one of us who wasn't flat chested. She had genuine perky twins from an early age. When she was brushing her teeth, I'd sneak up behind her and pretend I was going to milk them as if she were a cow. She'd yell at me to scat.

But she did show me exercises that she insisted would help me in my desperate desire to blossom. I crossed my arms, each hand holding the other forearm, and proceeded to rhythmically squeeze my forearms—one, two, three, squeeze, squeeze, squeeze. Despite my faithfully performing my routine, alas, my boobs grew like root vegetables, inward rather than outward.

Maimie, the fourth girl and four years older, was my best-friend sister, closest in age and heart. Every afternoon we did our homework together and then raced outside to get in a round of play. We'd roller-skate, jump rope, or mark the sidewalk with chalk for hopscotch. If Maimie was invited to a birthday party, my mother made her bring me along. And though my sister obeyed, she rightfully grumbled about it. I was a burdensome appendage.

* * *

Though my sisters and I were immersed in American culture, in our family home, we were as Chinese as we could be. At home we spoke English *and* Chinese, ate homemade Chinese cooking for dinner every night, and, for the most part, associated only with Chinese people. To make ends meet, my parents even took in a couple of Chinese college students as boarders.

My parents spoke with thick Chinese accents—my mother in particular. Often people looked at her cockeyed and told her they could not understand her. Since I did, I'd feel obligated to repeat what she'd said. I cringed from embarrassment for her and for me. My three older sisters also spoke with accents. But since Maimie was only two when she came to the US, she and I talked just like any American.

My father worked at the Chinese embassy until 1949, when the Communist Party under Mao Tse-tung turned the old China into the People's Republic. That's when the embassy dissolved, forcing Daddy to re-create himself. Armed with his elegant chiseled wood abacus, he became an accountant for the United Nations Food and Agriculture Organization (FAO). His colleagues marveled at how he could come up with the same answers with a few quick clicks of his ancient, exotic counting device much faster than they could with their clunky adding machines with buttons and handle levers.

In search of better pay, Daddy jumped to become comptroller at the Institute of Scrap Iron & Steel. To supplement that week-day income, he started a weekend job as an accountant, auditor, and bookkeeper at the Brighton Hotel in Washington. It was hard enough for my father to keep up with rent, utilities, food, and other essentials for a family of seven. But because of our race, finding a house posed an even greater challenge. In 1950s Washington, some landlords simply would not rent to Chinese people. Somehow, Daddy managed to find a row house at 1622 Decatur Street, in a white neighborhood in northwest DC.

I loved that house and its perfect little front yard planted with blue hydrangeas, small backyard, and large side yard. Knowing my father was strapped for money and caring for a big family, the kind manager of the Brighton helped fill our house with furniture she no longer needed at the hotel—handsome, classic four-poster beds with headboards, mahogany bureaus, and vanities from the fifties that made our home look warm and cozy. I still have a few of those pieces, and they remind me of my happy childhood.

While Daddy was working, my mother spent her days, as most housewives did, cooking, cleaning, making beds, washing clothes, and even mowing the lawn. Her routine was far from that of her cushy days in China. My sisters helped her with the endless chopping and prep work required for Chinese food. She indulged Daddy's desire for homemade soup, served, in the Chinese tradition, *after* the main course at dinner. Labor-intensive specialties made from scratch, like wonton soup, dumplings, and dim sum, were reserved for weekend lunches. Despite nightly delicious multicourse dinners, I refused to eat. I was a rail-thin waif. My mother was incredibly patient, sitting with me after everyone else had left the dinner table and pleading with me to please eat something, anything.

I didn't eat much at lunchtime either. Every morning my mother made us sandwiches for our school lunch boxes. Sometimes I was hesitant to let any of the other students see what I was eating because I knew that if I was having, for example, a Chinese egg sandwich, the white of the boiled egg would look light brown, having been cooked with beef in soy sauce. Creeped out and curious, the kids asked, "What is *THAT*?" I found it awkward to explain.

But *after* school, if my mother treated us to fresh glazed doughnuts from the grocery store bakery, I'd devour one, along with potato chips and a Pepsi. The combination of sugar and salt was irresistibly tasty.

\* \* \*

With money so tight, we could not afford a washing machine or dryer. I watched Mommy scrub laundry on a washboard—every piece of clothing for seven people—and lug it in a hamper up our steep, dark basement steps, through the kitchen, and out the back door to hang on clotheslines to dry. Maimie and I would run between the sheets as they fluttered in the breeze, laughing as we played hide-and-seek. My mother would yell at us in Chinese to stop it, lest we dirty her hard work. Only in the most freezing temperatures would she resort to hanging the wash in our cold basement. Determined to get the stains out of dirty rags, she'd boil them, stabbing them with a chopstick and lifting them to see if the soiled areas had melted away. In deep winter her hands were perpetually rough and chapped. My insensitive father would rudely brag about how smooth and soft his hands were, which was, of course, because he did not do any chores at home.

Witnessing my mother drowning in the drudgery of unending housework left a firm imprint on me. Here was a very smart woman consumed with menial tasks and unable to put her natural intelligence to work. While I inherited her perfectionist tendencies, obsessive, compulsive neatness, and the desire to have everything in life orderly and fastidiously uniform, I knew as a girl that keeping house was not going to be the center of my future life.

I felt my mother was not only unhappy with her lot in life but even more embarrassed that she could not read or write in Chinese, much less English. Unable to jot down a shopping list, Mommy simply made a mental inventory of what to buy. She recognized iconic American brands by their labels: Campbell's soup, Miracle Whip, Crisco, Green Giant peas and corn and, of course, Wonder Bread. Should I need a sick note for school, one of my sisters or even I, myself, wrote one in adult handwriting and signed "Mrs. Chung" for the unsuspecting teacher.

Though I was only eight years old, somehow I was assigned the difficult job of teaching my mother how to read so she could get her US citizenship along with the rest of the family. For our reading sessions, Mommy would take a break from her daily chores as she and I settled into a soft armchair together. While other mothers typically curled up to read books to their children, here our roles were reversed. I used my stash of children's books to teach her. Given her frustration and my inability to teach an adult how to read, we both struggled. I could only imagine how uncomfortable she was so I told myself I must muster all the patience I could.

My father encountered other hurdles as he navigated what turned out to be a six-year citizenship process. (Since I had been born in the US, I was automatically an American citizen.) Immigration officials conducted an exhaustive investigation of my family, interviewing our neighbors, the manager at my father's weekend job, and many others. They asked if we belonged to subversive organizations, had any Communist ties, or had ever made derogatory comments about the US. The most emotionally wrenching requirement for my parents was having to cut off all communications with their relatives in China since they were living under Communist rule.

Despite my mother's inability to pass her tests, an empathetic immigration official waved her through. On June 13, 1956, the members of the Chung family were extremely proud to raise their hands and take their oaths as American citizens.

Though we lived like a "typical" happy American family, with picnics in Rock Creek Park and trips to Marshall Hall and Glen Echo Amusement Park, we were also keenly aware that certain places, like some beaches, were off-limits because we were not white.

Thankfully, we did not encounter racism close to home. Our wonderful neighbors were instrumental in the Americanization of the Chung family. Our favorites in the row house next door were Miss Esma Maybee, her mother Mrs. Maybee, and Esma's son, John. Esma and my mother enjoyed a quaint formality when addressing one another. She called my mother Mrs. Chung. Mommy called her Miss Maybee. Esma took Josephine under her wing and taught her how to cook American dishes like meatloaf, roast beef, mashed potatoes, lemon meringue pie, meatballs, and spaghetti. Soon my mother was also making burgers and fries, chili, tuna fish sandwiches, and peanut butter and jelly sandwiches on Wonder Bread.

Another group of neighbors, the DeMarco family, inspired my sister Charlotte. When she picked up Maimie from a playdate with their son, she noticed Mrs. DeMarco's beautiful table setting for Sunday dinner, which included a tablecloth, carefully folded cloth napkins, crystal goblets, and silver flatware. "I said to myself, 'I'm going to do that when I grow up,'" Charlotte told me. At Hecht's Department Store, where she worked, Charlotte wandered to the china department, eyeing the formal tableware and memorizing how to set a proper dinner table.

For Western-style meals, we used cheap flatware from the five-and-dime, but my family wanted a fancier set that could be acquired in an enterprising manner. If we saved a certain number of cereal box tops, we could trade them in for one silver-plated uten-sil at a time. As each new piece arrived, I ripped open the box and announced it with great fanfare. "Another fork! Another knife! A teaspoon!" That's how we slowly pieced together place settings for twelve.

When it came to American holidays, our favorites were Thanks-giving and Christmas. One time, my mother tried to cook a tur-key with soy sauce. It was dreadful. From then on, my oldest sister, Josephine, cooked the bird, following Miss Maybee's recipe. Our Christmas tree was always placed between the living room and the dining room. The holiday wasn't a religious celebration for us. All we wanted to do was exchange gifts and sing carols.

The day my sisters brought home not just the new sensation, a television, but a washing machine for my mother was the moment the Chungs moved into the big leagues of 1950s Americana. It was all thanks to Charlotte, who had the privilege of a 20 percent dis-count because she worked at Hecht's.

I was more enthralled with the TV than the washer. Already a multitasking female, I had a habit of doing my homework, read-ing a book I'd borrowed from the library, *and* watching my favor-ite TV shows, from *The Little Rascals* to *The Mickey Mouse Club*. As they called the roll, I would pretend I was a Mouseketeer: "Annette! Bobby! Cheryl! Connie!" If only I could sing and tap-dance, just like them, I assumed I could be a Mouseketeer too.

When I was nine, we moved—though I was never clear why—to a small house on a hill at 3825 Warren Street, in a white neigh-borhood in northwest Washington. There I entered a new public school, Phoebe Hearst Elementary. It was scary to switch schools midyear, but having gotten older, I was no longer shy and timid. School became fun for me, which allowed me to emerge from my shell. The academics came easily and so did the social events. Since I loved to dance, I was ready for square dance parties and birthday parties, especially the ones thrown by boys I had crushes on. At one party, I even imitated Elvis, shaking my hips and pantomiming *Jailhouse Rock*.

Each morning, our class would stand and recite the Pledge of Allegiance from memory. Back then, prayer was allowed in public school, so we'd also say the Lord's Prayer and the Twenty-Third Psalm. Around this time, the US Supreme Court ruled that racial segregation in public schools was unconstitutional. District of Columbia schools were ordered to desegregate. There may have been other minorities in my school, but I don't remember them. What I do remember is being asked by one of the kids, "Can you see the ceiling and floor since your eyes are such tiny little slits?" Without flinching, I replied, "Yes, of course, I can see everything—just fine." I didn't think a lot about being different.

We weren't different from so many other families who came to the US from different cultures. While we were assimilating, we were also holding on to our native culture. We were fortunate to be able to cherry-pick the best of both worlds.

We played Monopoly, Parcheesi, and Pick-Up Sticks but also stayed up playing mah-jong all night.

We listened to Sinatra, Elvis, Doris Day, and Nat King Cole, but our parents took us to see Chinese opera too.

With a used Singer sewing machine, we made all our American clothes, while my mother hand-made us traditional Chinese dresses—those slim-fitting sheaths with modest slits, stand-up collars, and beautiful decorative frogs.

Charlotte transformed our straight Chinese hair into fifties-style bouncy curls using home permanents out of a box, called Toni.

There was one old-school Chinese tradition that was ironclad. My parents expected my three oldest sisters to marry Chinese men. My parents threw "Chinese dance parties," a not-so-subtle way of parading the Chung sisters before young, eligible Chinese men, most of whom had come to the US for college. Our family would roll up our dining room rug to expose a hardwood dance floor. We'd spin records on our phonograph and jitterbug, tango, samba, cha-cha, and fox-trot the night away, and we'd even form a conga line, snaking through the house. (That's how I learned to do all those ballroom dances.)

The Chung sisters were not only the hosts but the darlings of the parties—the most sought after. They were chatty, charming, and smart. And they lived up to the Chinese adage about their birthplace: "All the most beautiful women were born in Suzhou." It wasn't just hyperbole. They were quite striking. Who would be so lucky as to marry one of them?

Simply being Chinese was not enough for my mother. She stipulated that the men must not be from Canton, a southern region of China. A busybody Chinese woman my mother knew in New York had poisoned my mom's mind with the idea that Cantonese men clustered in Chinatown and opened such déclassé businesses as restaurants and laundries.

One day, it became clear that my oldest sister, Josephine, and her boyfriend, Bill Chen, were thinking of getting married. Uh-oh. But he was Cantonese! Josephine assured our mother that Bill, who was a biochemist, had no such plans. When they had been married sixteen years and had three daughters, they uprooted to Kissimmee, Florida, where Bill opened a Chinese restaurant and a diner—both successful. Do you think my mother said I told you so?

Josephine was the only sister who had a career later in life as president of her local school board and as a political activist in Osceola County.

Charlotte married Ming Chang, who, after college, joined the US Navy as an ensign. As he moved up the ranks, he suffered unthinkable discrimination, as several navy captains did not want a "Chinaman" as their weapons officer. Despite that racism, he ultimately rose to be the first Chinese-born American to be an *admiral* in the US Navy.

My third-oldest sister, June, married a lawyer, John Fugh, who joined the US Army in the Judge Advocate General's (JAG) Corps. He climbed the ranks to become the top lawyer in the army, *the* Judge Advocate General, and made history as the first Chinese-born American to become a *general* in the US Army.

My sisters were with their husbands every step of the way—loyal wives who were instrumental in driving their husbands to professional success. Had they lived in a different era, they could have had spectacular careers of their own.

Thanks to my parents, my four sisters were strong, ballsy, competitive high achievers who set a high bar for me.

## CHAPTER 5

# Beginning to Break Out

For the seventh grade, I found myself in a spanking new world—the great Lone Star State of Texas. As a naturalized American citizen, Daddy was able to get a job with the US government as an auditor for the Federal Power Commission. This meant my parents, Maimie, and I had to relocate to Houston for his two-year assignment. Not having lived anywhere but Washington, I was a bit wary.

Indeed, Houston was a whole new ball game for me. Entering the seventh grade at a public junior high school, I felt childlike because I was still a head on a stick, still skinny, short, and flat chested, standing side by side with voluptuous preteen cowgirls—big, bouncy darlings who already had boyfriends.

Fortunately, I met a kindred spirit in Carol Sama at school. She had short, dark hair, a gentle Texas accent, and a knack for style. She lived in a modest apartment with her mother, a warm, strong, independent woman. Carol's father was not in her family picture, but Carol never complained about his absence, nor did she complain about anything else in her life. She was a no-drama gal, a positive person, always cool and calm.

Carol was proud to be a Texan, and after a while I was feeling the infectious spirit of the state's proud history. In school, we were required to study Texas history, Texas geography, and the state's efforts to secede from the US and become an independent sovereign state.

In Houston, I felt as if I'd seceded from the Land of Bossy Sisters, breaking out of my wallflower stage. Pairing up with another girlfriend, I even performed "Honey Bun" from *South Pacific* for some silly school talent show. Just like Mitzi Gaynor in the film version, we donned oversize male sailor outfits, trying our best to mimic Gaynor's dazzling song and dance. I sang off-key, but I could dance.

While my dad was busy at work and Maimie and I were at school, Houston was a trial for my mother. Before Houston, in DC, Mommy had been surrounded by our growing family. My two sisters who were military wives and their babies had spent chunks of time living in our home with us while their husbands were out on tours of duty. Mommy loved doting on her grandchildren. And my parents still had Chinese dinner parties. With their flair and showmanship, they thrived on entertaining their friends, chatting in their native language, and remembering "the old days" in China.

Now, in Texas, all that came to a stark end. Bereft, my mother would sit alone and smoke menthol cigarettes all day long in our sparse garden apartment with rickety rented furniture. Our furniture had been put in storage in Washington.

The emptiness that my mother felt aggravated something a busier time had masked—the unhappiness of my parents' marriage.

Growing up, I watched them engage in intense verbal fights, yelling, screaming, and even breaking dishes. Because I was the youngest, my sisters would order me upstairs. Of course, that didn't insulate me from the sounds of the heated arguments. They shouted in Chinese, and there were certain words I'd hear only when they were arguing that I assumed were swear words. I was too embarrassed to ask anyone to translate them. As I got older, I realized my parents had a fractious relationship. Their only bond was the Chinese tradition that they remain married.

In 1960, after two years, my father's stint in Houston was over. We were happy to move back but discovered white flight had changed Washington. Following the whites to the suburbs, we rented a furnished rambler in Maryland. My father continued his job at the Federal Power Commission and later worked at the Maritime Administration.

I entered the ninth grade at Takoma Park Junior High School. Wanting to be a cheerleader like my sister Maimie, I tried out and made it. Takoma ended at ninth grade, so we moved to be close to Montgomery Blair Senior High School for tenth grade.

My dad found a nice new top-floor apartment in a brick building at the dead end of a residential street. One bedroom for my parents, another for Maimie and me. There were shiny parquet floors and sliding glass picture windows. My father had not been able to keep up the payments for the furniture in storage, so most of it was gone.

A creative woman, Mommy invented a way to fill the empty place. In the living room, she angled two rollaway twin beds against the walls. With some old bedspreads and strategically placed sleeping pillows, she pretended we had a corner sofa. On a flimsy rolling stand sat our black-and-white television with rabbit ears. I was terribly embarrassed to bring anyone home. For the longest time, I just could not. But eventually I did. I fibbed that our furniture was stuck in a storage facility because of some dispute.

In a space that was intended for a dining room table, Mommy placed a small, worn Formica-and-chrome table and four chairs with peeling plastic seats and backs. Against one wall was a metal bookcase my mother used as a china closet. I think all of that furniture came from the Salvation Army. She made do in a small, windowless kitchen, cooking dinner every night on a very tight budget.

Money had always been a problem, but now we were in dire financial straits. I did not know why. One memory is particularly vivid. My father took us on a most excellent weekend road trip to the New York State Fair—an inexpensive but wonderful vacation. I had finally outgrown my winter coat, and any hand-me-downs, which I would have gladly put on my back, were too worn. We went to a department store basement, cheaper than the main floors, where I tried on a coat with a fur collar. I loved it. But my father told me we could not afford it. As we left the store, I began crying on the street.

Shortly after the shopping trip, I overheard my father on the phone with a bank. He was anxious, stuttering, practically begging for a loan. I was overcome with shame that I had cried about a stupid coat. I would not make that mistake again. Hearing his desperation made me understand all too quickly the stress my father had been facing. I tucked that in my mind, vowing that when I was an adult, I would never be in such a financial bind and that I would never allow my parents to suffer that fate again either. One day I would shower my mother with luxuries like a nice dining room set and a genuine china closet with glass doors.

For tenth grade, I started at my new high school, one of eight hundred students at Blair High School in Silver Spring, Maryland. Though the school was integrated, the student population was mostly white. There were some minorities, but I didn't know them or anybody. It didn't matter to me because throughout school, most of my friends were white, anyway.

Fortunately, I met Laurie Gates, who lived in our apartment building. She was a nice, tall teen with frizzy blond hair. We walked to school together, and through her I met Nancy Sorrells, an all-American blond with sweet written all over her face. Nancy and I glued ourselves to each other throughout our years at Blair—literally walking the halls shoulder to shoulder.

Every Friday night, my father drove Nancy, Laurie, and me to Teen Club at the Nolte Recreation Center, a classic record hop where a DJ spun music of the day. The boys were shy or didn't know how to dance the Lindy or jitterbug, which left the girls to partner with each other. Nancy would take the male role, allowing me to take the female role. One night when a guy named Jerry asked me to jitterbug, I almost keeled over. He was outstanding. Oh boy, I thought, this guy can really do the Lindy—can't wait for the next time. Never happened. I assumed it must be because I was Chinese or because I was too skinny.

So be it. If I did not have a male dance partner, I'd conquer a different extracurricular activity: student government. After starting small as president of my homeroom in my sophomore year, I won the vice presidency of my junior class. In my senior year, I was elected to a position on the student government legislature.

For me as a teenager, participating in governing was fun, but what captured my attention was Walter Cronkite reporting about who was governing our country. Every night my parents had us stop whatever we were doing to watch Cronkite's *CBS Evening News*. I recall my father pointing out Nancy Dickerson, the first female reporter at CBS. Perhaps something subconsciously registered in my mind then.

We witnessed the Vietnam War on television, the first war Americans experienced on the small screen from the safety of our living rooms. I watched young male war correspondents crouched on the ground, dodging bullets, and thought how brave they were. Later I learned that a few students at my high school were joining their parents to protest the war and racial discrimination. I knew then that I would not be a participant in news. I preferred observing.

However, one day in particular is fixed in my memory, one in which all Americans found themselves emotionally involved. I was walking back to my homeroom after being inducted into the National Honor Society, a special certificate in hand, a rose and small ribbon pinned to my lapel. November 22, 1963. I heard a commotion in the hallway and people crying as we were hustled into our homerooms to hear our principal announce the shocking, unthinkable news over the public address system. Our young President John F. Kennedy had been shot and killed. I read and watched every account, every new detail. Who didn't?

And in 1964, during my senior year, President Lyndon Johnson signed into law the Civil Rights Act. At the time, I had no idea that important piece of legislation would have a huge effect on my life.

# CHAPTER 6

# Makeup, Beer, and Boys

I n the summer of 1964, after high school graduation, I met a new person in my mirror, thanks to the magic of makeup. My sister Maimie and I began experimenting with different products and eye makeup tricks. I filled in my eyebrows, drew a thick black line on my eyelid, and lined the lower part of my eye. Think raccoon. Suddenly my eyes popped! The transformation was miraculous.

My oldest sister, Josephine, helped me get my first genuine summer job, at the Interior Department, where she had worked. Riding with my father in his carpool to DC, I'd arrive bright and early every morning in downtown Washington. As a secretary in the public information office of the Bureau of Land Management, I was earning money to pay for my college tuition come fall.

I shared a tiny office with a rather old gentleman where I filed several stacks of paper in a small row of metal file cabinets. All day long, people came in and out of that closet-size room. The door slammed loudly. Finally I said to him, "Doesn't the sound of that door bother you?" He said, "Whaaaat????"

Up until now, I had dated only young Chinese men, most of whom had been born in the US to friends of my parents. We went to Chinese dance parties, where we were all...just friends. They were all nice, but I wasn't interested in any of them.

But at a gathering for summer interns at work, I met a handsome law school student from out of state, the first white American I had ever dated. Work was mundane but he wasn't. We had lunches and dinners, talking about government and politics—enjoying a great summer together. That is, until he casually mentioned he was engaged to a woman back home. I dropped him instantly.

Come fall, I was lucky enough to go to college at the University of Maryland, which had low tuition and easy admission standards. The running joke in those days was that if you lived in the state, all you needed to get in was a heartbeat. Now Maryland has transformed into a highly coveted institution, competitive with the best. I certainly would not be able to get in today.

Maimie, who was in her senior year at Maryland, drove us to the sprawling campus in the family car, a black four-door Ford Falcon. She'd park in one of the vast concrete parking lots on the fringe of school, and at the end of each day, we'd wait for each other to go home. When I did not have enough money to buy my books, my sister June came through for me. While her husband was traveling for the army, she was living with us to save money. She gave me a couple hundred dollars to buy used texts. I was so grateful.

Maimie and I had cut each other's hair, copying the style created by Vidal Sassoon that we saw in magazines. With a new hairstyle and makeup, I was ready for more than just classes. Quickly I discovered B&B: beer and boys. Curves took shape, thanks to the beer.

My favorite watering hole was the Rendezvous, or, as we students called it, the "Vous." I'd meet friends there to drink draft beer. Then we'd shuffle off in our Bass Weejun loafers coated with sawdust that littered the bar's floor. Even then, I was already trying to be like a guy and drink the boys under the table. I sort of pulled it off.

After my sister graduated, my father bought me my first car, a used putrid-green two-door Ford Falcon. Never mind that it was a clunker. I was thrilled. If I wasn't meeting the guys at the bar, I would go to the Student Union and play pool with other male buddies or join a girlfriend for a meal.

When I ran for a seat in the freshman legislature, I had to get creative. Others who were running represented their fraternities and sororities, but I didn't have money for the luxury of belonging to one. So how could I compete with students who had the might of these social powerhouses? Solution: I would represent my community—the commuters. Maimie and one of her girlfriends helped me silk-screen campaign posters. Using strokes as in Chinese calligraphy, we spelled out "Connie Chung for Legislature" and plastered them all over campus. I was playing the race card, which was terribly politically incorrect. But in those days, there was no such thing as PC.

My secret campaign weapon was a guy I was dating, Paul Savanuck, a Maryland sophomore who knew the ropes of campus politics. Paul had full lips and a sweet puppy-dog face. When he raised his eyebrows, they'd move high in the middle of his forehead so that they pointed down toward his ears, making him appear sympathetic and compassionate, which he was. He walked me around to his fraternity and to other Greek houses, where I delivered my campaign speech. Thanks to Paul, I won seats in the freshman and sophomore legislatures.

With my experience in student government, I found myself taking on a bold attitude. I cannot remember the specific issue, but I recall bucking the president of the sophomore class, saying out loud what all the student legislators were thinking—that he was "trying to pull the wool over our eyes." Whatever he was trying to bulldoze through the student legislature was wrong, and I surprised myself with my audacious pushback. I was no longer the little sister who just observed and stayed mum. Now I had gumption.

By popular vote of the frosh students, I was also crowned freshman queen. I had never been a queen before. College became what high school wasn't.

The keg parties at various frat houses were my introduction to raucous nights of dancing and drinking. When the live bands took their breaks, a DJ would play the Rolling Stones' "(I Can't Get No) Satisfaction," the Kingsmen's "Louie Louie," and everything from the Beatles. Unlike Paul, who would dance a subdued version of the pony, I was an exhibitionist, combining the jerk and the pony with a bit of the twist thrown in.

Toward the end of the night, the couples, all draped over one another, shuffled to "House of the Rising Sun" by the Animals. We all knew that when we heard the line "There is a house in New Orleans they call the Rising Sun…," it was time to crawl to the exit.

All this partying and all these extracurricular activities came with a price. My grades were tanking. I had started college as a biology major, only because I'd excelled in that subject in high school. But now I found the labs deadly boring. I switched to the business school. Since I was great in math, maybe I'd become an accountant, just like my father, minus the abacus. But accounting was a different animal. I tried it, but it didn't click for me. Even with the determined help of a classmate, I flunked.

As I was flailing around, wondering what career was in my future, all I knew was that I had to get serious and stop partying. My parents were not concerned. My father was still trying to make enough money to stay afloat, and my mother was back to helping my married sisters with their babies. They had their hands full.

My Texas girlfriend Carol Sama, whom I saw annually when she spent summers with relatives in New York, visited me in DC. I took her sightseeing, including a day on Capitol Hill. As we walked the hallowed halls I had toured before on student field trips, Congressman Seymour Halpern, a liberal Republican who represented Queens in New York, stopped us to introduce himself. Frankly, both Carol and I thought that was creepy, but we were courteous when he gave us his card.

This random encounter proved to be a turning point. The next summer, after my junior year, I needed a summer job, so I dialed the number on the card. I wound up going to work as a seventy-five-dollar-a-week intern in Halpern's office. This experience exposed me to a new world. My fellow interns were young brainiac nerds from Harvard, Yale, and other Ivy League schools. Watching members of Congress as they conducted the business of government was a heady experience, like a brush with greatness on par with the sighting of a rock star.

Halpern, who happened to be a former newspaperman, assigned me to write press releases and briefing papers on issues. I watched reporters chasing members of Congress and grilling them with challenging questions. I could feel the pulsebeat of news events affecting the actions of politicians and Americans' lives. This was the world in which I wanted to live. I wanted to be a journalist.

What kind of journalist wasn't clear to me. My news junkie father had exposed me to broadcast news every night and three newspapers a day. But in the late sixties, as nightly newscasts started to become dominant news sources for the American people, newspapers were beginning to struggle. Writing for print did not come easily to me. I had always been more wired for the visual. As a kid, I'd painted Chinese watercolors, sketched buildings, and dabbled in photography. Combining the visual with verbal storytelling seemed a good fit for me. Television journalism was growing in reach and importance. I thought perhaps there would be more room for a female in the burgeoning industry of television news.

My switch to a journalism major in my senior year meant I had to attend college for an extra year. The good news was that another year gave me a chance to report and write a bit for the school newspaper and also to seek tips from the students working at the campus radio station. A part-time weekday job as a secretary at the Naval Ordnance Laboratory close to home helped me pay my tuition and contribute to the family finances as well.

My eyes were wide open. I knew every experience was helping to prime me for the future, including my first encounter with political malfeasance. After my summer internship with Congressman Seymour Halpern, I received an additional paycheck from the US Treasury Department. It was dated after my departure. I called Halpern's office and was told to cash the check and write one back to someone who worked for the congressman. This seemed mighty suspicious, so I asked my father what to do. He smelled a rat and instructed me to send the check back to the Treasury Department. Two weeks later, I received another paycheck. I sent that one back too.

Funny—if I had been working in the news business at the time, I would have salivated to break the story.

# CHAPTER 7

# The Doctor

It was the 1960s. I was in college, and the sexual revolution was in full swing. The exact date and year are fuzzy, but details of the event are vivid, forever seared in my memory. No matter how hard I've tried to bury it in the dark recesses of my mind, I cannot.

I was sexually molested by our trusted family doctor, but what made this monster even more reprehensible was that he was the very doctor who had delivered me on August 20, 1946.

I was a cool coed, dating whomever I wanted. I was still a virgin but had advanced to the so-called heavy petting stage, short of intercourse. I assumed I would become sexually active and would need protection from pregnancy, so I went to this doctor for birth control pills, an IUD, or a diaphragm.

The doctor practiced out of his home in the Georgetown section of Washington, DC, an exclusive, tony section of the city where the wealthy and well-connected lived. I drove there from our family home in Maryland, parallel parked on the street, and walked the cobblestone entry to the front door.

Like many of the homes in the area, his was a creaky old structure. The front door opened to an entryway, a staircase, and an antiseptic smell. To the right was a sitting room, where patients waited on worn Victorian velvet-covered furniture. I sank into an armchair that needed a new cushion, my arms resting on doilies. The windows were covered with old lace curtains.

Off the sitting room was a door to the basement, where the doctor's wife spent her days. When we were kids and Mommy took us for regular checkups, she'd motion to us to greet the doctor's wife. She would smile back, meekly, from behind her Coke-bottle glasses, always seeming a bit confused, especially in her later years. My mother would shake her head and utter a Chinese version of tsk-tsk, adding under her breath, again in Chinese, "How sad."

That fateful day, I was alone in the waiting room. The doctor emerged from his office to the left of the front door. He typically wore a round headband mirror strapped to his forehead and a stethoscope around his neck. He ambled toward me with his gray hair and a kindly smile, his steps creating squeaks on the uneven hardwood floors.

He ushered me through large glass double doors covered with ruched curtains for privacy. The office was large, divided by a full-length curtain. Half of the room served as his office, the other half as his examination space. He drew the curtain, asking me to remove my clothing below my waist while he walked to his desk by the bay window. When I was ready, he entered the examination area and installed stirrups on one end of the cushioned exam table.

I had never had a gynecological exam before, nor had I seen

exam stirrups. It was all new to me, but I followed his instructions. I found it extremely odd to spread my legs and dig my heels into those cold iron stirrups.

Not understanding or knowing what he was doing, I stared at the ceiling. With his right index finger, he massaged my clitoris. Simultaneously he inserted his right middle finger in my vagina. He moved both fingers rhythmically, coaching me verbally in a soft voice, "Just breathe," he said. He mimicked the sound of soft breathing, "Ah-ah," and assured me, "You're doing fine."

Suddenly, to my shock, for the first time in my life, I had an orgasm. My body jerked several times. Then he leaned over, kissed me, a peck on my lips, and slipped behind the curtain to retreat to his office area.

I did not say a word. I could not even look at him. I quickly dressed and drove home. I may have told one of my sisters. I don't remember what she said to me. I certainly did not tell my parents, and I did not report him to authorities. It never crossed my mind that reporting him could protect other women. I was in my twenties and knew nothing about sex, embarrassed at my naivete. All I wanted to do was bury the incident in my mind and protect my family. I told my mother that the doctor lived too far away for us to see him. She did not drive, so she was fine if I chose someone else to take care of us.

I kept my dirty little secret to myself until many years later, when I told Maury. Was it before or after we were married? I don't remember. I just wanted him to know. He was appalled.

Five decades later, #MeToo was born thanks to the superb reporting of Megan Twohey and Jodi Kantor of the *New York Times*, along with Ronan Farrow's story for the *New Yorker*. That prompted my experience to rush to the front of my mind.

## Connie

On October 3, 2018, I broke my silence, publicly.

At age seventy-two, I found myself in the hospital with a broken collarbone from a fall caused by a severe reaction to a new medicine. As I recovered, I was held captive by the drama unfolding on a squawking television: the gavel-to-gavel coverage dissecting the nomination of Judge Brett Kavanaugh to the US Supreme Court.

A college professor named Christine Blasey Ford had testified before the Senate Judiciary Committee that the nominee had sexually assaulted her when they were teenagers. Her testimony was wrenching to watch. Kavanaugh's vehement denials appalled me. Reading the reaction to her story in newspapers and online, I was offended by how many did not believe her. Her detractors pointed to her inability to remember certain details of the assault. I, too, could not remember the day, the season, even the year of my assault.

What we women remember is what happened and who did it to us. In fact, we never forget. We can see the scene perfectly. I wanted the public to know that minuscule details were not important. I hoped I might sway any doubters with whatever residue of credibility I had from my long career of telling the truth and reporting the news.

I had already written a draft of the account because I had begun writing this book. But I was not sure if I wanted to take the big step of revealing something so deeply personal. In journalism, the golden rule is never to become involved in a news story. We do not take sides. We do not express our opinions. If we do have an opinion, we ignore it. We must get all sides of the story and report them evenly. We never cross the line!

Though I was no longer working in the news business at that time, I still abided by the canons of journalism. I talked it over with Maury. He urged me to sleep on it for a night or two. But I couldn't sleep. I'd wake up scratching out barely legible notes, using my writing hand that was barely functional because of my broken right collarbone.

I asked Maury to bring my laptop to the hospital, determined to tap out my story. I went over it with him and then emailed it to my dear sister-in-law Lynn, who was a senior editor of *Newsweek* and editor in chief of *Working Woman* magazine. Both of them had only minor suggestions. I checked with our longtime devoted family lawyer and dear friend to make sure I would not get myself in any legal trouble.

My open letter to Christine Blasey Ford appeared on the editorial page of the *Washington Post* on October 3, 2018. After recounting what I've just shared with you, I continued:

> I think the doctor died almost 30 years ago in his 80s. I've driven past his home/office many times but refused to look at it. Just yesterday, I found the house on Google Maps. Seeing it again, I freaked out.
>
> Christine, I, too, am terrified as I reveal this publicly. I can't sleep. I can't eat. Can you? If you can't, I understand.
>
> I am frightened, I am scared, I can't even cry.
>
> Will my legacy as a television journalist for 30-plus years be relegated to a footnote? Will "She Too" be etched on my tombstone instead? I don't want to tell the truth. I must tell the truth. As a reporter, the truth has ruled my life, my thinking. It's what I searched for on a daily working basis.
>
> Christine, I know the truth, as you do. Years ago, my husband read a novel by Rita Mae Brown called

"Six of One." He told me, "There's a great line in this book. 'The advantage of telling the truth is you don't have to remember what you said.'"

I wish I could forget this truthful event, but I cannot because it is the truth. I am writing to you because I know that exact dates, exact years are insignificant. We remember exactly what happened to us and who did it to us. We remember the truth forever.

Bravo, Christine, for telling the truth.

After the op-ed appeared, I was surprised at how many people wrote to me about their incidents. But the call I'd never expected came from one of my sisters. She said the same family doctor had molested her, years before my incident. She, too, had not told anyone, including our parents. All I could think was, "How terrible for her." My husband took it another way. He said he wished she had protected me by making sure I did not go see that doctor after what had happened to her.

Later I learned how this man came to be our primary care physician. Apparently, people at the Chinese embassy in Washington had referred him to my father. One of my sisters believed that many embassy employees went to this doctor for medical help too. How many other women had he abused? Now, of course, I regret not reporting him to authorities. The doctor is dead and gone, but I can still see his face as hard as I try to erase it.

Sometimes I wonder if that incident served to toughen me up so that I could handle any blatant sexual situations. I was no longer naive in that department. I was plenty naive about a lot of other matters, but I experienced a rude awakening.

In telling my story, I crossed the invisible line I had assiduously avoided my entire career. Shielding my personal thoughts and biases, especially in my news reporting, was crucial to my credibility. Never had I joined a so-called movement. My journalism had to be pure, free of any taint.

But with that *Washington Post* op-ed, I became a participant in the news. I felt, with more conviction than ever, that members of the Senate Judiciary Committee who were about to vote on the confirmation of Kavanaugh needed to be persuaded to vote against him. Since I was no longer working in the news business, I felt free to even call the senators who were still wavering on which way they would vote.

You know what happened. Kavanaugh was ultimately confirmed to a lifetime appointment to the highest court in the nation.

CHAPTER 8

# "You'll Never Make It in This Business"

"Beat the June crunch." That's what a journalism professor told me the semester before I graduated from Maryland.

"In June," he advised me, "there will be a flood of graduates applying for their first jobs. Before you graduate, get a part-time job for a semester to get your foot in the door. Then when you have your diploma, you'll already have your feet planted in the newsroom as your competition is knocking on the door." It was the best advice any college student could receive. Armed with my thin résumé and no experience, I made the rounds of all the local television stations in DC.

It was January 1969, a propitious time for me to seek a first job in television news. The Equal Employment Opportunity Commission had been one result of the 1964 Civil Rights Act. Groups advocating for women and racial minorities were loudly demanding equality in the workplace. Corporations were beginning to hear the persistent drumbeat and heed the calls to diversify their staffs.

At the time, I didn't think about the fact that I was a double minority, but no doubt it was a unique time for a young woman who was Chinese.

Eager and determined, I plotted my plan of attack. The four local Washington TV stations were in the same neighborhood of northwest Washington. Three of them were affiliated with the networks CBS, NBC, and ABC. Metromedia Channel 5 was an independent station.

First stop: I barged into the Channel 5 newsroom. I daresay no one could do that today—they'd be arrested at the front door. I asked to speak with the news director, who turned out to be a young blond man, Mike Buchanan. He didn't have an office, so I sat with him at the assignment desk in a big bustling newsroom with the staff of reporters, writers, and editors working around us. Despite never having worked in the news business, I boldly touted my energy and willingness to learn. "I will do anything!" I pleaded. "I don't have any experience, but I am a fast learner! Just let me come help two or three nights a week as I finish my last semester in college." I was loud and boisterous—everyone in the newsroom could hear my pitch. But Mike told me he did not have any openings for me.

Undaunted, I moved on to the next station, the CBS affiliate WTOP-TV.

There I met with Jim Snyder, a much more formal news director, in his office. He resembled comedian and talk show host Steve Allen but appeared more serious. He was not only the news director at the TV affiliate but the head of news for all the Post-Newsweek Stations, which were owned by the *Washington Post*. Snyder had enjoyed notoriety in Washington news circles for hiring one of the first Black anchors on local news and launching the tremendously successful all-news WTOP AM radio, the station I always listened to in my car. Knowing that, I had brought along an audiotape of a radio newscast I'd recorded at the campus radio station, WMUC, as my lame attempt at an audition tape.

When he played the tape of my mini newscast, he declared, without a moment of hesitation, "You'll never make it in this business." Yes, my tape was that bad.

For some reason, he gave me a grunt job anyway. I was assigned to work the graveyard shift two nights a week, helping out on the radio side. The hours were lousy, but my foot was in the door.

I took the job and completed my first eight hours overnight. It was deadly boring, and it was odd to go home as the sun was rising, but I was happy to have made my entry into the world of journalism.

The next day I received an unexpected phone call. I picked up, still a little loopy from the lack of sleep, and was surprised to hear the voice of the blond news director I had met the day before—Mike Buchanan at WTTG-TV Channel 5. He cheerfully told me, "Everybody in the newsroom got a collection going after you left. They want me to hire you...so you're hired! Come in two or three nights a week after classes."

What had I done or said in my pitch to endear myself to the staff? I wasn't about to ask. Mike was offering better hours, so I quit my overnight job and scurried off to my new position as a copy person. I didn't know what that meant—but it didn't matter. I was so driven, I just knew I could prove Jim Snyder wrong. No matter what he said, I was determined to make it in the news business.

Every time I saw Jim over the course of our careers, he laughed, remembering his prophetic assessment of my career potential. The higher I climbed, the more he beamed with pride.

## CHAPTER 9

# Channel 5 Family

I ntoxicated with my future in journalism, I sprinted into WTTG-TV Channel 5 thinking I could actually hear the staff cheering, "Hire that girl, now!" What better launching pad could I have imagined?

Mike Buchanan turned out to be the perfect mentor, an old-fashioned gumshoe reporter happy to teach me his trade. When a story broke, I marveled at how he galvanized all of us in the newsroom to a fever pitch in pursuit of it. His thirst for news was infectious.

Mike was as wacky as John Belushi. Once he jumped on the assignment desk and stripped down to his skivvies. Why? Did it matter?

Later he left management and went back to his roots, becoming the best police and crime reporter in the city. It was Mike who broke the story that John Hinckley Jr. had shot President Reagan because of Hinckley's infatuation with Jodie Foster. And it was Mike who uncovered the fact that local basketball star Len Bias, picked for the Boston Celtics, had died of a cocaine overdose.

After classes, two nights a week, I went to my job as newsroom "copyboy." In that era of newswire machines, stories from around the world came to newspapers, television, and radio stations from news-gathering companies: the Associated Press, United Press International, and Reuters via big, black, loud-clacking, free-standing teletype machines that spit out the latest news on cheap scrolls of paper twenty-four hours a day. I ripped the wire copy off the machines and stabbed them on nails in the wall under signs marked, "NEWS," "SPORTS," "WEATHER." If urgent breaking news crossed the wires, I'd tear off the copy and rush it over to the anchors, reporters, or writers.

Everyone at Channel 5 was surprisingly willing to nurture and guide me and offer me valuable advice, even though I was just a gofer—as in "go for" coffee or anything else they told me to fetch.

The head of Metromedia News, Ed Turner, was a corporate executive who cared about journalism and who would often deliver rapid-fire rallying speeches to the newsroom troops. Just below Ed in management was Tom Maney, the burly general manager at Channel 5. He had a big smile, smart suits, and a hearty hail-fellow-well-met demeanor. Every executive was a white male with a liver that could withstand lots of liquor. Even the Channel 5 lawyer was a red-faced, freckled, tall Irish redhead who could outdrink *Mad Men*'s Don Draper on a bad day.

The nightly news broadcast, *The Ten O'Clock News*, was anchored by a popular team of white men: Alan Smith, who diligently wrote much of his own copy; John Willis, who had a smooth, dulcet voice; Fred Knight, a friendly weatherman; and Maury Povich, a young, tall, dark, very handsome sports director with rapid-fire delivery and a devilish personality.

Ah. Maury Povich. He was well known and popular, son of the legendary *Washington Post* sports columnist Shirley Povich, who was revered in the nation's capital. From noon to two, Monday through Friday, Maury also coanchored a successful live daytime talk show called *Panorama*, must-see TV. It was a classic meaty talk show that featured news; interviews with politicians, members of Congress, authors, novelists, and biographers; serious issues; and light cooking segments with Julia Child. Because it was a Washington talk show, politics dominated the program, especially during the unfolding drama of Watergate, when the acrimony spilled into live debates. When one member of Congress leveled a charge on *Panorama*, another would demand to appear with a counterattack. From their offices on the Hill, congressional staffers tuned into *Panorama* as religiously as they watch cable news live in those same offices today.

The format gave birth to political punditry as we know it today. Maury is rightfully proud that he first put on the air such notable reporters as David Broder, Haynes Johnson, and Juan Williams of the *Washington Post*; Wolf Blitzer, then a young, unknown reporter for the *Jerusalem Post*; *Time*'s Bonnie Angelo; the *New York Times*' Richard Reeves; political journalists Jules Whitcover and Jack Germond; Nixon's Pat Buchanan; the *Los Angeles Times*' Jack Nelson; syndicated columnists Roland Evans, Robert Novak, Cal Thomas, Jack Anderson; and countless more. (I know my list is endless, but I want to give Maury his props.) These commentators offered viewers solid, fair analysis—not the combative, vitriolic, partisan opinions television news offers today.

Viewers loved Maury's unpredictability and mischievousness. He was like Peck's Bad Boy, the fictional character created by humor journalist George Wilbur Peck. Maury's coanchors on *Panorama* were John Willis from *The Ten O'Clock News* and a revolving door of women. For a time, the woman was Barbara Howar, a tall, thin, saucy southerner with a mouth that never stopped—perfect for a talk show. Barbara had befriended LBJ when he was president and had become a Washington socialite. She was living and playing the part of a "social X-ray" even before Tom Wolfe coined the term in *Bonfire of the Vanities*.

When I delivered Maury's wire copy to his desk, I was lucky if I got a thank-you or a nod. Surely, he could talk to me a little bit, like everybody else? No, he was strictly business. I couldn't help but notice he was happily married with two adorable daughters who sometimes came to the station to hang out or appear on his talk show. His lack of communication didn't bother me, though. There were plenty of single men in the field. Since I was free and sassy, I lived by the old maxim: "So many men, so little time." Besides, I was more focused on work than on love.

Susan Olney was the only woman reporter at Channel 5. A pioneer in local news, Susan had a solid reputation as a reporter who scooped other reporters, thanks to her sources at DC's city hall. She was a pistol of a woman, not even five feet tall, with a pretty face and a wide smile. As an experienced reporter, Susan became a big sister to me. It wasn't that Susan gave me advice. I simply watched her and admired her as an example of a woman who had made it. She had battled with the boys for years and made her mark, commanding their respect. If she didn't get it, she'd tell them off with salty language.

The executive producer of *The Ten O'Clock News*, Stan Berk, I called my "rabbi," the man who took it upon himself to mold me into a good reporter. His claim to fame was creating *Evans & Novak*, which starred syndicated columnists Roland Evans and Bob Novak.

With no makeup person at Channel 5, Stan asked me to apply pancake foundation to their faces. I bit my tongue and reluctantly did it. Years later, in social situations, Roland Evans would tell anyone and everyone, "Connie used to put on my makeup." I'd grimace and wish he'd get over it.

These were the days of film that had to be developed in a darkroom—before the luxury of videotape, which could be rewound and viewed instantly. Channel 5 employed two couriers on motorcycles to grab the film just shot in the field and speed it back to the newsroom to be developed, then edited in time for the news.

If the couriers were swamped, I became the designated messenger, scooting out in a four-door Ford sedan that looked like an unmarked police car. As a fill-in, not only did I learn how to navigate the streets of DC, I also absorbed an eye-opening taste of life in neighborhoods that were nothing like the crimeless white neighborhoods where I had grown up. For the first time, I saw the other side of Washington, DC, the underbelly, the depressed areas of the city. I found the stark sight of poverty that was gritty and sad. Murders, burglaries, the aftermaths of fires, shabby housing, schools in dire need of repair had been alien to me. At the time, I did not know I would spend the next three decades reporting about the sordid side of life all around the globe, from Bangladesh to Natchez, Mississippi.

One night, I was reading the wire services, as I always did. A young local man from Baltimore, Maryland, had been killed in Vietnam. To my horror, it was Paul. Paul Savanuck, my first boyfriend in college. He had dropped out and joined the army as a journalist, a writer for *Stars and Stripes*. I had always feared that he was unhappy about our breakup and had left college for that reason. Now he was a fatality of war. I was devastated. It was the first death in Vietnam of someone I knew very well. The Vietnam War suddenly hit home.

*Connie*

When I graduated from Maryland in June, the only job Mike Buchanan offered me was as a newsroom secretary. That's the way it was in those days. Men were not relegated to secretarial duties—it was women's work, commonly called pink-collar jobs. I took the offer anyway, confident I could parlay this nothing job into something better. Since Channel 5 was such a small, scrappy operation, I'd have to fill in on the assignment desk from time to time—listen to the police radios and watch for breaking news. I was determined not to be pigeonholed.

There was one lazy reporter who'd balk when I'd call him on the two-way radio and ask him to check out a story. One time, exasperated with his unwillingness to work, I asked him, "How about if I cover the story and you come in to watch the assignment desk?"

He was fine with that. I was thrilled. I wrote the story for the anchorman to read. Mike, my boss, wasn't pleased about my unilateral decision. But he couldn't help but notice how aggressive and hungry I was.

Another time, it was the worst allergy season Washington had experienced. I was asked to find out more about it and write a story for the weatherman. I wrote something like "a weed that won't give you a high—it will give you a sneeze." The weatherman, Fred Knight, smiled and said, "I really like this, Connie, it's clever!" Granted, it wasn't Hemingway heaping praise on me—nonetheless, it was an attaboy that encouraged me.

A few months after I started as newsroom secretary, a position opened for a writer for anchorman Alan Smith. Alan could have been the model for Ted Baxter on *The Mary Tyler Moore Show*. I could hear him clearing his throat in his office, practicing his lead out loud: "Hah-rumph. Good evening. Hah-rumph. Good evening," he repeated. Did I want to write for him? Of course! With his deep voice, he'd make my copy sound good. Besides, this was a step up the ladder.

The head writer, Tom Slinkard, a pipe-smoking, fast-writing worker bee, had been allowing me to write stories for the anchormen here and there. Under his tutelage, I'd learned enough about how to write news copy to apply for the job. When I asked Mike to hire me as a writer, he was blunt. He still needed a newsroom secretary, someone to replace me. That was my cue to come up with someone I thought would satisfy the ongoing pressure to hire women and minorities.

I ran across the street to the bank where I cashed my paycheck every two weeks. I always went to the same teller, Toni Taylor, a sharp, smart, pretty, young Black woman who could count out my measly wages in a flash. "Toni," I said, "do you want to be a BIG star at that TV station across the street?"

She did not hesitate: "Yes!"

I dragged her across the street to meet Mike. He hired her as newsroom secretary on the spot. And I moved up! Later Toni rose to become a producer.

When Mike allowed me to become a writer, it paved the way for the next step, to reporter. I kept nagging him to promote me. He gave me a few tryouts on *The Ten O'Clock News*—and after only a few months of writing, he relented.

There I was on June 1, 1970, with only two years in the news business, signing my first television contract as an on-air reporter for $300 a week, a little more than $15,000 a year before taxes. It was a three-year deal. The second year, I'd get a twenty-dollar-a-week raise, and then I'd get another twenty dollars a week the third year. I was so happy, I probably would have done the job for no pay.

Channel 5 seemed like a graduate school in broadcast television. My favorite "class" was film editing. Not a surprise since I tilted toward the visual. I wanted to learn everything about it. Now that I was a reporter, I had my chance. Editors Denzil Allen, a handsome man whose hair was beginning to thin, and Joe Rizzo, a fuzzy-haired, fuzzy-bearded sweetheart who years later became news director, were more than willing to show me their craft. After covering a story, I'd view the film on a Moviola to choose sound bites. They would hang the film strips by their sprocket holes on wire hooks, then splice the sound bites on an "A" roll and pictures on a "B" roll. You've probably heard the term "B-roll." That's its origin. But I will stop there because I assume you are getting bored.

I soon learned the art of marrying words to pictures. TV reporters do not need to describe what the viewer is seeing, such as the batter stepping up to the plate. They need to give information that may not be obvious to the eye, like "His first at bat surprised fans and even his teammates." Choosing the pictures in addition to the sound bites was part of the storytelling. Some reporters left producers to make the visual choices for them. Not me. I was obsessed with sitting beside the editor and producer, choosing sound bites and shots, even down to how many frames and whether to dissolve or cut from one shot to the next.

I began covering stories all over DC, working sometimes six days a week, and always on Saturdays. Often members of Congress held hearings or released information on Saturdays, because weekends were slow news days, which would guarantee coverage on television news and in the Sunday newspapers.

My early days covering Capitol Hill presented golden opportunities for me to rub elbows with political notables in Washington, from Massachusetts Senator Ted Kennedy and Wisconsin Democratic Senator William Proxmire (whose signature mission was eliminating wasteful government spending) to Supreme Court Justice

William O. Douglas. I covered Justice Douglas's hike on the Chesapeake and Ohio Canal with his young, pretty, blond wife Cathy to draw attention to preserving the canal. They were known around town because people were curious about Douglas, at sixty-seven having married Cathy as his fourth wife when she was twenty-three. She became a lawyer and their marriage lasted until he died at age eighty-one. Incidentally, Douglas was the longest-serving justice in the history of the United States Supreme Court.

I created relationships with political figures that proved invaluable to me during the Watergate years—from the iconic North Carolina Democrat Sam Ervin, who sealed his name in history as chairman of the Senate Watergate Committee, to Maryland Congressman Larry Hogan, the first Republican to break from his GOP colleagues on the House Judiciary Committee and vote for the first Article of Impeachment of President Nixon.

I even got to meet President Richard Nixon. In June 1971, members of the White House News Photographers Association were meeting with the president to celebrate their anniversary. The gathering was what was called, in White House parlance, a photo op. Our Channel 5 news crew, which would normally be posted at the White House briefing room, was out covering another story and could not join the Oval Office event.

Channel 5 was entitled to two passes. Anchorman Alan Smith and I were the only ones in the newsroom at the time, so Mike, our news director, pointed at us to go. I leaped at the opportunity! How exciting to stand in the Oval Office and meet President Nixon. Afterward the White House press office sent me a photo of the president shaking my hand. But John Yuro, my archival producer for this book, contacted the Nixon Library and discovered an even better photo from that day in the Oval Office. I am standing next to

President Nixon, who must have said something that caused everyone to look my way. Everyone else in the shot is a white male.

\* \* \*

Since I was a cub reporter, inevitably I'd be sent to do stories no one wanted, often on the "women's beat." One of the first stories I was assigned for *The Ten O'Clock News* was on Asian influence on fashion. I was told to go to a local department store and "model" the clothes. I grudgingly did the story. Being young, green, and grateful to have a reporting job, I simply did not feel I was in a position to object, as degrading as it was. I longed to be like Channel 5 reporter Susan Olney, so tough and seasoned she could avoid such silly stories.

"I hate fashion stories," I vented in an August 1971 *Newsweek* article on the "New Crop of Female News Reporters." I continued, "Give me a tear-gas, rock-throwing riot anytime." (I had covered many anti–Vietnam War protests by then.)

It was the first time I hit the national scene in print. At only twenty-five, I wanted to be sure anyone who read the article knew where I stood. The story pointed out that despite the inroads women were making in local TV news, many of us were disparaged as "house chicks" and relegated to fluff.

Michele Clark, a Black reporter in Chicago, said, "Some males have an ingrained belief that there are certain things a woman cannot do or understand." Michele was later hired by CBS News around the time I was hired.

Veteran Nancy Dickerson, who paved the way for all of us, was quoted too: "Every station in America feels it must have one Black and one woman." She was right. Channel 5 had one Black reporter and one woman reporter when I arrived. The problem was executives hired the obligatory "one of each" and were "done."

But by far the most important quote in the article was from a television executive who summed up the roadblock women faced. Reuven Frank, then president of NBC News, told *Newsweek*, "I have the strong feeling...that audiences are less prepared to accept news from a woman's voice than from a man's." More than a decade later, in 1983, Reuven Frank proved himself wrong by hiring me to anchor the Saturday *NBC Nightly News* and *NBC News at Sunrise*.

It seemed impossible for me to break out of the women's fashion beat. Stan, the executive producer, asked me to do an hour-long special, airing in prime time on Channel 5, on the frivolous controversy over the lengths of women's skirts: mini versus midi. I was just too appreciative that he was keeping me on his front burner to say no. Again, I relented.

I spruced the story up with some well-known people, Barbara Walters and First Daughter Tricia Nixon, who both agreed to be interviewed. And, I thought, maybe I could lure the outspoken wife of Attorney General John Mitchell, Martha, to do an interview? She loved cameras and was famous for lacking a filter. Surely, she would utter something quotable. I sneaked into the Mitchells' exclusive apartment building in the Watergate complex and boldly knocked on their front door. The maid answered, graciously taking my card and a letter I had handwritten to Mrs. Mitchell. When Mrs. Mitchell called and said yes, I was surprised and delighted.

Barbara Walters met me at the south entrance of the White House. It was the first time I had ever seen her in person. She wanted to chat with me about my interview before scheduling our sit-down. Barbara was already on NBC's *Today* show and well known for it.

Her limousine rolled up. We slid in, my first time in a stretch. Her assistant sat in the front passenger seat, rattling off questions, diligently jotting down notes as Barbara batted back answers, machine-gun style. I was taken aback. Barbara seemed so business-like, responding in a rat-a-tat rhythm, "Yes," "No," "Next?" It was like a scene from an old Rosalind Russell or Bette Davis movie: a woman executive barking orders to an underling. I thought to myself, "If I ever get to that point in my career, I'm going to throw in a lot of pleases and thank-yous."

On June 12, 1971, First Daughter Tricia Nixon was to have a fairy-tale wedding in the White House Rose Garden. It was hardly a surprise when I was assigned to that typical women's page story. On a bandstand on the South Lawn, I stood with microphone in hand in front of the glorious backdrop of the White House South Portico. Never mind that I could not see the Rose Garden from my position, and neither could any of the other reporters. To "describe the event," we had to use handouts from the White House Press office. What a joke! That was not what reporting was supposed to be. That was my first encounter with White House press manipulation, which every administration employs.

*   *   *

Several nights a week, after the newscast ended at 11:00 p.m., the Channel 5 gang made a beeline to Alfio's, an Italian restaurant across the street from the station, to unwind over drinks and din-ner. My favorites were clams casino and veal française with capers and lemon. I had never had either in my Chinese home. I graduated from the beer I'd downed in college to gin and tonics. Since I didn't have to be back to work the next day until 2:00 p.m., I could sleep it off.

Just about every one of the veteran cameramen, soundmen, and electricians at Channel 5 was kind and patient, showing me the ropes. But one cameraman, Billy, took every opportunity to tell me I had no business being a reporter. He was constantly berating me, telling me how wrong or green or stupid I was. I doubted myself because he was a talented cameraman. I took his criticism to heart, thinking maybe he was the only person telling me the truth. Perhaps he was right that I did not belong.

It was only as I was leaving Channel 5 for a new job that I realized what his real issue was. The gang threw a farewell party in the newsroom. Billy, a slight, wiry man with bushy dark hair, stared at me intensely. Fueled by alcohol, Billy gave me "the look." I could see the sperm swimming in the whites of his eyes. His long nose was pointing at me like a golden retriever's, his thin body shaking as dogs do when they are determined to chase a bird. It was easy for me to scamper away, the way squirrels outrun old dogs.

This was the first but not the last time a man in the news business would give me a hard time, then later put the make on me. I call that "he either wants to f*ck you or f*ck you over syndrome."

I did not dwell on it because one of my last stories at Channel 5 had opened the door to my next job, which launched my national career. I did a report on unsanitary conditions at Washington restaurants, including Le Provençal, an exclusive French eatery where power players lunched. When I barged into the restaurant with a camera crew to confront the owner, there sat CBS News Washington Bureau Chief Bill Small having lunch. Impressed with my doggedness, he gave me his card. Small later told author Sheila Weller, "Connie called twenty minutes later after I got back to the office. I hired her, and she became one of the most terrific reporters we've ever seen."

And so, my wildest dreams turned into reality. That's next.

CHAPTER 10

# CBS: Connie's Big Start

On October 1, 1971, I jumped into an ocean, having barely learned to tread water. I had been in the news business all of two years and on the air as a reporter for only one of them. Yet I was hired by CBS News, the most prestigious nationwide television network, led by the most trusted man in America, Walter Cronkite, the television anchorman I worshipped. Since no women anchored hard news, I had chosen Cronkite as my role model. I wanted to be just like "Uncle Walter," as he was known across the nation, the man my family and millions more tuned in to watch religiously every evening.

The Columbia Broadcasting System (CBS) was an empire created by William S. Paley, who was described by the *New York Times* as the personification of "power, glamour, allure and influence." He and his fashion icon wife, Babe, were the darlings of New York high society.

Paley was still chairman of CBS when I arrived at his doorstep. It was a thrill to meet the pioneering figure and his legendary right-hand man, Frank Stanton, president of CBS, who championed First Amendment rights on behalf of the entire television news industry. Whenever Washington tried to interfere in what television news was reporting, Stanton would eloquently testify on Capitol Hill, a stalwart defender of freedom of the press. I had only read about these legends in newspapers, and now I was working for them.

These were the glory days of broadcast news. CBS was called the Tiffany Network because it established the gold standard in entertainment *and* news. That's because Paley created a ratings juggernaut in prime time with shows that hauled in the money, like *I Love Lucy*, *Gunsmoke*, *All in the Family*, *Playhouse 90*, and *The Jack Benny Program*. He once told the CBS star correspondents at a dinner, "Don't worry about that"—meaning cost. "I've got Jack Benny to make money for me. You guys cover the news." Paley's shows provided the profits. His news division gave him prestige.

How did I get to plant my feet in this wonderland of respected journalists, where my idol Walter Cronkite was the lovable, trusted king? It was a dream that came true because of timing, a connection, and who I was—a woman and a minority.

Let's start with the Civil Rights Act, signed by President Lyndon B. Johnson on July 2, 1964, "the most sweeping civil rights legislation since Reconstruction," as the National Archives put it. The act outlawed discrimination in hiring because of race, color, religion, sex, or national origin. It also created the Equal Employment Opportunity Commission (EEOC) to hear grievances and to correct them.

Aspiring women writers at *Newsweek* magazine, including my future sister-in-law, Lynn Povich, took advantage of this new opportunity to redress inequities in their workplace. They were fed up with being relegated to jobs as researchers while men with the same experience were hired as writers, reporters, and editors—and, of course, paid more. As researchers, the women gathered the information only to turn their hard work over to the men who would write the stories. The most frustrating barrier for Lynn and the other women was that they were barred from ever being promoted.

In March 1970, Lynn and her fellow researchers met secretly in the ladies' room, hired a lawyer, and filed a class-action complaint with the EEOC. The sixty women who signed the complaint won a huge victory that ultimately led to Lynn's hiring as *Newsweek*'s first woman senior editor in 1975. She later wrote a book, *The Good Girls Revolt*, about the groundbreaking *Newsweek* case.

Women at *Time*, *Fortune*, and *Sports Illustrated* followed *Newsweek*'s lead, filing complaints the same year. Widespread news coverage goaded companies across all industries to rectify years of discrimination against women in the workplace. Even on Capitol Hill, the stodgy US Senate upended a 150-year tradition and hired females as Senate pages for the first time since 1820.

CBS News executives knew they needed to bow to civil rights groups and women's pressure groups. Washington Bureau Chief Bill Small was one of the first to take preemptive action.

Bill was a tall man with a quiet voice and hunched shoulders. His posture reminded me of a popular television host from my youth, Ed Sullivan. I was nervous as I arrived at his office with my résumé. But I shook it off with my spunky attitude: "Yes-I-don't-have-a-lot-of-experience-but-I-learn-quickly." Small asked me to write a short newscast to deliver from a tiny studio. Emerging after my momentous audition, I found him laughing out loud, guffawing at my amateurish delivery. Despite that, he hired me. I don't know how that was possible, but I was one happy person. If this job turned out to be the one and only job I ever had, I would be just fine. I had hit the jackpot.

At about the same time, CBS News diversified in one fell swoop, quickly hiring three other women in every permutation and combination: Michele Clark, a Black woman, based in Chicago; Lesley Stahl, a nice Jewish girl with blond hair joined me in DC; and Sylvia Chase, a gentile with blond hair in New York. We were a quartet of "affirmative action babies," as Lesley called us. Those old guard goats at CBS News probably thought, "Phew, we are *done*." Indeed, it wasn't until a full decade later that CBS hired a new wave of female on-air reporters.

For me, every day was a test. Would I measure up? My being a woman was a bigger challenge than my race. I wanted to be accepted and treated just like my male colleagues when we all covered the male-dominated world of politics at the White House, Capitol Hill, the Pentagon, and the State Department. Everywhere I looked, there were men. Since I wanted to fit in, I *became* one of them. In my mind, I could walk like them, talk like them, and be as tough as they. Why should I perceive myself differently?

How did the women who'd preceded me navigate the boys' club? It was complicated for me; I couldn't imagine what it was like for them. Still, it never occurred to me to call them and ask for their wisdom. I admired Barbara Walters; NBC's Pauline Frederick, the premier United Nations correspondent; ABC's Marlene Sanders; and Nancy Dickerson, the first female correspondent at CBS News. But who had the time? I assumed they were overloaded doing *their* all-consuming jobs. I myself was overwhelmed, trying to keep my head above water.

I was on the job only five days when I made my first appearance on the *CBS Evening News with Walter Cronkite.* It was October 15, 1971. I was sent to cover a congressional hearing that was not expected to be newsworthy. The surgeon general had recommended using phosphate detergent even though it would pollute the environment. But at the hearing, his subordinate dropped a surprise on his boss, directly contradicting him. That was news.

As I rushed from Capitol Hill to the bureau, my heart was racing. Fortunately, Bob Meade, the evening news producer assigned to work with me, was calm, but we both knew there was no time to waste. We were on deadline.

Bob and another producer, Don Bowers, chain-smoked and joked about sex. I thought all their sexual innuendos were funny, and I cheerfully played along—topping them with sassy, badass replies. There was nothing sinister about their banter, nor mine. Today, some would probably find it inappropriate in the workplace—but honestly, in those days, it was normal and cut the deadline tension. As we worked together, it was clear they were helping me hone my reporting, writing, and producing skills. They knew I was green, and they genuinely wanted me to succeed. I didn't care about the remarks. I cared about my work and the final product.

Bob viewed the film and recommended a structure for the minute-and-fifteen-second story. I broke a sweat as I sat down at one of the manual typewriters in the newsroom, trying not to panic. Anxious, I couldn't think clearly to write my script. "*I can do this,*" I assured myself. When I looked back at that script as part of my research for this book, I was shocked! I had written: "Should *housewives* ignore the danger to the environment and use phosphate detergents?" Oh my word! Sure, it was 1971, but was I really thinking like a Neanderthal? Only women—"housewives"—use detergent? Shame on me.

I was about to go to a small studio in our CBS News building to record an on-camera portion of my story when I was stopped by the producer, Bob Meade. My shoulder-length hair was tightly hair-sprayed into a bun, an attempt to look older and more serious. Bob suggested I take the bun apart and wear my customary teased flip. I am convinced he thought that since it would be my first exposure on national television, I should not look like Marian the Librarian. He may have envisioned I'd pull one bobby pin from my head and give my head a shake and my hair would fall to my shoulders in sexy slo-mo, a cascade of soft curls, just as in those L'Oréal commercials.

It was the first and the last time anyone suggested what I should do with my hair or clothes. Thank goodness, because I would not have taken kindly to that. Yet it was common for viewers to scrutinize a woman's appearance on the air, while men were allowed to be bald, fat, and ugly!

Our story done, I settled into a chair in the newsroom. Every night, all of us in the CBS Washington bureau would gather to watch Walter's newscast together. Cronkite's nightly newscast started with what we called a ticker. The sound of the rat-a-tat newswire machine was accompanied by a baritone voice that announced, "This is the *CBS Evening News with Walter Cronkite.*" And as the voice intoned the name and location of each correspondent who would appear that night, the name was typed on the screen as if on ticker tape. It was a thrill that first night when I saw and heard, "Connie Chung in Washington." I was only twenty-five years old. After my story aired, everyone in the newsroom applauded, even the star correspondents. How sweet it was.

That moment was a short honeymoon for this cub reporter. Bill Small fostered a climate of competition among the correspondents, encouraging us to compete not only against every other network and print reporter but also against each other. The team was unparalleled, intimidating as heck, and brutal. It was every man for himself. The head of CBS News Radio said, "His [Small's] team at CBS is considered second only in the annals of broadcast news history to Edward R. Murrow and the 'Murrow Boys' who invented the profession in World War II." That was a daunting bar for me to clear. I was over the moon to be among that vaunted group. But it was no easy street. According to television news legend, at NBC, the stains on the industrial carpet were just coffee, but at CBS, the stains were blood.

Small created a caste system, a hierarchy. At the top were star correspondents with important beats and big egos. Daniel Schorr was a take-no-prisoners, rumpled investigative correspondent whose mouthful of teeth caused him to shower me with spittle when he spoke. Schorr covered Watergate along with Lesley Stahl, who uncovered countless stories from her Watergate sources but was forced to give him the information. On top of that, Schorr was rude to her, refusing to acknowledge her work.

Marvin Kalb, a tall, distinguished man, was our diplomatic correspondent, covering the State Department and national security. His brother, Bernard, also worked at CBS News as a correspondent but as a general assignment reporter. Even though Bernie was older than Marvin, it was Marvin who had more stature. Maybe the story was apocryphal, but legend had it that even the Kalb brothers' mother knew which son "mattered." She would call the office and say, "This is Marvin Kalb's mother. May I speak to Bernie?"

Roger Mudd, the chief Capitol Hill correspondent, was a longtime CBS News fixture, known at CBS to be the heir apparent to Walter Cronkite. He had a long face and gigantic feet and hands—and a good sense of humor. Occasionally I'd ask Roger for advice because he was down to earth and approachable. He was always kind to me, although there was some tension when we both were at NBC News in the eighties. I was assigned to coanchor a magazine program with him, after he started the magazine program solo. I could tell just by the expression on his face that Roger was not happy about adding me to the roster, but he was not rude about it. He was much more accepting of me than Dan Rather would be a few years later.

Then there were the White House correspondents, who could count on being on the air almost every night. Robert Pierpoint, known to be an intrepid, aggressive reporter, had been on the White House beat until Dan Rather unseated him as the top dog covering the president—pushing Pierpoint to backup man.

Rather was a tall Texan who was always the gentleman. He had made his mark covering Hurricane Carla in Texas, tying himself to a tree as wind and rain whipped around him. His dramatic coverage of the weather caught the attention of CBS News.

Years later, after many successful, impressive assignments at CBS, Rather was offered a job by ABC News. Using that as leverage, he was hoping to replace Walter Cronkite as anchor of the *CBS Evening News*. Even though Cronkite had privately told CBS executives he was ready to leave the "daily grind" of anchoring every night, the newsroom and industry scuttlebutt was that Cronkite was encouraged to step down to make room for Rather. When Rather replaced Cronkite, in 1980, he leaped over Roger Mudd, who had long anticipated that seat would be his. The next year, Roger left CBS for NBC.

Meanwhile, we cub reporters, including Bernard Shaw, a Black reporter who joined Lesley and me in the Washington bureau, were just peons next to those star correspondents. We did not have offices, only small mailbox cubbies with no place to put our research files. We were forced to scrounge for a chair, telephone, and manual typewriter in the main newsroom in order to do our jobs. Eventually we were treated to the type of desk we'd used in grade school, where the desk is attached to the chair. These were placed in a back hallway, one in front of the next, just as in a schoolroom. A CBS News correspondent dubbed us "Minority Row" and complained that fried chicken, knishes, and egg rolls were ruining the neighborhood.

I was often asked to keep a seat warm for a beat reporter while the "star" went out to lunch or did who knows what. I did just that at the White House for Rather, the State Department for Marvin Kalb, the Pentagon for Bob Schieffer, and Capitol Hill for Mudd. I always hoped that news would suddenly occur on my watch—and that I'd be allowed to report it on Cronkite's news program. Unfortunately, that never happened. Always, I had to brief the star and turn the story over to him. That was called being "big-footed." I was imprinted with many wing-tipped footprints.

As far as I was concerned, Walter Cronkite could walk all over me anytime he wanted.

After just a few months on the job, I met my idol for the first time when he came to anchor the *CBS Evening News* from the Washington bureau. I felt as if I were meeting the pope. Seriously. He was such a giant in broadcast news, employees brought their families to watch him live, from just a few feet away. Afterward he circled the room, graciously shaking everyone's hand, asking questions of the children. He was kind, warm, friendly, down to earth, and never intimidating. His chuckle was better than Santa Claus's.

Walter Cronkite was a straight-talking, responsible newsman.

He radiated gravitas and humility, never behaving like the superstar he was. He was just plain nice.

Walter was also generous. If he thought I did a good story on his news, he would call me that night after he was off the air and give me an attaboy. Or he'd type a note on his manual typewriter and send it to me through interoffice mail—from New York to Washington. I prized the note I received in 1976 regarding the resignation of President Ford's campaign finance committee chairman, David Packard.

*Dear Connie,*

*Congratulations on the clean beat on the David Packard resignation. That's the kind of stuff that makes us all look good and for that deep gratitude.*

*Come up 'n see us sometime,*
*Walter*

And I did visit Walter if I was in New York, any chance I got. I loved my job. I felt incredibly privileged to be at CBS News and didn't want this ride to end, always hoping Bill Small had my back. After all, I was his investment. And I was investing in my future as an independent earner as well. No one—not my parents nor any husband—needed to take care of me. It felt good.

Despite my fear of screwing up and getting myself fired, every day I was determined to prove myself worthy, working long hours six or seven days a week. I was on top of the world.

# CHAPTER 11

# Good Girl/Bad Girl

L ike so many working women in the 1970s, I strove to be the good
girl, the Goody Two-shoes. I listened earnestly and obeyed the
orders of my superiors or those who supposedly knew better. As if
being female weren't enough, I was also Chinese, meaning that in me,
CBS got a double dose of obedient, respectful, and dutiful.

However, there was another side of me that the men did not antic-
ipate, that left them puzzled. I was like the girl Henry Wadsworth
Longfellow described in his poem "There Was a Little Girl":

> *When she was good,*
> *She was very very good,*
> *And when she was bad she was horrid.*

Well, maybe not horrid. Let's say snarky.

The devil-may-care baddie (who sat on my left shoulder) would taunt the goody (who placed herself on my right shoulder) for being stuffy and urge her to say anything that popped into her head. But the good girl resisted because she knew better.

The good journalist diligently did her job. Men in politics and government at the White House, Capitol Hill, the Pentagon, and the State Department would size me up from head to toe and greet me with a look as if I were an ice-cream cone or a little china doll. Newsmakers I approached for interviews often toyed with me. When I caught up with Nixon's Attorney General John Mitchell on Capitol Hill, he said as cameras rolled, "You look just as pretty as ever." Did he expect me to smile and thank him? I was there to do my job and proceeded with my questions. Same with Secretary of State Henry Kissinger. As I approached him with my microphone in hand, he'd flirt. There was little I could do or say to avoid those creepy old men.

But if I *knew* the men, I was the sassy bad girl. Before the dude could toss a sexual innuendo or racist remark at me, my modus operandi was to lob a preemptive strike. I did it to him before he could do it to me. The male would be so darn shocked, he'd laugh nervously. I am not saying my approach is advisable, but I owned it, and soon those who dealt with me knew that I could get to the bad side—faster, better, and funnier than they could. It worked. They would not mess with me when I was willing to offend first, then laugh it off.

If a man made a play for me, subtle or overt, I looked him in the eye and dismissed him. A swift "In your dreams" or blunt "Don't even think about it." "You are out of your league." "You must be hard up." A serious, quizzical "Really?" shut it down.

Never would I run to the ladies' room crying and shaking. A toughie, I determined there was no crying in news, just the way, years later, Tom Hanks shouted at his all-female team in *A League of Their Own*: "There is no crying in baseball!"

Maybe someone can figure out if being the only Asian reporter was a help or a hindrance. I still don't know. There was no doubt that the racism I experienced was as reprehensible as the sexism. Those who called me "dragon lady" or said to me, "You *slant* the news" or called my reporting "*yellow* journalism" thought they were so clever. Even men I knew would allude to my being Chinese, thinking it was funny. One referred to me as "OSE"—"Ole Slant Eyes." Another asked, "Where are you staying? Is it near Chinatown?"

At daily White House press briefings, an Episcopal priest, Lester Kinsolving, would shout outlandish questions at the press secretary from the back of the room. He worked for various small newspapers but was considered a pesky gadfly.

One day, as I sat in the White House press room, Lester asked me, "Is it true what they say about Asians?"

I snapped back with remarkable haste, "Is it true what they say about priests?"

I don't know what "they" say about Asians or priests but it didn't matter, he was speechless.

Whether it was sexism or racism, I'd beat them to the punch with a self-deprecating joke. One time, CBS News Bureau Chief Bill Small said to me, "Tell them why I hired you." I don't know what possessed me to reply quickly, "You like the way I do your shirts." Bill laughed uproariously. He repeated that story for years.

My approach to these derogatory remarks was the only way I could handle them at the time. It was tiresome and insulting, but I lived with it. If I'd obsessed about the issue, I could not have done my job.

My mother, Mah Pih-liang, in 1930s China. *(Author's personal collection.)*

My father, Chung Ling Jai-pao, in 1930s Shanghai. *(Author's personal collection.)*

Chung family at Glen Echo Park in suburban Washington, DC. Left to right: Dad, Mom holding Connie, Maimie, Charlotte, Josephine, and June. 1947. *(Author's personal collection.)*

Chung family gathered for a Christmas celebration. Left to right: Josephine, Charlotte, Maimie, Dad, Mom with her hands on Connie, and June. 1948. *(Author's personal collection.)*

Toddler Connie with red nail polish (!) holding Christmas stocking. *(Author's personal collection.)*

College student on campus at University of Maryland. 1969. *(Photograph by Mike Rosoff.)*

Working as a copy person for Washington's Metromedia station, WTTG-TV Channel 5. 1969. *(Photograph by Thaddeus A. Miksinski Jr.)*

Covering First Daughter Tricia Nixon's Rose Garden wedding on White House South Portico lawn. June 12, 1971. *(Author's personal collection.)*

All eyes, including President Nixon's, on Connie in the Oval Office. June 16, 1971. Discovered by researcher John Yuro. *(White House photo courtesy Richard Nixon Presidential Library and Museum, Yorba Linda, CA.)*

Questioning 1972 presidential candidate Senator George McGovern. Signed: "For Connie who never took no for an answer…" *(Author's personal collection. Photo Still from CBS Photo—Courtesy of CBS Broadcasting Inc.)*

With CBS News Washington Bureau Chief Bill Small, who hired me as national TV reporter on Cronkite's news in October 1971. *(Photo Still from CBS Photo—Courtesy of CBS Broadcasting Inc.)*

Chance encounter with President Nixon outside the West Wing during the Watergate scandal. October 18, 1973. *(White House photo courtesy Richard Nixon Presidential Library and Museum, Yorba Linda, CA.)*

Covering President Nixon's trip to Egypt in 1974. Pyramid and tape recorder over my right shoulder and notebook at the ready. *(Author's personal collection.)*

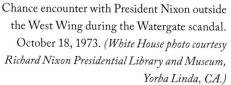

With my role model, Walter Cronkite, on Nixon's Middle East trip. Signed: "…so when you get to 35,000 feet just level it off…and you ought to be okay." Walter had a great sense of humor. 1974. *(Author's personal collection. Photo Still from CBS Photo—Courtesy of CBS Broadcasting Inc.)*

Covering Nixon's trip to the Middle East. June 1974. Why does that young Saudi Arabian man have his hand on his hip… *(Photograph by Dennis Brack.)*

…And why are these three guys mimicking me too? *(Photograph by Dennis Brack.)*

Interviewing President Gerald Ford. Center: New Jersey Congressman Peter Rodino. December 1974. *(Photograph by Karl H. Schumacher for the White House. Image courtesy the Gerald R. Ford Presidential Library.)*

Interviewing my favorite politician, Vice President Nelson Rockefeller, aboard Air Force Two. June 1975. *(Photograph by Jack E. Kightlinger for the White House. Image courtesy of Rockefeller Archive Center.)*

Covering the congressional hearings into the impeachme of President Richard M. Nixon. July 1974. *(Photograp by Dev O'Neill. Courtesy of th U.S. House of Representatives Photography Office.)* #mood

Maury and I coanchoring the news for KNXT-TV in Los Angeles. It was a short pairing on air, but our marriage is still going strong! *(Photo Still from CBS Photo—Courtesy of CBS Broadcasting Inc.)*

My parents at my apartment in Los Angeles. 1980. *(Author's personal collection.)*

With CBS executive Gene Mater and CBS President Frank Stanton. *(Photo Still from CBS Photo—Courtesy of CBS Broadcasting Inc.)*

With CBS Chairman and CEO William S. Paley in the KNXT-TV newsroom in Los Angeles. *(Photo Still from CBS Photo—Courtesy of CBS Broadcasting Inc.)*

*To Connie Cheung: With best wishes and thanks for what I hope turns out to be a good interview. William S. Paley*

*NBC News at Sunrise with my favorite and best executive producer, Gerry Solomon. (© by Marianne Barcellona.)*

President Ronald Reagan and Vice President George H. W. Bush at White House State Dinner for Chinese Premier Zhao Ziyang. January 10, 1984. *(White House Photo Courtesy Ronald Reagan Library.)*

In those early days at CBS, I was often saddled with light features and women's stories like an art exhibition, toy safety at Christmas, and new orangutans at the National Zoo. I lumped it, figuring that's what reporters had to do to earn their stripes. But there was something about covering a dreaded First Lady Pat Nixon nonevent that made all reporters, including the men, cringe. The guys refused, but I didn't have the chutzpah to turn down an assignment.

Somebody *had* to cover First Lady events as protective coverage—just in case something happened. She was a nice lady, but she had a stiff, fixed smile, as if she was the long-suffering political wife which she was. Would anything she was doing really make news?

Eager to make something of what I knew was nothing, I would think of a question that might elicit a comment. Unfortunately for me, Mrs. Nixon would reply with a pithy sound bite. My reward? I was sent to cover her again and again.

On December 1, 1971, the First Lady went Christmas shopping with her daughter Julie, three months before the president's historic visit to China. I asked Mrs. Nixon about her plans for the trip. She revealed that a friend had been teaching her Chinese. That bit of "news" made it onto Cronkite's broadcast that evening.

About two weeks later, Mrs. Nixon gave reporters a tour of the White House Christmas decorations. Naturally, I was sent to cover it. I asked her to say something in Chinese. She laughed. "Oh no. You're an expert. I don't dare practice in front of you." I pressed on, graciously but insistently. She demurred again.

What precipitated Nixon's extraordinary China trip was a simple exchange of table tennis players between the two superpowers. Those matches were known as "Ping-Pong diplomacy"—games that thawed relations and created a breakthrough in talks with China. I did not ask to cover the visiting Chinese Ping-Pong players. I was assigned to cover them, probably because I spoke Chinese.

But later, I was also assigned to cover the arrival of the Chinese pandas at the National Zoo, a gift from the People's Republic of China to the US. Why did that story end up in my lap? The possibility that the pandas might understand my Chinese was not likely.

When it came time for President Nixon's historic trip to China, *This time*, I thought, *how about if I do to them what they did to me? I will play the race card*. I pushed to be sent. My pleas were for naught. Too many CBS News executives were shamelessly angling to get their names on the trip manifest. The *Washington Star* newspaper in DC even noted the absurdity of my absence, saying CBS was "the only network with a Chinese American correspondent, Connie Chung, [who] would seem to be a natural choice, but apparently she was shanghaied somewhere along the line."

I watched on television as Nixon opened the doors to China after two decades of Cold War isolation. I could not help but chortle when President Nixon made an all-too-obvious comment as he stood before China's Great Wall and declared, "I think that you have to conclude that this is a great wall."

The president's success in normalizing relations with China had more of a personal impact on me than a professional one. My father had not been able to write to our relatives in China for more than twenty-five years. My parents did not know who was still alive. Letters flowed again, but my parents kept what they discovered to themselves, probably because none of it was good news.

\* \* \*

While China and diplomacy were left to experienced CBS correspondents, I was frequently sent with a camera crew on what were called "stakeouts," in which I'd ambush someone with questions while cameras were rolling. I begrudgingly did what I was asked, even though I agreed with CBS News State Department correspondent Marvin Kalb, who took me aside one day and said, "Stakeouts are *not* reporting." They were all about nabbing a sought-after interviewee, catching him off guard, and confronting him with a question he had been avoiding. It was known as "gotcha journalism." Mike Wallace of CBS's *60 Minutes* perfected gotcha moments in which his victims would squirm.

I was assigned to "get" Deputy Attorney General Richard Kleindienst when his nomination for the top job at the Justice Department was thrown into doubt over an antitrust deal.

One day, after his confirmation hearings were gaveled to a close, I ran outdoors to link up with a camera crew. I asked Kleindienst three questions. Each time, he answered with a version of "I don't wish to comment," all the while smiling, chuckling, and laughing.

Not content with his nonanswers, the crew and I gave chase on a raucous ride ten miles out of Washington to suburbia and the Burning Tree Club in Bethesda, Maryland. When Kleindienst ran into the golf club's front door, I was right behind him, following on his heels. The door slammed behind him, right in my face.

Undaunted, I burst into the lobby of the club. Much to my surprise, I was unceremoniously ejected. I felt like a character in a Bugs Bunny animated cartoon being bounced out the front door, tumbling and rolling in a ball, head over heels, down the driveway. I thought I was being booted because I was an inquiring reporter. But the actual reason was that the club was the exclusive domain of men. Burning Tree remains men only to this day.

The next day, I was once again poised to question Kleindienst, this time outside the hearing room. I was pleasantly surprised when he stopped and calmly answered every question I asked. Cronkite was mighty proud of my exclusive. That night, the *CBS Evening News* ran three long minutes of my interview, prized real estate on the broadcast.

I always thought Kleindienst stopped to answer my questions because he wanted to reward my doggedness. Maybe not.

Some fifty years later, at our yearly lunch, Lesley Stahl, my buddy from those CBS News days, remembered that Kleindienst interview completely differently. Lesley said she vividly remembers watching my first Q and A on television with the rest of us in the CBS newsroom, when he laughed off my questions. She believed Kleindienst knew he was seen unfavorably by the public and felt compelled to rectify his behavior the next day by cooperating with me instead of blowing me off. Lesley said it was a rude awakening for all male interviewees that they had to take *all* reporters seriously, including and *especially* female reporters.

There were two stakeouts with gruff old men who couldn't have cared less whether I was a man, a woman, or an aardvark. The powerful union leader, AFL-CIO President George Meany, was trading barbs with President Nixon. I chased him into an elevator with a hand microphone still physically tethered to the camera crew as the door closed. The cameraman, soundman, and electrician were stunned as Meany and I rode the elevator, just the two of us. Undaunted, I still questioned the labor leader, hoping the cameraman was still rolling on a closed elevator door. Unfortunately, the humorless Meany mumbled something unintelligible.

My other grumpy old man interviewee was FBI Director J. Edgar Hoover, who was famously reclusive in the face of the media. Still, every year he would emerge from his fortress at the

FBI building to appear before a congressional committee to make his budget request.

Because there were rumors that Hoover might retire, I was sent to accost him with cameras rolling. As he left Capitol Hill, I asked, "Director Hoover, are you planning to retire?" He answered with a simple sentence: "The wish is father to the thought." Taken aback, I repeated, "Yes, but are you planning to retire?" Without a pause, Hoover retorted, "I said the wish is father to the thought, and that answers your question." The camera crew and I looked at each other somewhat puzzled but chuckling. That night, Hoover and I appeared on Cronkite's *Evening News*.

With Washington stories dominating Walter Cronkite's *Evening News*, I was covering every burp and hiccup in government and politics. It was a privilege to know and interview people who were making history before my eyes. As I worked to develop trust with members of Congress, I hoped they would become sources and give me scoops. Those relationships became career-long bonds: with Republican House Minority Leader Gerald Ford, who later became President of the United States; with Senator Ted Kennedy, the best-known almost-candidate for president; and with my favorite, Michigan Democrat Philip Hart, a thoughtful, honorable, respected senator known as the "Conscience of the Senate." He took me seriously, which I could not say about all the men on the Hill. I could always depend on him for everything from an unbiased analysis of an issue to background explainers.

Bureau Chief Bill Small was sculpting me into an experienced reporter who would cover every story and subject necessary. One day I would be covering a congressional hearing on drunk driving; the next day baby crib deaths; the next passage of a foreign aid package or budget bill. I covered complicated economic issues, trade legislation, and the intricacies of diplomatic and foreign policy. I was a jack-of-all-trades, master of none, as the phrase goes.

Small even chose me to question newsmakers on the highly respected Sunday interview program *Face the Nation*. When I was a kid, my family had spent Sundays watching the interview programs— NBC's *Meet the Press*, ABC's *Issues and Answers*, and *Face the Nation* on CBS. I had always thought veteran correspondents were chosen for the three-person panel, so I was honored each time I was asked to appear on *Face the Nation* to question the likes of Vice President Nelson Rockefeller, Agriculture Secretary Earl Butz, Senate Majority Whip Robert Byrd, and Ford Campaign Chairman Howard "Bo" Calloway.

Despite my covering important stories, including the forced resignation of Vice President Spiro Agnew, machinations of the Nixon and Ford White Houses, secret bombing raids in Cambodia, and anti–Vietnam War and antibusing demonstrations, there was one producer in the Washington bureau who always made me feel as if I did everything wrong. I knew I had a lot to learn, but surely, I was not the failure he made me out to be. This man would quiz me every morning to see if I had read the *New York Times* and *Washington Post* from cover to comics. If I told him I had not seen a particular story, he'd rip me apart for being ill prepared even if it was an insignificant story.

His behavior was classic hazing, and still, I hoped one day I would meet his approval. Years later, when I was working in Los Angeles, he was in town and asked me to dinner. I wondered why he would ask me to join him and quickly realized what his MO had been. It was the old "he either wants to f*ck you or f*ck you over syndrome." He put the make on me but didn't press it, thank goodness. I was surprised but wrote it off for what it was.

The truth is that the hazing probably worked to challenge me into clearing the high bar Small had set for me. I put my nose to the grindstone, demanding excellence of myself. Those formative years laid a foundation for me, one in which I learned how to be a journalist from the CBS masters of the craft, covering important, serious, significant national and international news.

I knew the good girl could succeed, as long as I could curb the enthusiasm of the sassy one.

CHAPTER 12

# Three-Martini Lunch

E ven though I was just a cub, Bill Small plucked me for a plum
assignment—covering a presidential campaign in 1972. I was
truly shocked to be tapped because a presidential election was the
Super Bowl of politics. Reporters who covered presidential candidates
had tickets to every game, shadowing the quarterback and even sitting in on huddles. Only leading correspondents were entrusted with
covering the race for president because if the candidate made it to
Pennsylvania Avenue, the reporter might be crowned White House
correspondent, a ticket to news stardom—not that I thought that
shiny beat was remotely possible for me. I was part of a team covering McGovern. Two veteran male television correspondents hovered
above me. I was the third banana, assigned primarily to CBS Radio.

Still, I couldn't believe I was getting a beat usually reserved for
experienced political reporters. I presumed the boss wanted me to
get my teeth into some red meat. I devoured the opportunity.

Make no mistake—it wasn't as if I were assigned to cover someone who was actually expected to *win* the Democratic nomination, let alone the White House. The candidate I tailed was Senator George McGovern of South Dakota, considered the *least* likely to win. Whoever the Democrats chose would face the daunting Republican incumbent, President Richard Nixon, fresh off a major foreign policy feat: reestablishing relations with China. Off I went, living out of a suitcase for one long year, chronicling McGovern's fledgling campaign. It was exhausting but exhilarating, one of my best years as a reporter.

McGovern was the son of a Methodist minister, a tall, awkward, and self-effacing man. He was neither a dynamic speaker nor a political persuader. Rather, he often sounded as if he was whining. He did not have an engaging personality, yet he enjoyed an extremely passionate following. As a liberal, antiwar candidate, he galvanized vocal supporters by promising, if elected, to bring all US soldiers home from Vietnam. That polarizing war was an issue that created a vulnerability for Nixonites. They tried to dismiss McGovern, neatly packaging his supporters as far-left hippie radical peaceniks who smoked dope and dodged the draft. Both political parties underestimated how much the divisive public sentiment for and against the Vietnam War would drive the 1972 election.

CBS spent money galore on coverage for a full year before Election Day, sending out with the candidate not only three-person film camera crews and producers but three reporters.

Often the leader of our pack was CBS News political correspondent Bruce Morton, a quiet, cerebral man—a writer's writer. Newspaper reporters thought television reporters were glamour boys, but Bruce was exempt from that derision. They respected his intellectual insight and could tell he wasn't just a show horse—he didn't act like one. I felt inferior in Bruce's presence, probably because I assumed he thought I was a dumb kid. Years later when I ran into Bruce, he said, "I am a fan." I was surprised, and immensely flattered.

If Bruce wasn't covering McGovern for CBS News, correspondent David Schoumacher was the designated lead. He had a deep, booming voice and a walk that looked like a waddle. Yet he possessed a macho confidence and a laugh that made him charming. In his memoir, *The Place to Be: Washington, CBS, and the Glory Days of Television News*, CBS News correspondent Roger Mudd revealed something I had never known: that Schoumacher had been asked by our boss, Bill Small, to take me around to "train" me. Instead Schoumacher told Mudd, "I found her on the phone behind my back selling [pitching] stories to the *CBS Evening News*."

Oh dear, that was verboten. I suppose I was a tad too aggressive. We cubs were supposed to pass any information, including story ideas, to our big bear correspondent. But I was quite hardheaded and driven. I sulked at being "big-footed" just because I was less experienced. Why should I bow to his seniority?

Today I am amazed that I had the audacity to believe I deserved equality with the veterans when I had been at CBS less than a year. Oops.

While Roger noted in his book that my aggressiveness was not overlooked, he described me this way: "Most of the men got along with Chung, because she had a robust sense of humor and was not afraid to play their game. Chung says she played the game because, 'I was trying to get rid of them so I could just do my job. They were always chasing me.'" Mudd continued, "But she was also easy to work with. She was smart enough to say, 'I need help.'" And in asking for help, I got a lot of it.

As the third-string correspondent, I rarely got any airtime

on television. Only occasionally I'd appear on Walter Cronkite's *CBS Evening News* or the *CBS Morning News*. Radio was my responsibility.

How I transmitted my radio reports to New York was old-school broadcasting. I would record my report on my Sony tape recorder. My favorite radio producer, Lane Vernardos, gave me a professional Electro-Voice microphone that made everyone sound like Walter Cronkite. I'd use a regular old-fashioned telephone so I could unscrew the mouthpiece. Inside were prongs that I attached to small leads or wires like jumper cables that attached to my Sony recorder. Phone lines magically transferred my report. Pay phones were very difficult to unscrew. Often I would borrow a large wrench from a radio reporter pal to open the darn thing.

We campaign reporters were like a band of brothers, spending more time together than with our families. Being cynical sorts, we were happy to pass judgment on the campaign family members we did not like. We tended to agree that two were especially insufferable because they took themselves much too seriously: R. W. (Johnny) Apple of the *New York Times* and Adam Clymer of the *Baltimore Sun*.

However, being surrounded by other veteran print reporters such as David Broder (*Washington Post*), Jack Nelson (*Los Angeles Times*), Jim Naughton (*New York Times*), Jack Germond (*Baltimore Sun*), Marty Nolan (*Boston Globe*), and Walter Mears (Associated Press) was, I felt, invaluable to my growth as a reporter. Their questions were intelligent and probing, their writing accurate and fair, their knowledge of politics vast.

Since I was a constant presence on the McGovern campaign, Lou Cannon of the *Los Angeles Times* and Bill Greider of the *Washington Post* and *Rolling Stone* magazine would look to me to give them background as they dipped in and out of coverage. That was mighty flattering.

Another veteran print person who followed McGovern from time to time was the great Mary McGrory, a genteel woman with gray hair and a thick Boston accent who was an exquisite writer and political analyst. I had read her columns for years in the *Washington Star* and later in the *Washington Post* and had long wondered how she managed to write such superb pieces.

While covering McGovern, she and I were often the only ones still working into the early-morning hours in the campaign press room. I didn't dare bother her. There, out of the corner of my eye, I caught a glimpse of her writing process. Mary toiled away for hours writing and rewriting on her manual typewriter. I yearned to look over her shoulder and ask what she was thinking, but I had the good sense not to interrupt her. Meanwhile, I was trying to just get something coherent down on paper that would be at least acceptable for the *CBS Morning News*.

Being a reporter came more easily to me than writing. I was always on my toes and never slacked off because I was too afraid I'd miss a story. Every morning, from whatever godforsaken town we'd spent the night in, I'd call the overnight assignment desk at CBS in Washington to find out what news had broken while we were sleeping. This was long before the internet and smartphones would give us the latest news at our fingertips.

My diligence did not go unnoticed. In Timothy Crouse's book about the adventures of the campaign press, *The Boys on the Bus*, he observed, "Few TV correspondents ever join the wee-hour poker games or drinking. Connie Chung, the pretty Chinese CBS correspondent, occupied the room next to mine...and she was always back by midnight, reciting a final sixty-second radio spot into her Sony or absorbing one last press release before getting a good night's sleep." The next morning, Crouse noted, I would be "bright and alert, sticking a mike into McGovern's face" with pointed questions, while the print reporters, after spending the night drinking, stood bleary eyed, listening, just in case McGovern should say something newsworthy.

Tim was right. I said to myself, "I will not engage in such debauchery." At the time, I haughtily thought, "Those reporters are just a bunch of drunkards."

But when I woke up, I'd discover the *New York Times* or the *Washington Post* had broken an important story. Someone from the McGovern campaign had leaked an inside story to a boy on the bus! How did one of those drunks get that story? Then it dawned on me. The reporters were drinking with lubricated McGovern aides who then spilled their guts. How stupid could I be?

So much for staying in my room. No more good girl tucked in bed early. I joined the boys in the bar, just as I had in college. Yes, that made it harder to get up bright and early the next day—but I was not going to miss a scoop.

Tom Oliphant, a reporter for the *Boston Globe* who wore owl-like glasses, distinctly remembers one of our many nights at the bar. Oliphant, one of the younger reporters, hired by the *Globe* fresh out of Harvard, described something I said as "by far the best comeback to a drunken stalker I ever heard in a saloon."

"This guy keeps trying to horn in on our conversation, standing right over you," Oliphant recalled when I interviewed him for my book, "slurring words and lamely trying to evoke something. Each time, you graciously ignored him. But eventually it got bothersome, and I was just getting ready to stand up and try to shoo him off when you gave him a truly disdainful gaze."

Oliphant recalled how I threw all caution and political correctness to the winds and he quoted me as saying to the drunk, "Look, you don't want to go to bed with me. You'll just be horny an hour later." Oliphant said, "There was immediate applause from the table, and the guy slunk off. From that instant on, you could never do wrong."

If the boys on the bus were perennially horny, I was perpetually tired and hungry. One of the rules of the campaign trail I quickly learned was to eat a big breakfast because it might be my last meal until midnight. Before bed, I'd fill out my breakfast order, checking "Orange juice" and "Steak and eggs," and hang it on the hotel doorknob. A hearty breakfast got me through the day.

The press flew on what was called the "zoo plane." We were the animals on our own luxurious plane with first-class seats front to back. The 747s were leased from Pan American World Airways (Pan Am) or Trans World Airlines (TWA), big airlines with wide-body planes that all no longer exist. My radio producer, Lane Vernardos, and I always grabbed the bulkhead seats right behind the bathroom and the pilot's cabin. That way, we could race off the plane first. I used my flight time to write news reports on my Olivetti manual typewriter.

As experienced and wise as I was becoming, I was equally naive and clueless. I didn't realize until I read Tim Crouse's book that people were smoking dope on our zoo plane with the infamous *Rolling Stone* writer Hunter S. Thompson. Surely, I could smell the grass? Nope.

\* \* \*

After a few months, I was beginning to feel as if the boys on the bus and McGovern's aides were finally taking me seriously. McGovern's press secretary, Dick Dougherty, was quoted by a *Newsday* reporter as grumbling about a male reporter, "That so and so. He's the Connie Chung of the male press corps." In his story, the *Newsday* reporter continued, "The reference was to CBS's Connie Chung, the beautiful China doll of the campaign, who has a reputation for asking tough questions." I didn't think I was beautiful, but I was beaming because the writer declared I knew how to ask good questions.

I was beginning to get my props as an old hand, as if I were just one of the guys. There was something called a "pool report." If the candidate was not allowing the entire press corps to cover an event, only a handful would attend. One reporter would write up a report to be shared with all the others. In his pool report, I was amused that Jim Naughton of the *New York Times* mocked a reporter new to the campaign for asking a question of the candidate. Naughton wrote, "It was Connie Chung's responsibility to thrust microphones into McGovern's face."

McGovern dragged us from city to city. The daily schedule was always the same—from 5:00 a.m. until after midnight. Meet in the hotel lobby, board the bus, board the zoo plane, land in a city, board the bus, watch McGovern deliver his stump speech, which we fondly called "The Three-Martini Lunch." Same speech, different city. We could recite it with him: "There's something wrong with a tax system that allows a two-hundred-thousand-dollar-a-year corporate executive to deduct the price of his three-martini lunch, when a working guy can't deduct the cost of his bologna sandwich." When McGovern wrapped up his appearance, we'd run to the press room, file our reports, get back on the bus, back to the airport, back on the plane. Groundhog Day.

When the press arrived in a given city, our luggage would be dropped off in a big room at whatever hotel we were spending the night in. McGovern's campaign logistics person, John Gage, would have all of our room keys in hand. As he shouted out our names, we would take our keys and retrieve our luggage to drag to our rooms.

"Connie Chung," John would bellow in a boffo radio voice. The male reporters would shout back, "Here, here, I'll take it!" "In your dreams," I'd snarl.

Once, on the McGovern campaign trail, I was talking on a pay phone in an old-fashioned booth at the Biltmore Hotel in Philadelphia. The booth had a folding door, a small attached seat, and a large, vertical black wall phone. I was talking to a fellow I had dated back home in Washington. (Yes, I did have dates here and there.) Two rascals—Jim Naughton, a short, nice-looking blond and a superb *New York Times* reporter, and Jules Witcover, a sharp, always-hungry-for-a-story reporter for the *Los Angeles Times*—approached my phone booth. Witcover always had a cat-that-ate-the-canary smile on his face. Together they barged in, pushing the door open as they pressed their noses into the booth. What did they want? I immediately assumed they were harassing me! Sexually harassing me like junior high school boys. What could I do to get rid of them? Sitting there, my eyeballs staring at their belt buckles, I swiftly pulled down their flies. They hightailed it out of my view.

For his memoir, CBS correspondent Roger Mudd called me to ask if that story was true—because Naughton and Witcover had both told him about it. To my surprise and delight, Naughton had told Mudd that I was up earlier and stayed at it longer than anyone else and was "always nosing about the campaign's edges." Witcover told Mudd he thought I must be working on a major story. Mudd wrote, "In an attempt to tease Chung about her intense work habits, Naughton says he and Witcover started mugging for Connie's benefit." Oh my goodness, I completely misread them. I suppose I was underestimating their view of my reporting and overestimating my sex appeal.

All the hijinks on the campaign trail were more fun than

annoying. We were a raucous bunch who enjoyed the competition and behaved like juvenile delinquents.

The celebrity McGovernites who latched on to the campaign made life even more engaging. Actor/director/producer Warren Beatty was a political junkie who often joined the traveling road show as the opening act. It was a good way for McGovern to attract more people into his tent. When Beatty showed up, it would cause quite a stir. The notorious ladies' man chased any skirt he could spot. But there were very few women reporters on the campaign trail. I was happy to flirt and joke with him, but I was determined not to succumb to his charms.

On one trip, Beatty brought his girlfriend, actress Julie Christie. She had just come off a string of notable movies, including *Dr. Zhivago* and *Darling*, for which she won an Academy Award. McGovern invited me to join them for dinner at his Maryland shore retreat on St. Michael's Island. I was the only reporter sent by any news organization to St. Michael's for what newspeople called the "death watch." CBS News preferred to call it "protective coverage" in case something happened to the candidate.

I was hesitant about the invitation. McGovern's wife, Eleanor, wasn't going to be there since she had not joined him on the island. It seemed quite peculiar—just the four of us. But I accepted, hoping he might reveal some information regarding his campaign. Maybe I'd get a scoop. Instead, I got an eye-opening experience.

We had a quiet, uneventful dinner. At one point, I excused myself to go to the guest bathroom. As I made my way back to the dining room, I encountered McGovern in a dark, narrow hallway. He stopped me and tried to kiss me. I was shocked. I stepped back. He quickly took the cue and stepped back too. It was not an aggressive act. Just a surprising one.

When I got home, I told the fellow I was dating at the time. He rolled his eyes. I told no one else. It never happened again. I was accustomed to a lot of talk, but very few men tried anything more, unless it was obvious that I was interested in them. That was the part that was puzzling to me.

The only other time something similar occurred with a prominent person was in the 1980s. I was seated at a black-tie dinner next to former President Jimmy Carter. At one point during the dinner, his leg and knee pressed against my leg under the table. I immediately looked at him. He smiled. Oh dear. This incident happened after President Carter had told *Playboy* magazine he had "looked at a lot of women with lust" and had "committed adultery in [his] heart many times." I think I saw that look.

Having a job that put me adjacent to power showed me that presidents and presidential candidates were just human beings with pimples and blemishes, flaws and foibles, who put their pants on one leg at a time. But at the same time, they possessed overblown egos and were just arrogant enough to believe they could lead the free world.

When McGovern returned home to Washington to keep up with his senatorial duties, I toddled back to my parents' home for R and R. Yes, I was in my midtwenties and still living with Mom and Dad. I was embarrassed that I had not gotten my own apartment, but I was always honest and did not keep it a secret. Everyone at CBS in Washington knew I was still living with my parents.

Meanwhile, Lesley Stahl, my CBS buddy, was a sophisticated single. She threw a party at her tony Watergate apartment in Washington, DC, which was filled with furnishings from her first marriage, yellow love seats and a bookcase lined with books and whatnot. She greeted me at the door in a slinky black dress. I felt like a child by comparison. When my dates came to pick me up (some were even bachelor members of Congress), they would drive to my parents' suburban Maryland home, forty minutes from Capitol Hill, where they were greeted by my father before I walked out the door with them.

While I was on the campaign trail with McGovern, my father suffered a heart attack. I rushed home. His health scare prompted him to retire from the federal government. From that moment on, at age twenty-six, I became my parents' parent. The transition was instant and dramatic. Suddenly I had become not just the breadwinner of the family but the emotional caregiver as well. My parents had become my children. Every payday, I'd hand over my check to my father so he could pay the mortgage and other expenses, just as my sisters dutifully had done. He insisted I put a small amount in a savings account. I didn't want to, but I did what he thought was best.

My sisters were neither able nor willing to help support our parents. They were out of the house and had built their own families and lives. I would have thought that since all four of them had been born in China and three were married to Chinese men, *fealty* of parents would be a big part of their DNA. Only after my father wrote them letters, noting that I should not have to carry the financial load alone, did one other daughter contribute a small amount each month and a son-in-law offer a monthly stipend to my parents.

Now I knew I absolutely could not screw up at my job and be fired. I needed my paycheck to support my parents and me. I felt the pressure and weight but proceeded on my career path with a vengeance. I was more focused, ambitious, and driven to succeed than ever. "Besides," I thought, "I'm single with not much of a personal life." I had to get back to work.

\* \* \*

I flew to Miami to cover my first Democratic convention in the summer of '72. Today, party conventions are coronations of the candidates, but back then, conventions could dissolve into contentious food fights. McGovern was the presumptive nominee, but he was too far left for the Democratic old guard. He needed to make a critical choice for his number two, picking a running mate who could bring the party regulars on board.

His first choice, Senator Edward Kennedy, was an adamant no. McGovern turned to two Senate colleagues, Connecticut's Abraham Ribicoff and Wisconsin's Gaylord Nelson. Both said no. McGovern settled on a relatively unknown senator from Missouri, Thomas Eagleton, who wasn't even on his short list. The trouble was that McGovern and his staff never asked Eagleton if he had any skeletons in his closet, not even conducting a quick background check. Big mistake.

The convention turned into a debacle. It was so poorly orchestrated that McGovern did not deliver his acceptance speech until three in the morning. I had been waiting with a camera crew all night to get a word with him as he left his Doral Beach Hotel room for the convention floor, but he rushed by me. Why was he in such a hurry? America was asleep. That was no way to launch a presidential campaign.

Only a few days after the convention, an anonymous tipster called McGovern's headquarters in South Dakota, revealing that a decade earlier, Eagleton had been hospitalized for "nervous exhaustion" and had electroshock treatments for clinical depression three times. Unlike today, depression was discussed in hushed tones. The revelation rocked the campaign.

Eighteen days later, McGovern dumped Eagleton.

McGovern was once again in search of a running mate. Senators

Hubert Humphrey, Frank Church, Gaylord Nelson, and Walter Mondale all said no before they could be asked. And Senator Ted Kennedy, again, made it clear he wasn't interested.

After I kept needling McGovern aides to tell me whom he had chosen, I learned that Maine Senator Edmund Muskie had been asked and had turned him down too.

Finally word came to CBS that the prospective choice was arriving in DC on a private jet landing at midnight. We suspected the passenger might be Sargent Shriver, husband of Eunice Shriver, President John F. Kennedy's sister. A CBS News crew and I staked out the air terminal. We knew that if there were any telltale black sedans with men in suits talking into their thumbs, that meant the Secret Service was in place to meet the person.

Sure enough, a small contingent of black cars pulled out of the terminal. We gave chase. Where were they going? We knew our city well and could see where we were headed—Arlington National Cemetery. When the cars stopped at the entrance of the cemetery, the gate swung open and closed before I could hop out and accost the car with the mystery man. The entourage disappeared into a dark hole.

Larry Windsor, who was working for McGovern, told me years later that he was in the lead car with the Secret Service. They warned him, "If we have to block Connie Chung and her CBS car, hit the floor!" Larry wondered what the Secret Service had in store for me. Me too!

We were successfully blocked in our tracks. The camera crew and I circled the cemetery, checking out the exits, but we still could not find the entourage. They must have slipped out a different exit. We lost them.

It was about one in the morning. If the passenger was Kennedy in-law Sargent Shriver, it made sense that he would go to the Kennedy gravesites at Arlington Cemetery. I asked the crew to go to Hickory Hill in Virginia, the home of Robert Kennedy's widow, Ethel Kennedy, to see if there were any lights on or any Secret Service cars roaming the grounds. Nothing.

So I came up with the harebrained idea of asking the crew to drive to the home of McGovern's good friends George and Liz Stevens. George Stevens was the son of famed Hollywood director, producer, screenwriter, and cinematographer George Stevens Sr. I knocked on the door at the outrageous time of 2:00 a.m. Remarkably, George answered. Out of either pity or amusement at my chutzpah or admiration for my ingenuity, George told me where I could find McGovern—at the town house owned by Henry Kimmelman, McGovern's head fundraiser.

The crew and I sped to Kimmelman's in minutes. I knocked on the door and was greeted by a smiling Kimmelman, who basically said with his eyes, "You've got a scoop, kid." He said, "Just wait a little longer and McGovern will come out."

Hours later, McGovern emerged at the front door. We shined a light and pointed a camera at his face. He told me Sargent Shriver was his new running mate. My mother watched my exclusive report on the *CBS Morning News* that morning and was mighty proud of my scoop but told me, "You look tired."

"But," I noted, "you could only see my hand, holding the mic." (The rest of my report was a voice-over.)

As only a mother could, she replied, "Your hand looked tired."

CHAPTER 13

# Watergate

O n what turned out to be a pivotal day in history, I was following candidate McGovern on the campaign trail in Buffalo
and then Albany. He ended his day downstate, in New York City,
where he met with Mayor John Lindsay. As we ran all over the state,
we had no idea that events taking place down in Washington, DC,
would alter the course of the nation.

At 2:30 a.m. on June 17, 1972, five men were wiretapping tele-
phones at the Democratic National Committee Headquarters in
the Watergate office building when a security guard, making his
overnight rounds, noticed that a door was taped open and alerted
police.

That bungled burglary gave birth to the infamous scandal
known as Watergate, my most memorable story ever. But before all
the shocking layers of the conspiracy were laid bare, President Nixon
had won reelection, beating McGovern in a landslide victory.

The day after the burglary, two young, dogged *Washington Post* reporters, Bob Woodward and Carl Bernstein, began investigating Watergate and methodically turned up crucial evidence of not only Nixon's connection to the crime but also his attempt to cover it up.

Every other reporter in Washington, including me, tried our best to keep up with the headline-grabbing revelations they unearthed, but we were no match.

I was assigned to the courthouse, where the Watergate burglars faced District Judge John Sirica. There I began a cordial relationship with James McCord, the burglar described as the best "wireman." (He was an expert at rigging undetectable eavesdropping devices.) McCord quietly promised me he would give me the first copy of the book he was writing, titled *A Piece of Tape*. I thought I had found the key to the inside story of Watergate, but months before he finished the book, McCord wrote a blockbuster letter to Judge Sirica that blew the lid off the conspiracy. McCord's bombshell letter said that he and his fellow burglars had committed perjury because of "political pressure" and that higher-ups were complicit. McCord's allegations were vague and did not name names. Still, it was enough to send the media scrambling for more details. I wished I had somehow squeezed that information out of McCord. When he finally gave me his book, I was disappointed that it contained nothing scintillating.

Much more juicy information emerged before the Senate Watergate Committee hearings, which were carried live, gavel to gavel, on daytime television, creating riveting drama far better than soap operas. As I sat in the large hearing room, I found myself witnessing a true-crime story of historical proportions as it unraveled live. Later, as the plot thickened, with testimony closing in on President Nixon, Americans could not tear themselves away from the hearings, now on prime-time television. North Carolina Senator Sam Ervin, the captivating committee chairman, had twitchy eyebrows that were a joy to watch because they telegraphed his suspicions when he felt witnesses might be lying.

Half a dozen or more of us in the Washington bureau were assigned to cover various angles of the Watergate story. CBS investigative correspondent Daniel Schorr and his second banana, Lesley Stahl, were the primary reporters. Lesley routinely handed over tips and scoops she had uncovered to Schorr. He would use the information as his own, regurgitating it to the viewers with nary a thank-you and certainly never giving Lesley credit.

"Deep Throat" was *Post* reporter Bob Woodward's mysterious anonymous source whose leaks eventually took down the presidency. Woodward told his editors that Deep Throat was Deputy Director of the Federal Bureau of Investigation Mark Felt but kept it secret from the public for thirty years. That's what reporters do. We protect our sources unless our editors need to know their identities.

Unnamed sources were commonplace. For instance, anytime reporters read "a senior State Department official" or "a senior diplomatic official" or "a senior national security official," we could assume the anonymous leaker was Nixon's Secretary of State Henry Kissinger.

We at CBS knew the rules of journalism, but because leaks were the only means of eking out the truth about Watergate, CBS created an unusual special Watergate unit to keep a record of who said what and when they said it, to assure accuracy. Knowing the presidency was at stake, Small was adamant that no one he oversaw would make a mistake. Small established strict standards: If information came from an unnamed source, we must have at least *two solid first-person sources*—meaning two (not just one) reliable people who had firsthand knowledge of what had happened. If we had a third person confirming the information, that person could be a *secondhand source.* We could not run with any story without fully verifying every part of it.

Sometimes I'd prowl the halls of Capitol Hill at night, looking for my own Deep Throat, perhaps one of the Watergate committee members or staffers who was working late and who might be tired enough to inadvertently give me a tip I could develop into a story.

This meant late nights that collided with early mornings. One time, I was scheduled to do a *live* report at 7:00 a.m. on the *CBS Morning News* from the top floor of one of the congressional office buildings. With only a couple of hours of sleep, I drove like a maniac the forty minutes from home to Capitol Hill, camera ready (as always). The camera crew was set up and ready for me, but with no cell phones, there was no way for me to assure them I was en route.

When I reached the elevator, I discovered it was broken. So in my four-inch heels I ran up thirteen stories of marble stairs and slid into camera position with only fifteen seconds to air. The camera crew and control room were mighty relieved to see me.

But by the time I clipped my microphone onto my lapel and popped in my earpiece, I was so out of breath, huffing and puffing so hard, I could not speak. It took me another ten seconds or so, panting on camera, before I could proceed with my report.

Picking up crumbs Woodward and Bernstein left behind, I found a few small scoops. Nixon had taped his Oval Office conversations but refused to make them public because the recordings showed his complicity in the cover-up. When the US Supreme Court forced him to release transcripts of his tapes, I discovered that the White House had omitted a full page of presidential conversations. In the missing transcript page, Nixon revealed his disdain for the *Washington Post* by pledging to challenge the license renewals of *Post*-owned television stations. President Nixon said, "The main thing is the *Post* is going to have damnable, damnable problems…the game has to be played awfully rough." Sure enough, three months later the White House had filed license challenges against two *Post* television stations in Florida.

Nixon also believed not only the *Washington Post* but certain individuals were out to get him, so he compiled what his counsel John Dean called an "Enemies List," people Nixon thought were his detractors or opponents in the media, including CBS's own Daniel Schorr.

I was assigned to get reactions from those on the list, one of whom was a Washington socialite named Joan Braden. By the time I dug up her home phone number, it was 3:00 a.m. I threw my hesitation to the wind and called her despite the hour. She was so furious, she gave me an earful and slammed down the phone. I always wondered what upset her more: that I woke her up or that she had made Nixon's Enemies List.

I often started my day as early as 5:00 a.m., assigned to accost a Watergate figure at his home before he went off to work, then I'd cover the Senate hearings, and afterward I'd chase witnesses all the way home.

The crew and I pursued White House counsel John Dean almost every evening after he testified. Dean, the young blond lawyer who had bravely told Nixon there was a "cancer" growing close to his presidency, drove a speedy Porsche that could outweave our clunky Ford town car. We could not keep up. In addition, Dean used a remote-controlled garage door opener, giving him precious seconds to disappear just as we pulled up behind him.

One time, Lesley Stahl had the clever idea to crouch in front of Dean's front door and interview him through his mail slot. Our boss, Bill Small, proudly regaled reporters who covered media with the lengths to which Lesley and I would go for our interviews. He would trot us out as examples of "what makes good reporters," namely, as he put it, "immense appetites to get a story."

ABC's Sam Donaldson, a friendly competitor, was often side by side with me on stakeouts. One sunny weekend, the two of us approached Nixon Domestic Advisor John Ehrlichman at his home as he was mending his fence.

Sam cheerfully asked, "Can we help?"

Ehrlichman was a wily man with a smirk perpetually plastered across his face.

"Yes," Ehrlichman replied, hammer in hand. "Put your finger right here."

The CBS assignment editor often sent me to the home of Nixon Chief of Staff H. R. Haldeman at 5:00 a.m., and my pal Sam would be there too. Haldeman would open his front door, wave at us, reach for his *Washington Post* on his doormat, and close the door. Then, as he emerged from the front door to drive to the White House, I would rush forward, camera rolling, mic in hand. "Did you...did you...did you?" He would not say a word, briskly slamming the car door in my face.

One Sunday, the assignment editor summoned me. I was apprehensive because I could tell he wasn't happy about what he was about to ask me to do. *Newsweek* had just reported that President Nixon and Haldeman had told John Dean they were pleased with the cover-up. That was the first time both Nixon and Haldeman were linked to the scandal. "I want you to talk to Haldeman as he goes to church."

"Aw no, no, you don't want me to do that. Come on, no, not on his way to church," I pleaded.

He would not back down. "That's your assignment." I knew what his reasoning was. It was the only chance to catch Haldeman; otherwise he could duck our cameras by simply staying behind the closed doors of his home.

I made my way with a crew to Haldeman's Christian Science church, spotted his distinctive crew cut, and approached him as he walked with his family from their car to the church. His wife shot me an eviscerating look. I was mortified, certain that God would strike me dead with a bolt of lightning. I excused myself profusely for the distasteful intrusion and asked, "Would you be kind enough to speak to me?"

No doubt taking pity on this reporter, who was clearly just following the orders of an irascible assignment editor, he said, "Meet me at my house and I will stand there for questions, after services."

Back at his house, in a fourteen-second sound bite, he told me he intended to fully cooperate with the grand jury and authorities. It was an exclusive.

Two weeks later, Haldeman gave me another exclusive interview on his front doorstep, in a driving rain. In one hand I held an umbrella for both of us and in the other my microphone. For the first time, he flatly denied that President Nixon had had any involvement in the Watergate bugging attempt or cover-up. Later, evidence showed that was a lie.

Then one day, at the peak of the unfolding Watergate saga, an unfathomable incident occurred. Nixon had been assiduously hiding from the press. As incriminating tidbits kept emerging about what he knew, his only refuge was to stay mum.

I was told to go to the White House to keep the seat warm for White House correspondent Dan Rather. That meant Dan wasn't around and CBS needed a warm body, aka me, in the White House press room in the event that news broke. I had covered for him many times and it usually yielded nothing.

Entering the White House grounds through the northwest gate, I showed my official press pass to the guards at the kiosk and made my way toward the West Wing, where I would veer left to the press room.

It was a nice, bright day with no one around, until…

Imagine my shock to see, in the driveway outside the West Wing portico—none other than President Richard Nixon!

As I calmly but swiftly walked toward him, the Secret Service swarmed around me.

I started to ask the president a battery of questions, desperately trying to recall my copious notes from covering the Senate hearings. I did not dare take out my pen and notebook, which I feared would scare him away.

The White House press room did not have a direct view of the West Wing driveway where Nixon and I were standing. But somehow curious White House reporters must have noticed some commotion outside. They began to pour out into the sunshine with notebooks and pens, but Secret Service held them back. I was ecstatic I had an exclusive with the embattled president!

Or did I? Nixon proceeded to artfully dodge all my questions. Then, looking directly in my eyes, he asked *me* a question that came out of left field.

"How much money do you make?"

I was startled. "Excuse me?"

He repeated the strange question. I launched into a lengthy explanation: "I make a base salary of about twenty-six thousand dollars a year, but if I do a report for the *CBS Evening News with Walter Cronkite* or one for the *CBS Morning News*, I am paid an extra fifty-five dollars. And if I do a radio spot, I get an extra twenty-five dollars for each.

"And if I rack up a lot of radio spots," I proudly added, "I can bring my salary up to as high as twenty-eight thousand dollars a year."

The president proceeded to offer me his thoughtful wisdom.

"Just remember this: you have to make *more* money."

With that, he turned on his heel and strutted off to the West Wing with his Secret Service detail following close behind.

I walked back toward the press room, flummoxed, trying to make sense of what had just happened to my scoop. Before I could get through the door, Helen Thomas of United Press International, the dean of the White House press corps and my hero, rushed to me, dogged reporter that she was.

"What'd he say? What'd he say?"

To this day, I have no idea what he said about Watergate, if anything. So much for my exclusive.

\* \* \*

When the Senate Watergate Committee completed its hearings, the evidence against President Nixon was turned over to the House Judiciary Committee for impeachment hearings. As chairman of the committee, a little-known congressman from New Jersey had the unenviable task of leading the proceedings. Peter W. Rodino, diminutive in size, a self-effacing, unheralded member of Congress, had to lead a forum in which partisan politics might interfere with the rule of law. No one was sure he could rise to the occasion for this heavyweight bout, but rise he did, distinguishing himself for the first time in his forty-year career. His trusted administrative assistant, Francis O'Brien, provided him with strength and a resolute determination, guiding him into history.

I was one of the few women in the press corps covering the House Judiciary Committee hearings. Each day, I'd arrive early at the large, elegant hearing room where the thirty-eight committee members sat behind their nameplates on a two-tiered dais. Only two members of the committee were women, both Democrats, Texas Representative Barbara Jordan and New York's Elizabeth Holtzman.

After the hearings adjourned for the day, all the reporters would rush to the dais to ask members about the day's dramatic testimony. A photograph of the room, taken by Capitol Hill photographer Dev O'Neill, shows me looking as if I had "had it," surrounded in every direction by men. I don't remember feeling weary, but that is what is written all over my face. I always called that iconic photo "Sea of Men."

The male members of the House impeachment committee in the photo have their backs to the camera. The elbow on the left in a checkered blazer is Maine Republican William Cohen, who later became a senator and secretary of defense. The man on the right is Maryland Republican Larry Hogan, who was the first Republican to announce he would vote for impeachment.

In 2020, CBS News correspondent Vladimir Duthiers found the photo and gave it to his journalist wife, Marian Wang, a senior news producer on *Last Week Tonight with John Oliver*. She posted it on her Twitter account and wrote, "I keep this photo of a young Connie Chung in my office. It's a 'mood.'" In today's lexicon "mood" means "That is relatable" or "That is so me!" Her tweet blew up! And the comments were priceless:

**Vivian:** Such a #mood. The things she must have gone through.

**Cary Barbor:** Wow. I can't imagine the amount of B.S. she put up with.

**Chris Valentino:** Literally me when I walk into my workplace.

**June Doe:** I feel her mood in my soul. She looks so tired of their shit.

**Joe Raimonde:** I can smell the Brut and Royal Copenhagen from here.

**Tracy Paeschke, MD FACC:** All women know what she's thinking.

My worst fears about today's workplaces were realized. I felt sad for the lack of progress but extremely happy for the camaraderie!

Impeachment was on the front burner. That heat was too much for Nixon. He found the escape hatch presidents used when faced with a domestic scandal, namely a foreign trip to divert attention away from troubles at home.

The White House carefully orchestrated positive coverage for Nixon during a nine-day trip through the Middle East. Walter Cronkite, Dan Rather, Robert Pierpoint, and I were assigned. It was my first White House trip, but once again, my primary job was to cover for radio and tag along with the First Lady.

Our first stop was Salzburg, Austria, for talks with Austrian Chancellor Bruno Kreisky, then on to Cairo, Egypt, where President Nixon was greeted by throngs of wildly cheering crowds that veteran reporters said were *staged* along his motorcade route.

It was a whirlwind trip from Salzburg to Cairo and on to other stops in Riyadh, Saudi Arabia; Jidda, the country's diplomatic capital on the Red Sea; Damascus, Syria; Tel Aviv and Jerusalem, Israel;

and Amman, Jordan. Every stop was a carefully staged photo opportunity. In one of the cities, I recorded what is called a "stand-up"
sign-off for a *CBS Morning News* report. I said, "Connie Chung,
CBS News, where am I?" One for the blooper reel.

The Nixon White House was phenomenally organized, provid-
ing reporters with loose-leaf books containing detailed itineraries,
research information, and even weather reports. Our handbook
advised us, "In Saudi Arabia, women should take particular care to
dress conservatively. Sleeveless dress, pantsuits and short skirts are
strongly discouraged." Even though miniskirts were the style at the
time, I heeded the guideline—to an extent. I wore long sleeves but I
did not have any long skirts. Mine were above the knee, the style of
the day.

I was a spectacle in the Arab world. Photographers covering
the president could not resist taking a photo of me in a cream-
sicle dress in which I literally stopped traffic to help our camera crew
get through crowds. I don't know why, but the crowd that gathered
stared at me as if I were a Martian.

Even more amusing are photos of me in the same dress being
mimicked by young Arab men. In one photo, a man has his hand on
his hip, just like me. In another photo, my left forearm is covering
my waist and my right elbow is resting on my left hand. My right
hand is holding a pen up near my chin, as if I'm saying to myself,
"Hmmmm." Three young men are pictured in the background doing
the same. Every time I look at those photos, I chuckle, wondering
what they were thinking.

My first encounter with ABC's Peter Jennings was on this trip.
He was a suave Middle East correspondent who would later become
the number one anchorman on *ABC World News Tonight*. He looked
as if he'd come out of central casting to play the part of a dashing,

debonair, trench-coated foreign correspondent who could sweep women off their feet.

When we had some downtime, I joined other reporters on a shopping adventure. Some came back with outrageous purchases—carpets they planned to haul home on the press plane. (Yes, it *was* allowed.) The goodies I bought were far more portable, like a small, skinny sculpture and a vase. When Peter asked how much I'd paid for each item, he was aghast at my answer, declaring I had been "taken." He insisted we return to the souk and get my money back. We did. He was very pleased to have rescued this damsel in distress.

President Nixon's feet had barely touched the ground when the White House planned another trip, this time to Brussels, Belgium, for a North Atlantic Treaty Organization meeting and then on to Russia for Strategic Arms Limitation Talks (SALT II) with Soviet leader Leonid Brezhnev. I was part of the White House press corps, along with Dan Rather. Once again, my primary responsibility was to cover First Lady Pat Nixon. But I also filed radio reports about the actual summit.

I was a bit trepidatious and wide-eyed because I had never visited a communist country—the Soviet Union was my first. We were bused from the plane to Moscow's Intourist Hotel. We diligently kept to our tight schedules, not wanting to be left behind in Communist Russia. NBC White House correspondent Richard Valeriani offered to be my buddy to ensure we didn't lose track of the entourage and go missing. I was grateful that Richard's room was just a few doors away from mine, especially after I eyeballed the zaftig woman posted on our floor. She was the keeper of our room keys, which we could not pocket, nor would we have wanted to, for they were attached to an extremely heavy ball I feared would someday be locked to my ankle if I didn't abide by her rules.

The first night in my hotel room, I was having trouble getting to sleep. Fearing the hefty key keeper might want to visit me, I pushed a bureau in front of the door. When Richard knocked on my door the next morning to make sure I was on schedule, he could hear me moving the bureau out of the way.

"What are you doing?" he shouted through the door.

For breakfast at the hotel dining room, longtime Moscow Bureau Chief Murray Fromson kindly invited me to join other CBS News members and crew. I was flattered that he included me. Not knowing what to order, I thought a soft-boiled egg would be a safe choice. The egg arrived in an elegant eggcup. Nice Chinese girl that I was, I had never seen an eggcup before. I picked up the egg—thinking it was just like a hard-boiled egg—in my right hand, and, like a pitcher winding up for a fastball, I was about to bang the egg on the tablecloth.

"Nooooo!!" Fromson shouted.

Just in time! Thank goodness Murray showed me how to tap the shell as the egg was perched in its cup.

While Nixon and Brezhnev held their summit, I wandered around in search of a ladies' room and ran into Lloyd Shearer, who wrote Walter Scott's Personality Parade, which appeared each week on the inside front cover of *Parade* magazine.

He asked me how I was faring on my first trip to Russia.

I replied with the utmost confidence, "Very well, Lloyd, I've got this."

He couldn't resist saying, "Then what are you doing in the men's room?"

Nixon and Brezhnev were planning to meet at the Black Sea. I was sent ahead to do a story for Cronkite's news about the beach where privileged Russians went on vacation. When I got there, I discovered wall-to-wall sunbathers, men and women lined up like bacon strips sizzling on a sandy skillet. The assignment was worth a feature story on the *CBS Evening News.*

Somehow I learned that Soviet dissident physicist Andrei Sakharov was willing to be interviewed by the visiting American press. My heart started pounding. Could I handle this important interview? Would Cronkite news producers allow *me* to conduct it? Then I realized I had best be a dutiful worker bee and turn it over to Murray Fromson. Murray deserved the exclusive. After all, he'd saved me from getting egg on my face at breakfast.

On this trip, I reported a few stories on the *CBS Evening News* about First Lady Pat Nixon, but there was little news of consequence for any of us. The entire trip was just one big photo opportunity—expensive, perfunctory, and uneventful.

\* \* \*

Back in the USA, I covered every development during the House Judiciary Committee Hearings, appearing frequently on the *CBS Evening News.* Finally judgment day arrived. The committee was to vote on the first article of impeachment.

But before that first vote was taken, Maryland Republican Congressman Larry Hogan announced he would vote for impeachment. It was an emotional moment. As I watched his breathtaking announcement, Hogan appeared to be on the verge of breaking down. I knew Hogan well, having covered him for local news when he was a Maryland county executive. Even though I'd had no inkling he was going to pull the impeachment trigger, I knew him to be a brave and principled man, so I wasn't surprised he was willing to be the first Republican to stick his neck out.

There had been a lot of handicapping during the day, but finally the first vote on the first article of impeachment was called. It was carried live on prime-time television. I covered it live on CBS Radio, speaking into a big desk microphone set up for me in the committee room.

The cavernous committee room was hushed as Chairman Rodino called upon each member to cast his or her vote.

"Mr. Donohue. Aye."

"Mr. Brooks. Aye."

Clutching my tally sheets, I listened anxiously, checking off each aye and nay. Some members were barely audible, seeming to whisper their important vote. My heart was racing because of the gravity of the moment. I was witnessing history unfold before my eyes.

The ayes had it on all three articles of impeachment—obstruction of justice, misuse of power, and contempt of Congress. The committee's recommendation to impeach Richard M. Nixon was subsequently sent to the floor of the full House, yet no vote was ever taken because the president realized it was all over. He did not have the votes to avoid impeachment in the House and conviction in the Senate. He had no choice but to resign.

On a hot August night in 1974, America was poised for his resignation speech. My assignment was to wander around on the street and inside the White House grounds to see what I could sniff out.

The star White House correspondents from all three networks stood like tin soldiers on separate platforms two feet high and three feet wide in Lafayette Park, across from the White House, with the North Portico entrance lit and perfectly framed behind them. Huge klieg lights flooded Pennsylvania Avenue as if it were an old-fashioned Hollywood movie premiere.

Outside on Pennsylvania Avenue and in Lafayette Park, I saw throngs of people gathered, cheering, chanting, and celebrating.

It was a bizarre scene—a street carnival outside—yet inside, in stark contrast, the White House appeared funereal. Normally 1600 Pennsylvania Avenue glistened with bright lights shining out, but on this night the windows were dark. The only room that was buzzing with life was the press room, which was packed to the gills with reporters from all over the world.

I was anxious to see if I could find any preresignation information. I was walking from the northwest entrance of the White House when I suddenly encountered the president's assistant, Steve Bull, the young man who was always at Nixon's beck and call, appearing out of the darkness.

I whipped out my reporter's notebook, thrilled at the possibility I might break some news.

"Have you been with the president? What is his mood? Have you read the speech he's about to deliver to the American public? How will he couch his resignation? Is he angry? Upset? Sanguine? Guilt ridden? Is he going to admit he ordered the Watergate break-in?"

Understandably protective of his boss, Bull told me Nixon would recount his accomplishments in the five and a half years of his presidency and that Vice President Gerald Ford would become president effective the next day, when Nixon's resignation was official. Bull would not reveal if President Nixon would admit wrongdoing. (He did not.) But did describe the president's mood as somber.

Information in hand, I rushed over to Dan Rather's platform. I dutifully looked up at him. "Dan, I just talked to Steve Bull. Here's what he said."

Would Dan do what all the star CBS News correspondents did—simply take the information and report it on air?

No, Dan looked down, somewhat paternally, and generously said, "Well, step right up here. I'm about to go back on the air. You tell them what you found out."

Surprised, I stepped up on the platform and stood next to the White House correspondent. Dan looked into the camera and said, "CBS News reporter Connie Chung has just run into White House aide Steve Bull, who has been with the president. Connie, what did he tell you?" I recounted the quotes, pleased that I had a mini scoop.

"Thank you, Connie," he said, approvingly.

It was the first time we appeared on camera together.

## CHAPTER 14

# Rocky

"Our long national nightmare is over." With those words, Gerald Ford grasped the reins from Nixon, becoming the thirty-eighth President of the United States. Ford, who had been a decent and honorable member of Congress for a quarter of a century, made it his mission to heal the country, but first he needed to choose his replacement.

Traditionally, the vice president doesn't do anything of consequence besides serve as backup to the president. He presides over the Senate but may not vote, except to cast a tiebreaker. And the veep shows up for funerals of heads of state the president has neither the time nor the desire to attend.

Nelson Rockefeller, who had turned down other presidential candidates who offered him the opportunity, calling the vice presidency "standby equipment," this time accepted the nomination. He had aspired three times to the presidency, in 1960, 1964, and 1968.

Now it was 1974, and it would be the closest he would come to leadership of the Western world.

Rockefeller was a smooth politician with a scratchy voice, rectangular glasses, and a superfriendly demeanor. Rocky, as he was affectionately known, had a signature greeting: "Hiya, fella!" But he had not grown up just another ordinary fellow. Nelson was the grandson of the onetime wealthiest man in America, Standard Oil magnate John D. Rockefeller Sr., and was no political novice, having served in the administrations of FDR, Truman, and Eisenhower in Washington. He was a liberal/moderate Republican who had successfully won election to four terms as New York's governor.

CBS named me the first woman to cover a vice president, and that meant the Rockefeller beat was all mine! No big-footing correspondent hovered above me. Finally I had arrived. When I did my due diligence, researching Nelson Rockefeller's background, I couldn't help but notice that he had said he was "not cut out to be a number two kind of guy." I thought, "I have something in common with this man."

My coverage of Rockefeller started with his confirmation hearings before congressional committees. The vetting process, expected to be pro forma, was anything but. Rocky was not happy about opening the books of his fortune, which he felt was nobody's business.

Nonetheless, investigators on the committees uncovered questionable campaign practices and evidence that Rockefeller and his family had given millions of their vast wealth in gifts, interest-free loans, and political contributions, some to curry political favor. All the revelations piled up to a heap of trouble. I became a walking encyclopedia of all money matters Rockefeller.

Surprisingly, Rockefeller's confirmation for a position that he was not keen about anyway was on shaky ground. Would he be forced to withdraw? Not a chance. Nelson Rockefeller liked a good fight. Bring it on. He welcomed combative encounters with members of Congress, and he was anxious to defend his family name. Ultimately, after a four-month drama, Rockefeller was confirmed and sworn in as Vice President of the United States.

Rocky turned out to be no ordinary, run-of-the-mill veep. He was unfiltered, terribly unpredictable, and liable to shock, much to my delight. What promised to be a dull event could suddenly turn into a food fight because Rockefeller had said something unscripted.

At one appearance, hecklers gave Rockefeller the finger. He returned the favor, extending his middle finger to them. The unstatesmanlike gesture became known as "the Rockefeller salute." He refused to apologize for it.

The training wheels I had worn over the years at CBS were off. I appeared often on Cronkite's news and the *CBS Morning News*. And earning the trust of experienced political reporters like Lou Cannon of the *Los Angeles Times* bolstered my confidence. Lou thought I knew more about Rocky than anyone else on the beat. He even recommended that reporters assigned to the vice president check with me for accurate background information.

Feisty as Rocky was, he'd become annoyed when I nagged him about whether he still itched to be president, but I did not take his anger personally. He understood the relationship between politicians and the press. It was adversarial, not intentionally antagonistic. We were not out to "get" anyone. Our job was to challenge politicos and ask tough questions. If I asked one, Rocky responded with a tough answer. That's why he was my favorite politician—I relished the sparring.

Over the years, I had come to categorize politicians in three buckets: those who feared scrutiny, did not trust the press, and were less than candid, like Nixon, who considered us the enemy; those who tried to befriend us, hoping to own and control us, like Kissinger, who tried to manipulate reporters to give *his* version of a story; and those who were honest brokers, who didn't roll over easily yet believed the Fourth Estate was a necessary and important part of our democracy. Rockefeller fell into that category.

My belief was that because of his vast wealth, Rockefeller did not feel the need to follow anybody's rules. He would do and say as he wished—because he could. He was a leader in his party— liberal and moderate members of the GOP were known as "Rocke- feller Republicans." But Rocky could not appease the conservative wing and frankly did not want to. To me his independence was refreshing.

Gawking at his material wealth up close was fascinating. At a Republican fundraiser at his house in Maine, he took the press on a tour before the party started. He was especially proud of having cor- doned off a section of the ocean, which he heated for swimming. We reporters shook our heads in disbelief at what it must have taken to heat an ocean. At another GOP fundraiser at the sprawling Rocke- feller family estate in Pocantico Hills, New York, he showed us some of his jaw-dropping art collection and a Japanese-style house he had built. Those were just two of his many properties.

Covering him on the road meant bouncing from city to city for speeches, fundraisers, and meetings, ending the week in New York, where he spent his weekends. He and his wife, Happy, never moved to Washington, even though they had two houses available for them there—a personal home they had owned for years and the official vice president's residence on the grounds of the Naval Observatory. Though they redecorated the official residence with priceless art, they never lived there. Rockefeller, an avid modern art collector, put a $35,000 Alexander Calder bed in the master bedroom. Calder's modern artwork was a peculiar addition to the traditional Victorian house, but no matter. Rockefeller always did what he wanted.

President Ford was oblivious to whispers from his supporters that his strong-willed number two might wrestle him for power. A confident President Ford named Jim Cannon, a trusted, longtime Rockefeller aide, domestic advisor, a key White House position. That appointment gave Rockefeller unprecedented influence with his old confidant advising President Ford about important policy. Since a vice president did not have the president's ear, Rockefeller could use Cannon as a conduit to Ford. But I knew Jim Cannon, a former journalist, to be an honorable man who was honest and loyal to both men, and, I might add, a valuable, trustworthy source for me.

Rockefeller tried to maintain a low profile, saying he was nothing but a "staff assistant," meaning he just did what he was told, but none of us who followed him truly believed that. He had a habit of inadvertently breaking off on his own and getting himself in trouble.

More than two months into his vice presidency, Rockefeller committed his first self-inflicted wound. He was presiding in the Senate during an intense debate about the filibuster rule when he refused to allow a member of his own party, a leader of conservative Republicans, to speak, which helped liberal Democrats in the contentious verbal battle. That whipped the conservative GOP members into a frenzy, prompting a devastatingly harsh attack by his fellow party members, who threatened, in retaliation, to refuse to cooperate with the Ford administration in the future.

Weary from the drama, Rockefeller flew to Detroit to deliver a scheduled speech. On a late-night flight home, in a long Q and A with reporters, Rockefeller became irritated with questions about his presidential ambitions.

"Why do you think you are not, as you put it, one of the competing rising stars in 1980?" I asked.

He looked directly at me. "Because I don't think anyone gives a good goddamn, if you'll forgive me, about 1980 politics."

Pointing his finger at me, he continued. His anger was palpable.

"And I think you make a tremendous mistake even thinking about it...and I resent it as a politician that people think that all I'm interested in is politics."

Our gaggle of reporters gulped at how blunt he was.

As for failing to allow a conservative senator to speak, Rockefeller had to make peace with an apology on the Senate floor. But the peace did not last long. Rockefeller continued to utter comments that offended conservatives and devolved into petty party politics. He had always been a moderate elephant who leaned toward moderate donkeys, leaving him in a pile of dung.

As the 1976 presidential election approached, the conservative wing created a loud drumbeat of calls to dump Rockefeller as Ford's running mate. Up-and-coming conservative star Ronald Reagan was waiting in the wings to challenge Ford for the Republican nomination, so the right wing demanded Ford replace Rocky with a rock-solid conservative.

Less than a year after he was sworn in as vice president, Nelson Rockefeller scheduled a news conference. Even though I had never anchored anything, I boldly asked our new CBS News Bureau Chief Sandy Socolow if I could anchor Rockefeller's likely withdrawal from the '76 Republican ticket. It would be a live, televised *CBS News Special Report*, and I was confident I could do it. Sandy, whom I respected and trusted, actually considered my request but decided that veteran anchorman Roger Mudd should sit in the anchor chair, and I should attend the televised news conference. I understood. I knew it was a big ask, and Roger had years more experience.

As anticipated, Rockefeller announced he would not be Ford's running mate in 1976. The reason, he said, was political.

On live television I asked, "Was it clear to you that conservative opposition to you was so great that you would be a liability to the president? And was it clear to you that you would probably be dropped from the ticket if you did not withdraw yourself from it?"

Rocky responded, "No, I don't agree. Let me, let me explain. It's a minority of a minority"—(meaning the conservatives in the GOP). "And I don't think the opposition, if I use your word, quote, unquote, is basic. But it is an issue and subject of concern to those who are responsible for the president's campaign and nomination. And it's just not worth it."

If I may try to interpret what he was saying: though the Republican conservative wing was a minority, it was influential enough that Ford's campaign team feared it was too risky to choose Rockefeller as his running mate this time around.

When I arrived back in the Washington bureau, Sandy said, "I knew you would ask a great question! I made the right decision." I agreed.

As for Rockefeller's future ambitions, a reporter at the news conference asked him about his "longtime quest for the presidency."

A classic Rockefeller reply followed: "Well, I'd have to say, I'm closer right now than I've ever been." (Room laughter.)

As Rockefeller resumed his nonduties as vice president, he kept playing coy about whether he might challenge Ford for the presidential nomination in 1976 or beyond, but in the end he was "fatalistic," as he put it, about the presidency for himself. It eluded him. His political career was over. During an interview, Rocky said to me, with a smile, "I won't have anyone to argue with anymore."

A few years later, in January 1979, when I was a news anchor in Los Angeles, I was reading the wire services. A bulletin announced, to my shock, that Rockefeller, only seventy years old and retired from public life, had died of an apparent heart attack while sitting at his desk at his office. It had happened at 9:20 p.m. in Los Angeles, 12:20 a.m. in New York.

I felt pangs of sadness. He had been such a vibrant, self-assured man, full of energy.

After thinking about it for a while, I thought to myself, "*Wait. Nelson Rockefeller working at his office after midnight? I don't think so.*" That seemed highly out of character.

The time sequences in the initial bulletin were later revised several times. The story kept changing as details dribbled out, each one murkier than the last. Even Rockefeller's loyal spokesman, Hugh Morrow, struggled with each conflicting revelation. Rockefeller had apparently collapsed an hour earlier, and it had occurred not at his office at 30 Rockefeller Plaza after all, but at a town house he owned in midtown Manhattan that he supposedly also used as an office.

He had been working with Megan Marshack, a blond twenty-five-year-old staffer who curated his collection of books on his beloved art. She lived right around the corner in a cooperative apartment and had met him at his office in a long black evening dress.

When Rockefeller collapsed, Marshack tried to resuscitate him to no avail. She called her neighbor, Ponchitta Pierce, a local on-air newsperson, who then called 911. It was an hour from the time Marshack witnessed Rockefeller's collapse before the 911 call. What was going on in that hour? No one could explain the time gap. Once emergency crews arrived, they tried to revive Rockefeller, but it was too late.

The circumstances of Rockefeller's death became fodder for the tabloid press and late-night comedians, who conjured up all sorts of scenarios about what Rockefeller was doing when he had his heart attack.

But in the end, tributes came from every luminary in Washington politics, from presidents to rivals—like Nixon, Ford, Carter, Reagan, and Barry Goldwater.

He left most of his estate to his wife, Happy, and their two sons. His four older children from his first wife were given smaller provisions because they had been taken care of by earlier gifts provided by Rockefeller and his father, John D. Rockefeller Jr.

He forgave several loans, including $45,000 to Megan Marshack for the purchase of her cooperative apartment a few doors away from the town house where he had died. More than a month later, his older children released a statement saying that they believed Marshack had done her best to save their father and it would be wrong to continue to debate over the details.

By then everyone, including me, had moved on to other news, which is what occurs in journalism. On to the next story.

CHAPTER 15

# Go West, Young Woman!

After covering McGovern, Watergate, and Rocky, it was hard for me to find a news story that seemed as important, challenging, or significant. For five years, I had been privileged to watch history unfold firsthand. Now anything I covered seemed routine, almost mundane.

One day, CBS News President Richard Salant summoned me to the network news headquarters, a building that had once been a dairy in Hell's Kitchen on Manhattan's west side. What could the meeting be about? I was nervous. Such a command appearance in the Big Apple was rare and intimidating. Salant greeted me with his infectious Cheshire cat smile. Sitting with him was a younger-looking suit, as we called management types, with light hair. Chris Desmond had just taken over as general manager of the CBS-owned-and-operated station KNXT-TV Channel 2 in Los Angeles.

Desmond offered me a job to anchor his local newscasts. He went through the proper CBS hierarchy, asking his higher-up, Salant, if he would be willing to give my transfer his blessing. I thought, "Is this how baseball players feel when they are traded?" The good news was that if I accepted the offer, I would still be in the CBS family—at the network where I wanted to spend my career. But did I want to leave national news?

The normal route for a television news reporter was to advance *from* local news *to* national network news, but I had already achieved that coveted stature. I'd be going *from* network news *to* local news—a step in the wrong direction. Would leaving make any sense?

One reason to go local was that I could get more anchoring experience. But by 1976, I had been a substitute anchor on the *CBS Morning News*. Often I coanchored with either CBS News' Morton Dean, a superb correspondent, or Hughes Rudd, a wonderful curmudgeon. But in those days, no one watched the *CBS Morning News*. If anyone was up and wanted a breakfast companion, they tuned into the popular *Today* show with Barbara Walters. Anchoring the CBS early-morning broadcast was like going into the Witness Protection Program.

Friends would ask me, "Where have you been? Have you been sick? On vacation? Off on assignment in Sri Lanka?"

"Uh, no," I'd reply, "I have been getting up at one in the morning Monday to Friday, anchoring the *CBS Morning News*. You haven't been watching?"

To my great surprise, CBS offered me that coanchor job on the *CBS Morning News* if I stayed. That was a big deal because the early-morning competition for American eyeballs was heating up. Barbara Walters and her appeal demonstrated that people who got up with the rooster enjoyed TV with their coffee.

I had been at CBS News for only five years. A coanchor job at the number one news network was significant. Why didn't I take the offer? It has always nagged at me.

Part of my reasoning was that I would be coanchoring a straight news program. Unless CBS changed the format to compete directly with top dog *Today*, I did not think that job had much promise. If I chose to stay, I needed to find out what CBS had in mind. I had more tossing and turning to do.

Feeling torn, I weighed the fact that people at CBS in Washington probably saw me as a kid. Certainly in my role as a reporter, I was in no way a child—I was going head-to-head with powerful men. Yet everyone at CBS knew that at age twenty-nine, I was still living under my parents' roof. I was ashamed that I had not moved to my own place years earlier, wondering how I could possibly be taken seriously as a grown-up in the news business. I concluded I had to leave my professional home, CBS, to be seen as a major player.

But my most important reason for leaving CBS in Washington was deeply personal. After my father's retirement in 1972, I had become the breadwinner in my family. I was holding down the fort, footing the bills, feeling incredible financial pressure and, frankly, feeling put-upon, especially when my sister Maimie, my best friend, asked me for $8,000—every cent in my savings account. She and her second husband wanted to buy a house. I gave her the money.

Since I was now the head of the household, I felt intense heat to make more money, and at the same time, I was suffocating under my parents' roof. All my life, I had been the "good daughter" who never rebelled, even in my teen years. All my sisters had married and left town. Now, with a chance to break out, I was ready to get out of Dodge. I wanted my independence and freedom, to live on my own.

The Los Angeles job would more than triple my salary, from $29,000 a year to $100,000. It would have taken me years to earn that much had I stayed at CBS in Washington.

I needed the money, and taking this offer was my way out. My leaving town would surely force my sisters to step up to the plate and share the responsibility for our parents, especially emotionally. They were not calling enough to suit my parents. I was the only one listening to my parents' complaints. I promised Mom and Dad I'd still meet my familial obligations, but for me, the personal freedom of moving across the country was as crucial as the money.

CBS News threw me a lovely goodbye party where all the competition melted away. My parents were invited too. I was embarrassed about that, but I knew I was cutting the apron strings, and it would not be long before I'd be on my own.

CBS President Frank Stanton, who had retired, sent me a note, handwritten in boxy and stylish printing like an architect's. "We will miss you and your superb reporting from 2020." (The address of the CBS Washington bureau was 2020 M Street.) "Los Angeles is fortunate indeed." I was honored Stanton had taken the time to write.

Flying to California, I felt a weight lift from my shoulders. Rebellion at age twenty-nine seemed a bit ludicrous, but better late than never.

CBS in Los Angeles put me up at the legendary Beverly Hills Hotel, home of the Polo Lounge, where Hollywood stars and dealmakers rendezvoused. I was given a glorious suite on the first floor, just to the right off the lobby. It had its own spacious patio. It was always sunny and seventy-two degrees. I felt as if I was living la dolce vita.

I ordered room service for breakfast before going to work—and snacks at night when I got home. Room service was open all weekend too. Life as Eloise at the Plaza couldn't possibly be any better than this.

For months, after paying my parents' expenses, I saved much of my hefty paycheck while CBS picked up the tab for everything at the hotel, until company accountants woke up. I was firmly encouraged to get a place of my own. "Oh yes, of course," I said with a wry smile.

My first apartment was my dream come true at 8720-B Shoreham Drive, a small two-bedroom condominium on the second floor of one of a tidy cluster of brick town houses named The Shoreham. A charming brick wall surrounded the small buildings, and pathways snaked through the cobblestone courtyard, which was lined with flowers and a small pond. It was perfect.

The entrance had a buzz-in locked iron gate that made me feel safe given that the complex was just a block from Sunset Strip in West Hollywood—a neighborhood known for sex, drugs, and rock and roll and not considered ideal for a single woman. "How can you live there?" alarmed friends said. "Prostitutes walk the strip every night!" Those gals never bothered me.

Just two blocks away on Sunset Boulevard was the Roxy Theatre, the legendary music venue where crowds of fans (some probably stoned) jammed the street on weekends to catch a glimpse of Neil Young, John Lennon, Alice Cooper, Ronstadt, Zappa, Cocker. It was a hot hangout where the established and wannabes mingled, including fresh faces Leno and Letterman testing their stand-up routines.

The apartments had been built in 1937 by Metro-Goldwyn-Mayer Studios for its contract megastars and starlets during Hollywood's Golden Age. Real estate agents claimed Janet Leigh (*Psycho*), Olivia de Havilland (*Gone with the Wind*), Ava Gardner,

Veronica Lake, and even Katharine Hepburn and Marlene Dietrich had lived there.

My condo was rumored to have been occupied by Vivian Vance (*I Love Lucy*'s neighbor Ethel Mertz) and handsome actor Farley Granger. I bought it from the daughter of Red Auerbach, the legendary coach of the Boston Celtics. Don Robinson and Hal McGuire, a gay couple, lived below me on the first floor. A lovely older couple had just sold their third-floor apartment to John Hinkel, a single gay man. I felt safe having gay men above and below me, although I was not happy when one of them stole one of my boyfriends, with whom I had never gotten past first base.

Across the way from me, a single gay man owned the entire town house. Some nights, I could peek into his second-floor window and watch a delightful sliver of a peep show. How outrageous and rude of me. I'd quickly admonish myself and pull down my shade.

An apartment or so over lived David Niven Jr., son of the charming British actor. The son, the spitting image of his father, was quite a bon vivant and drove a British roadster with the steering column on the right side of the car. He was always gallivanting into the entrance of our small garden complex with a tall, beautiful woman on his arm. It was like watching an old black-and-white movie—they'd throw their heads back and laugh as they bounced their way into his apartment. I could imagine them drinking French champagne and popping chocolate-covered strawberries all night.

I loved my condo. It had a sun-drenched living room with a large bay window, sparkling white shutters, and built-in bookcases flanking a fireplace. Across from the fireplace was a wall-to-wall mirror that made the room look twice as large. All the walls were painted a warm, funky taupe and had creamy white molding.

My bedroom had many windows begging to be opened for an

incredible crosswind. On Friday and Saturday nights, I'd often hear a helicopter circling above the open field that my apartment overlooked at the dead end of Shoreham Drive. I'd look out the window and see a big search spotlight, like the ones in movies when a prisoner escapes. The light would scan the area for the runaway criminal. "Come out with your hands up," a voice on a bullhorn would shout.

I was determined to concentrate on my work, so it was never a priority to create a home with furniture. I left my apartment almost empty for about a year, with only one soft chocolate-brown chair that looked like a structured beanbag in the living room, a small Parsons table in the kitchen, and a couple of straight-backed bentwood chairs for breakfast. My dresser and bureau were the same ones that had been in my high school bedroom. They were furniture my father's hotelier employer had given our family back in the fifties and were classic Art Deco.

I'd bring men I dated home, inviting them into my living room. As they looked at my one chair, they'd be taken aback. My refrigerator was always empty too. I could tell they were thinking, "What's with this woman?" I found it amusing and hardly a big deal. The guys probably didn't have anything in their refrigerators either.

Finally my neighbors Don Robinson and Hal McGuire insisted I get serious about being a grown-up. Since they were professional decorators, they couldn't wait to get their hands on the project. Soon I had two suede love seats, two soft armless side chairs covered with Fortuny designer fabric, an antique coffee table, a Chinese-style round end table, and an elegant six-foot-long old church altar table—all of which I still use to this day.

I finally felt like an adult. I had left home as everybody else my age had years before. At long last, I was a liberated woman.

* * *

My job was to coanchor the hour-long *5 O'Clock News* with Joseph Benti and the half-hour *11 O'Clock News*. I soon realized that anchoring local news meant having an intimate relationship with viewers. We nightly news anchors lived in our viewers' homes—not only in their living rooms but also in their bedrooms. Our late-night *11 O'Clock News* viewers were often prone, watching us between their toes. We were always told to speak into the camera as if we were telling our mothers what had happened that day. I needed to shed my stiff network delivery and abandon the straitjacket worn by national news broadcasters.

And I believe that viewers who watched us day after day, night after night, *knew* who we were, what we were like. Anchors cannot disguise who we are, and frankly, I think that's the way it should be. I was my normal down-to-earth self. Viewers know who is a phony and who is genuine.

Benti and his girlfriend of many years, Christine Lund, invited me to their home for dinner before our debut night. A very tall, lovely blond, Christine was a popular coanchor on the ABC local station—in direct competition with Benti and me. Odd, but if Joe and Christine didn't have a problem with it, why should I? I was overwhelmed by the warmth of their welcome.

*Working* with Joe was a different story. The experience was a live training ground and a foreshadowing of coanchoring with other insufferable partners in my future. Joe loved the sound of his own voice and had a propensity to hog airtime and oxygen. Anytime we were covering breaking news and had to ad-lib, he spoke incessantly. I could barely elbow my way into the coverage. I came to recognize it as a common male anchor habit.

Media articles had ballyhooed my arrival—so much so that Los Angeles Mayor Tom Bradley presented me with a key to the city shortly after I started. And I met California Governor Jerry Brown, the young, progressive eligible bachelor nicknamed "Governor Moonbeam" because of his out-of-this-world ideas. He was a hippie in a suit. My coworker Bill Stout, a respected former CBS News correspondent who delivered a nightly commentary on our news, invited me to join him and his wife, Peggy, for an intimate dinner with Governor Brown at their home. What a lovely gesture. It was especially memorable because Bill and Peggy had two large parrots that squawked four-letter words from their open perches throughout our meal.

And many of the correspondents and staff at Channel 2 invited me to their homes for weekend dinners. I loved being back in the warm womb of local news—which was far friendlier and more civil than the brutal, cutthroat climate of network news. Once again, I felt as if I was part of a professional family with no cutthroat relatives.

Management juggled my anchor partners throughout my seven years in LA, always on the hunt for a winning team. I would be coupled with one TV husband, then forced to divorce; then a new male would parachute into the anchor chair next to me.

Even Maury, my eventual real-life husband, coanchored with me. Since we had known each other before, there was a chance it might work, but the boss who'd hired Maury was fired. The new management moved quickly, designating Maury as last hired, first fired. Our television marriage lasted only a few months, not long enough for us to develop any on-air chemistry. Our real marriage is still going strong!

After Maury, I found myself once again aboard a merry-go-round of coanchors. They were in and they were out while I remained the constant. Mike Parker, a redheaded younger man with a full strawberry-blond beard, was a solid, serious journalist, but management moved on.

Thinking a two-woman team would be progressive, management lured Marcia Brandywine from San Francisco, where she was a popular anchor. But that didn't work either.

This was the era of "happy talk," when local anchors were encouraged to be chatty. I was not accustomed to it, but in that climate, I relaxed at the anchor desk and became less constrained, shedding my stoic network news persona.

Inevitably, happy talk led to mishaps. One night I tossed to our sportscaster Ted Dawson. Before he began his segment, he said, "You're not really interested in knowing about sports news, Connie." For the record, my love of sports started in Washington, when I was growing up with the Senators, our baseball team, and even extended to boxing because my father was a devotee of champions like Joe Louis, Rocky Marciano, and Sugar Ray Robinson.

At the conclusion of his sports report, I said to Dawson, "You think I don't like sports, don't you, Ted?"

Dawson replied, "It's not that I think you don't like sports, I just think you don't know anything about it."

That really ticked me off. He obviously didn't know I thought I was a jock in heels. I surprised him (and myself) with an uppercut.

"It's not that I don't like sports, it's just that I don't like you." (Why did I blurt that out?)

In turn, he said, "When is my laundry going to be done, Connie?" Oh dear. Remarkably, there was no fallout from that exchange, which is emblematic of how racism or sexism were viewed in the late 1970s. Dawson was eventually replaced by sportscaster Jim Hill, but not because of the laundry line.

The nationally popular lead anchor on CBS Sports, Brent

Musburger, decided he wanted to add local sports to his repertoire, and he cut a deal to come to Channel 2 in LA. Brent was CBS's premier play-by-play man for football, basketball, and anchor of *The NFL Today*. After a while as a sportscaster, he was tapped to co-anchor the news with me—even though he was not a newsperson and didn't pretend to be. He was a sharp, smart, amiable broadcaster with rapid-fire delivery and higher-than-a-kite energy who just read the news as it was written for him. I found myself speeding up my delivery to keep up with his pace. Brent was a fun partner but didn't have news-based credibility.

Finally the music stopped. No more musical chairs. Management raided Jess Marlow, the longtime news anchor at our competition, the NBC station, who became my perfect anchor partner. Jess was a reputable journalist with a warm smile and great sense of humor. To counter the happy talk craze, Jess liked to say, "Dare to be dull." He wasn't dull at all, just serious about news. We hit a comfortable stride largely because we supported each other, bailing each other out if needed. He never had a trace of big-shot-itis. We were never competitive, nor did we engage in one-upmanship. The viewers could tell, and it showed in the ratings.

I had a daring habit of playing chicken with the camera. Five or ten minutes before the news began, the stage manager would hustle the anchors to our desk. I was always late, wickedly enjoying the anxiety I cast: "Is she going to make it?" One time, I screeched into my chair with only thirty seconds to air. As I tried to clip my microphone onto my lapel, the safety chain on my wristwatch became caught on my mic. As the stage manager bellowed: "Five, four, three, two..." I fidgeted and twisted—but could not dislodge the darn chain.

I greeted the audience with a smile, "Good evening," with my limp wrist planted under my chin, dead center on my chest. Oh boy, what a bozo I was. My wonderful coanchor, Jess, not wanting *me* to appear awkward, planted a limp wrist firmly on his own chest and said, "And good evening." What a dear.

\* \* \*

From the moment I arrived at Channel 2, I declared I would not just show up to "read" the news as some lazy anchors did. My goal was to continue to burnish my reputation as a serious political reporter.

When major political figures made pilgrimages to tap deep pockets in Hollywood, I went out in the field to interview them for our broadcast. They were the usual suspects, like President Carter; Vice President Walter Mondale; Senator Ted Kennedy; his wife, Joan; and Tennessee Senator Howard Baker. It made for long days and nights until *The 11 O'Clock News* was over, but I was happy to work.

Among the reports I did were a two-parter grading Governor Brown's performance, another story on the race for state attorney general, and one on the cliffhanger reelection of California Senator John Tunney, son of heavyweight champion Gene Tunney and a former law school roommate of Ted Kennedy. (When I had covered Capitol Hill, I'd see Kennedy and Tunney trolling the hallowed halls like frat brothers, looking for mischief.) In 1980, I even convinced the news director to unchain me from the anchor desk to travel to New Hampshire, Massachusetts, and New York to follow Governor Brown, Kennedy, and Carter on the presidential campaign trail.

Along the way, I hustled the stories I had shot for local news, pitching them to Walter Cronkite's news (on a drought in the San Joaquin Valley and on California gray whales) and the *CBS Morning News* (on an open California congressional seat). I was so driven, I wanted to be sure I would not disappear from national news.

In May 1978, our assignment editor, Ted Savaglio, arranged quite a coup for me. I was one of only two news reporters allowed to cover President Nixon's book party at his home at La Casa Pacifica in San Clemente. Nixon was thanking those who had helped him with the publication of his autobiography, *RN: The Memoirs of Richard Nixon.*

President Nixon arrived in a golf cart at his buffet party at what once had been known as the Western White House. When he walked in the front entrance of his home, I greeted him with a cheerful "Hello, Mr. Nixon!" but he ignored me, not even looking my way.

The president then said a few words to the gathered, likening his experience of writing his memoirs to birthing a baby. After his speech, I tried a couple more times to talk to him, but each time, even when I stood very close to him, he stonewalled me. His aide, Jack Brennan, took me by the arm firmly and, leading me to the door, said with a smile, "It was nice to see you again, Connie."

\* \* \*

My favorite cameraman/editor, Paul Hammons, and I traveled to El Salvador at the height of the guerrilla war between the right-wing military and leftist guerrillas. It was my first exposure to a war zone. As we traveled a dusty road, we were told there were land mines buried along the way. Riding in a rickety truck, I fell asleep, which is a quirky reaction I have when I am frightened. Paul was incredulous. Here I thought I was brave, but just hearing the bullets whizzing in the air and the rat-a-tat of gunfire scared me away from volunteering for war coverage ever again.

Back home in Los Angeles, I was exposed to a different kind of danger. I did a story on a drug rehabilitation commune called Synanon that had started off as a respected program but morphed into a wacky religious cult. The commune's leader, Charles Dederich, was misusing money and violating the group's nonprofit status.

After I got an exclusive interview with Dederich, he began to threaten anyone critical of Synanon with violence. That's when I received bizarre telephone calls at the station. Our switchboard operator told me I was being warned to stop reporting negative stories about Synanon. Since I left work alone each night at midnight or later, my boss hired an off-duty police officer to accompany me home.

The off-duty officer, who ran the security service, was my escort for a while. One night his brother-in-law, also an off-duty cop, substituted for him. At my front door, he tried to kiss me. I reported what had happened and never saw the creep again.

After my three-year contract with Channel 2 was up, I hoped to return to network news but came up empty, so I renewed my contract in LA.

By then, my duties had increased to anchoring three programs: the half-hour *4:30 P.M. News* in addition to coanchoring *The 6 O'Clock News* and *The 11 O'Clock News*. And to maintain my ties to CBS News, my agent, Alfred, negotiated opportunities for me in New York to substitute for the *CBS Morning News* and the *CBS Weekend News* and to anchor the West Coast edition of *Newsbreak*, a one-minute news update in prime time.

So between *The 6 O'Clock News* and *The 11 O'Clock News*, I'd grab dinner and scoot to CBS's Los Angeles bureau twenty minutes away, where I'd write and deliver *Newsbreak*, and then I'd drive back to Channel 2 in time for the late-night news. I was busy and always working but still happy to be on my own.

My life changed dramatically when I received a call from my parents.

That's coming up.

# CHAPTER 16

# Ch-Ch-Ch-Changes

The bright California sun was shining on me every day, and I thanked my lucky stars that I was enjoying my work and was secure with my new contract.

Then my parents called.

With excitement in their voices, they informed me they were moving to Los Angeles to be with me.

What? No, they could not be serious. Yes, they insisted. My supporting them with my generous paycheck was not enough. I tried to find a way to tell them that I needed to live apart from them. "Please don't clip my wings," I desperately wanted to say. But I did not know how to say no. I knew this turn of events did not bode well for me.

After paying off the mortgage on their house in Maryland, I could afford to buy a new home I found for them in Van Nuys in the San Fernando Valley. Every week they expected me to join them for Sunday dinner. My mother would spend our time together complaining, ranting angrily about everything under the sun. I did not know why my parents bickered constantly. I could only surmise that their unhappiness was buried in the half century of their arranged relationship. Since I worked from early afternoon until midnight, they came to my apartment for lunch every Wednesday. I dreaded the routine.

The role reversal was more pronounced than before. I had two extremely dependent people whom I felt obligated to care for in every way—emotionally, financially, physically. On weekday mornings, before I went to work, I'd shepherd them to doctors' appointments I had scheduled for them, talk to their doctors, and keep their health records. I'd take charge when I realized that the doctors and their office workers did not treat my parents with respect unless I accompanied them. When they went to appointments alone, they were dismissed. Because they both spoke with thick Chinese accents, especially my mother, people claimed not to understand them. But as soon as I showed up, they received white-glove VIP treatment because people recognized me from television. How appalling that my name and face gave my parents an unfair advantage over other patients. And yet without me, they experienced blatant discrimination.

On Saturdays, I'd take them out to dinner, and I tried to think of ways to entertain them by taking them to events they might enjoy. As their recreation director, I tried to make them happy, always including them in anything I did, including a party I hosted for my work friends in the garden of my apartment complex.

Driving home from the party, they had a terrible accident. My mother, in the passenger seat, lost consciousness, but my father was not injured. By the time I got to the hospital, my mother was fine, but I knew I needed help.

Josephine, my oldest sister, who had always been there for me, came, along with Maimie, my closest sister. All they needed to do was stay at my parents' house to care for my father while my mother recovered in the hospital.

Maimie convinced Josephine to go to a bar. When I found out, I was furious. I wanted a helping hand—not more trouble. Thankfully, my parents recovered.

My father had bigger dreams than the house I had bought for them in the Valley. He wanted a house in Beverly Hills to brag about to his friends back East. He found a modest house and insisted on moving. Once again, I gave in, hoping they would be happier. That was a pipe dream.

Although I occasionally went out on dates here and there, I spent many Saturday nights alone, feeling intense anxiety about my impending Sunday dinner with my parents. One rare Sunday when I skipped the family dinner, I went to a barbecue at the house of Andrea Reiter, my best friend at work. I remarked, "Is this how *other* people spend their Sundays?" Unable to counsel my parents into having a better relationship and with all the other daughters far away, I was the only one left for them to cling to.

My father wrote scathing letters to my sisters, equating love with money and lauding me for supporting them financially. His tone and message were, "Only Connie is here for us." By placing me above my sisters, he almost succeeded in turning them against me.

I could not bear the conflict and drama. I now realize work was my escape. I could be the person I wanted to be—a worker bee who was strong and independent, who could compete in a man's world in a worthy profession. Thus, I did what men do. I compartmentalized my life. When I was working, I thought only about work. When I was not working (rarely), I allowed myself to wallow in my family mess.

At about the same time, Maury was fired from Channel 2, and his marriage ended in divorce. I could not imagine the double hit he faced. Maury always says, "Connie had to pity me in order to love me." I don't know where he got that insane idea. I never pitied him. Yes, I felt sorry that he was caught in a management shuffle that put him out the door, without a chance, after only a few months. I did not pry about his marriage.

Since I was one of the few people Maury knew on the left coast, we connected, sharing our familial stories of woe and our professional tribulations over the years. It was comforting. Neither of us had solutions to offer, but it was good to commiserate. In two months, he was hired to anchor the news and host a talk show in San Francisco. Now we had a budding relationship between LA and San Francisco. A long-distance romance worked just fine for both of us. He was newly single, and I loved playing the field and not being beholden to anyone. As we got closer, we felt comfortable enough to introduce me to Maury's daughters, Susan, a teenager, and Amy, a preteen. We kept these visits casual, just weekends of fun.

\* \* \*

Still working like a fiend, I did an investigative report on a doctor who had engaged in questionable practices. He must have been upset with my report. Unbeknownst to me, he hired a private detective to tail me to dig up dirt. Later, the private detective's office was raided by Los Angeles police for reasons that the authorities did not reveal to me. The police called to tell me they'd found a file with my name on it saying I went to work at the same time every day, returned home at the same time, did not have wild parties, and rarely went out on weekends. Essentially, I was a flat-out bore. What a depressing and thoroughly embarrassing report!

That did it. With all the Sturm und Drang of my family, it suddenly hit me. I had forgotten to have a personal life. Determined to no longer sequester myself, I gave myself permission to go out and have fun.

Next scene: the Beverly Wilshire Hotel, where I was exiting through a revolving door. Entering through the revolving door: Warren Beatty. We circled around a few times, laughing at the silliness. Remember Beatty? He was the one who chased every skirt on the 1972 McGovern campaign. I was a dedicated reporter who did not want anything to taint my reputation. I resisted his overtures.

Now I was in La-La Land and Warren was relentless. What the heck. He actually lived at the Beverly Wilshire Hotel in a small room on a top floor, tucked in the eaves. We went out a couple times and he called often. There were times when he rang me at my apartment when Maury and his daughters were visiting me. One day, either Susan or Amy answered my phone. Her eyes bugged out when she whispered to me that Warren Beatty was on the line. She added, "We won't tell Dad." How cute is that? From then on, if Warren called and the girls were at my apartment, they would say, "Connie, it's Walter!"—their code name for him. They were and are the best.

After Warren built a huge house at the top of Mulholland Drive, he threw a party to screen a current motion picture. That's how Hollywood celebrities viewed new movies—in the comfort of their homes, where they had large screening rooms. A projectionist would be hired for the night. Celebs no doubt believed going to movie theaters was for the masses.

Warren invited me to the party at his house in the Hollywood Hills. I could not help but notice that the women far outnumbered the men. Could it be that the women thought it would be a slumber party for two? I knew no one except Warren. While we watched the movie, I started to notice something strange. Why was everyone getting up, going somewhere, and returning just a couple of minutes later? They were missing the whole film. What was going on? Someone later told me they were probably doing cocaine. I was so naive about drugs.

I did not even know that a tube was used to snort coke, but I soon found out. A friend of mine, Karen Danaher Dorr, who had been an audio person at CBS News in Washington, was now living in Los Angeles and working as an executive in film. She called me after she experienced the trauma of being raped. Fearful to stay in her home, where the rape occurred, she asked if she could stay with me. Of course I offered her my spare bedroom. Knowing many people smoked marijuana then, yet not knowing if she did, as a precaution, I asked her to keep drugs out of my home. One night I had dinner with an old schoolmate, who joined me at my apartment afterward. The next morning Karen came to me with a small glass tube in her hand. I asked her what it was. "I found it in the Kleenex box in the spare bathroom," she said. I looked at her with a blank expression on my face, and suddenly her eyes widened. "You don't know what this is, do you?" That was how innocent I was. I did not know it was used to snort cocaine. She grinned.

Irving "Swifty" Lazar was a powerhouse dealmaker packed in a small man with oversize black-rimmed glasses. Lazar was a talent agent extraordinaire for stars and authors from Cary Grant to Lauren Bacall, Gershwin to Cher, Hemingway to Capote, and even Richard Nixon. Humphrey Bogart had nicknamed Lazar "Swifty" after the agent sealed three deals for Bogie in a single day.

Swifty was known for throwing legendary parties. After seeing me on the news, he and his wife invited me to a dinner party at their home in the Hollywood Hills. Their house was decorated as beautifully as a grand Fifth Avenue apartment, filled with lots of antiques and chintz. I was starry-eyed at the gathering of glitterati.

To my shock and delight, I found myself chatting with my ultimate heartthrob, Gregory Peck. I had probably seen every one of his motion pictures. Yes, his voice was as deep and his face as handsome as on the big screen. As I stood there with him, the newspaper reporter he'd played in *Roman Holiday* came to life before my eyes. His character snookers a princess, played by Audrey Hepburn, into a night out in Rome, creating a scandal for her and a scoop for himself. But he falls hopelessly in love with her and refuses to submit the damaging story for publication. "Oh my," I thought, "a journalist with a heart"—Gregory Peck and I had something in common! I certainly would have given up my princess-ship for him. Alas, Peck shook me loose from my daydream by introducing me to his statuesque, elegant wife, Veronique. I had never felt so short.

When I went to refresh my cocktail, there stood the great Billy Wilder. He was much more than a brilliant director, he was also an unparalleled screenwriter—*Ninotchka* starring Greta Garbo, *Sunset Boulevard*, *Stalag 17*, and *Some Like It Hot*, just to name a few. I had seen them all. Wilder told me he watched me on the news and was incredibly enthusiastic about meeting me in person. I could barely contain myself. He took me by the hand to meet Jack Lemmon, whom Wilder had directed in *The Apartment*. What a treat it was to shake the hands of Lemmon, his wife, Felicia Farr, and Walter Matthau and his wife, Carol Grace. We all sat in an enclosed patio with white latticework and chairs covered in Lilly Pulitzer pink-and-green fabric. The Odd Couple chatting it up with a little local news anchor.

All night, I kept getting glimpses of Ryan O'Neal, who was looking very *Love Story*–ish. Our eyes met several times during the night, but I never seemed to be able to gracefully weave through the stars to talk to him. Before I knew it, the night was over, and everyone was heading to the door to give hunky wannabe actors our valet tickets so they could run and get our cars. I found myself at the door just in front of Ryan O'Neal. I looked at him and a line from old black-and-white movies emerged from my lips: "Your place or mine?" O'Neal replied, "Up to you." With a subtle and casual glance back at him, I said, "Follow me." I hopped in my black Jensen-Healey convertible, gunned my motor, and scooted down the hill—waiting for him down the road. Feel free to use your imagination.

One night a girlfriend of mine and I decided to go to dinner at Musso & Frank, a small, funky restaurant on Hollywood Boulevard. We settled into a booth, just the two of us. Not far away, at another booth, were four guys. They asked if we wanted to join them. "Sure." We nodded, squeezing into their booth.

They seemed nice, smart, fun. I asked the guy I found most appealing what he did for a living. "I play in a band." At the end of the dinner, he asked me if I wanted to go to his house. "Sure."

In his cluttered living room, an upright piano took a prominent spot. "Would you play something you perform with your band?" I asked innocently. "Sure." He launched into "Hotel California." Gulp.

By this time, Maury, who had gotten an anchor job in San Francisco, had already moved on to the NBC affiliate in Philadelphia, where he was a news anchor, reporter, and talk show host. We were still a two-city couple, but the long travel time between LA and Philly slowed our romance. Still, we talked frequently. I called to tweak him: "I went out with an Eagle." Maury replied, "You mean the Philadelphia Eagles?" How I groaned.

Even though we both knew we did not have an exclusive relationship, Maury felt compelled to remark: "You are star-f*cking!"

I retorted, "YOU can't even remember the FIRST names of the women you are dating—let alone the LAST names."

When the movie *The Blues Brothers* was about to be released in 1980, a girlfriend and I were invited to a party to promote the film at a restaurant. We stayed until the end, disappointed that the two stars, John Belushi and Dan Aykroyd, never showed up. The restaurant was closing, and the waiters were trying to shoo us out. I looked up at the wall and saw a black-and-white silk-screened poster of Jake and Elwood, the characters they played. My girlfriend knew exactly what I was thinking. "No," she warned me. "No, you can't." It was large but light. Lifting it off the wall was easy. I asked my pal to just follow me. I pulled up in my Jensen-Healey convertible and assured her I was going to drive slowly and would she please hold the poster down so it would not fly away? It looked great framed above my fireplace in my living room. I still have it. It's the best. Shhhhh.

The seven years I spent in Los Angeles were the halcyon days of my single life, during which I made lifetime friends, but soon all those friends started leaving for the Big Apple one by one, because Channel 2 was rich with talent in front of and behind the camera. It was common for the networks to use Los Angeles stations as a farm team for poaching talent. Our competition did the same— NBC plucked news stars Tom Brokaw, Bryant Gumbel, and Tom Snyder from the local LA NBC station.

My best female friend, Andrea Reiter, who directed me, was the first to go to New York. Then my best male friend, sports producer David Winner, was lured to CBS Sports, and then Executive

Producer David Corvo was off and running to the CBS network in New York. I had one foot out the door, saying, "Wait for me!"

Professionally, I had become too comfortable and did not feel challenged anymore. I needed to be scared again. It was time for more of the heart-thumping moments I knew would help me learn and grow as a journalist.

Mary Kellogg, head of KNXT programming and later the executive who oversaw *Live with Regis and Kathie Lee*, gave me some valuable advice: "You have to *tell* management what you want. They can't possibly know what all their employees or job applicants want." Hearing that from Mary, one of the few women I knew in management, I realized none of the male managers in my career had given me a tip like that.

My lawyer/agent, Alfred, agreed that I could best represent what I wanted from prospective employers. I would negotiate the job description, and he would take care of the salary. Knowing I wanted to return to network news, I met with the CBS, ABC, and NBC News presidents to make my own case.

Before I left California for my next job, I made it clear to my parents that at thirty-seven, I wanted them to let me go on to my next chapter alone. Since two of my sisters had settled back in Washington, and Mom and Dad still had friends there, I suggested they return to DC. They balked, but I insisted. I assured them I would still support them and help them as I always had.

Channel 2 put together a goodbye tape for my last night on the air. To my surprise, the great Stevie Wonder was included!

Years later, Stevie Wonder and I both received honorary doctorate degrees from Brown University. I remember him well because he was paired in the processional with the president of Portugal, who was also being honored that day. The processional path we walked was not easy terrain. How endearing it was that the president of Portugal was helping guide Stevie every step of the way. I spoke at the graduation. Unfortunately for all of us, Stevie did not sing.

On my goodbye tape, Stevie said, "If you ever come back, remember, we have a blind date."

# CHAPTER 17

# Maury

B efore I take you to my next job in New York, I must pause for a commercial about my husband, Maury, and the seven years we slow-walked our relationship before we finally got married.

You may know my husband, Maury Povich, as the man who's been determining the paternity of every child in America. With his booming voice, he makes the big reveal to his anxious guests and audiences on his talk show, aptly named *Maury*.

"You *are* the father!"

"You are *not* the father!"

Now, if I may, allow me to introduce you to the Maury I know. He and I could not be more different.

He is a rule breaker. I am a rule maker.

He is fine with a mess. I am obsessively, compulsively neat.

He won't do any chores unless I ask. I love to organize and tidy up. (Chore-gasms, I call them.)

I multitask. He doesn't know how.

I want to discuss. He's into avoidance.

After a fight, Maury always wants to make up before going to sleep. I want to continue fighting the next morning.

Maury will take food into the bedroom. I wouldn't think of it.

He won't ask for directions. Of course I will.

I'm a worrywart. My girlfriend Nanci Nadimi says I can take a thread and weave a rug as big as Madison Square Garden. Maury moves on.

I am a perfectionist and a control freak. He has neither the time nor the inclination for anything of the sort.

He's a pro's pro. One take and done. I must do several, and I'm still not satisfied.

I am slow and have unending patience. He is always in a hurry.

When the going gets tough, he plays golf. For me, when the going gets tough, the tough go shopping.

Here's an example of one of his admirable but annoying traits. We were asked to anchor a health care panel together. Weeks before, we were given three-inch loose-leaf binders filled with detailed research. I studied it all, line by line, taking notes, preparing questions. "Let's discuss," I urged. Maury waved me off.

On the morning of the panel, Maury said, "OK, let's talk over breakfast." I gave him a list of the panel members he'd be introducing that I'd carefully prepared for him. I had my own list. "I don't need that," he said, and proceeded to skim the hundreds of pages of information.

Then, approaching the stage, he whispered, "Where's that list of the people I am introducing?" I handed it over, shooting daggers with my eyes.

We proceeded. Such a quick study, Maury shows off, citing

statistics from the research he just read minutes before. Picking up his wireless microphone, mingling, he proceeds to walk and talk to the audience, up close and personal. As I watch him ad-lib his way through the hour, I am beholden to my notes, trying my best to keep up with him.

I never want to work with him again.

For you to know Maury, I need to tell you how he grew up. Like me, he was born in Washington, DC. His childhood photos show that even as a kid, he had a perpetually mischievous look, as if he was thinking, "What trouble can I get into today?" Maury proudly cops to having been unruly, rebellious, and incorrigible. On his report card, a teacher describes him this way: "Maury has so much potential, if he would only apply himself." All he cared about at his all-boys prep school was a trifecta of sports: football (cocaptain), basketball (cocaptain), and baseball.

Sports was in his blood. He worshipped his father, the legendary reporter, sportswriter, and columnist Shirley Povich, whose fine work appeared in the *Washington Post* for seventy-five years. Yes, seventy-five years, and yes, his name was Shirley. He was born in Maine in 1905, and it was common then for men to be named Shirley or Marion. At one point in his career, my father-in-law was named to *Who's Who of American Women*. He was asked how he got along with his male colleagues. His response? "I just try to be one of the guys." (As you know, I did too!) Walter Cronkite wrote him a note asking him for his hand in marriage. Both were serious journalists with active funny bones.

Maury's dad was an erudite man who spoke in a clipped manner with an accent that sounded almost British. He was always properly dressed in a suit, button-down dress shirt, and repp tie (diagonally striped) topped off with a gray flannel fedora adorned with a classic grosgrain ribbon. Just like my father, Maury's dad would wear his fedora precisely right, slightly tilted.

As Shirley's son, lucky Maury became a batboy for the Washington Senators and met his heroes, like Joe DiMaggio, Ted Williams, and Stan Musial.

(A slight digression. Once Joe DiMaggio was watching one of my interviews and remarked to a friend, "I'd hate to be at the other end of one of her fastballs." What a compliment.)

And just like his father, Maury has always been a very good writer. At the University of Pennsylvania, he and a buddy each read half the required short stories—then briefed each other. At blue book exam time, a panic-stricken Maury nudged his pal and asked with urgency, "What's the story about?" The friend answered with a sentence or two. Maury scribbled furiously.

When the professor returned the blue books with grades, Maury's was the last to be handed out.

"Mr. Povich obviously did not read the short story," the prof stated with certainty, "but I gave him an 'A' for creativity."

Maury's mother, Ethyl, had grown up in Washington, DC, which in her day was considered a rather southern city. Her speech was tinged with a slight southern lilt.

"Maw-ree," she'd drawl, "are you still smoking?"

When he'd reply, "Yes, Mother, I am," she'd shake her head in disapproval.

"That's terrible, Maw-ree...then give me one." She'd enjoy her single cigarette, taking a long draw, just as my mother did.

While Maury's father enjoyed local and national acclaim, his mother seemed invisible. Articles about Shirley Povich always lauded the Povich children—Maury's older brother, David, a trial lawyer and partner in a prestigious Washington law firm; Maury, the star television news anchor; and the youngest, Lynn, the pioneering senior editor at *Newsweek*. Nary a word about wife and mother Ethyl. "Those poor motherless children," she'd lament, wryly and woefully sighing about her lot in life.

Maury was a local news star in the nation's capital for fifteen years as a news anchor, talk show host, and reporter covering Capitol Hill; the White House; the assassinations of JFK, Martin Luther King, and Bobby Kennedy; and anti–Vietnam War demonstrations. You name any story in the sixties and seventies, and he was there.

You may think I'm biased, but Maury was a darn good interviewer in his years as a traditional multisubject talk show host, whether he was questioning a diplomat (Abba Eban), a politician (Spiro Agnew), an author (Gore Vidal), an actor (Jack Lemmon), an actress (Shirley MacLaine), a Watergate figure (John Dean), an activist (Gloria Steinem), or the incomparable chef Julia Child.

But he had a bigger dream—he wanted to be Walter Cronkite, so he went on a five-city odyssey to Chicago, LA, San Francisco, Philadelphia, and Washington. He never captured the brass ring. Instead, he would help guide me to Cronkite's chair.

Our seven-year courtship was entirely long distance. During those years, we went on several vacations with his two daughters, Susan, a teenager, and Amy, a preteen. Amy kept tugging at me: "When are you getting married?" It was so nice to hear her say that, but neither Maury nor I was ready to take such a giant leap.

We continued our commuter relationship until he worked in Philly. He had married right out of college. Feeling his oats, he made up for lost years, putting into practice the old line: "So many women, so little time." I told Maury we needed to take a time-out. We took six months off from one another but continued to talk on the phone.

# Maury

The year 1984 turned out to be significant in my personal life. My old best friend from Texas junior high school days, Carol Sama, called and surprised me with big news: she was getting married. Just like me, Carol had been a single working woman until almost forty—the successful editor in chief of a magazine called *Houston Home & Garden*. Now she was finally ready to pull the trigger.

Coincidentally, my six-month hiatus with Maury was up. Time to reassess our relationship. Knowing Texas was midway between the West and East Coasts, I made him a fifty-fifty proposition: Would he like to meet me halfway at Carol's wedding in Houston? With that rendezvous, Maury and I were dating again, but still not exclusively.

Shortly thereafter, I moved to New York for a job, and Maury was back working in Washington, DC. We were only an hour's plane ride apart, an easy commute.

We had what we both believed was a perfect relationship. We were seeing one another while living in two different cities—working hard during the week and spending weekends together. Sometimes he felt ready to get married, but I wasn't. Then I was ready, and he wasn't. Our match was clearly love, but we wouldn't come to the net at the same time.

What followed was another unexpected call. My closest friend, Andrea Reiter, also my age, pushing forty, told me she was getting married. Andrea had been my best friend at Channel 2 in Los Angeles. She was the control room director of the news, her calm voice always in my wired earpiece when I was on air. And as my BFF, she has always been the one in my ear in my nonwork life.

My head was spinning: my two best pals had crossed to the dark side, one after the other. I had to sit down and collect my thoughts. I wasn't a spinster, but at thirty-eight I could no longer claim I was too young to get married. I'd been having such a grand old time working and dating, I'd forgotten to get married.

Maury believes we were on vacation in Italy when we talked, once again, about marriage. He says he popped the question. I don't really remember. When we returned stateside to our apartments in NYC and DC, I thought, "If we're going to get married, maybe we ought to set a date quickly, with elections and other stories to cover, we needed to plan our schedules. I better find something to wear now." I went shopping for something casual, maybe a long white sweaterdress. I couldn't find one, but I happened to find a slim antique lace wedding dress that fit perfectly. I called Maury to tell him we were good to go. I deny to high heaven that I was so superficial that once I found something to wear, I made the momentous decision to take the big step. Don't believe Maury when he claims otherwise.

We both figured this was an easy commitment. After all, we were living in different cities. It was not a giant leap into... m-m-m-marriage. Just an inch forward. We both liked the idea. Work all week and spend weekends together. We did not have to actually live together. That prospect was much too scary.

Maury was so wonderful and respectful. Despite being forty-five, he honored my traditional parents, asking them for my hand in marriage. The first thing my father said was, "Connie, you are still going to support us, aren't you?" I was never more mortified. How terribly depressing that my father could not muster some happiness for me. My money was more important to him than my happiness.

My mother was just plain relieved. About three years earlier, she had given me her most prized piece of jewelry, her dark green jade engagement ring, which she had saved for me, her youngest daughter. Mommy had parted with one of her precious jade pieces from

China on each sister's wedding day. She was so tired of waiting for me to marry, one day, she put her ring in my hand. "Please take it. I've been wanting to give this to you. It's yours." I was thrilled.

Ours was a small wedding in my New York apartment with Chung and Povich relatives and five friends each. I arranged tulips for the dinner tables, and instead of a cake, we had a few different pies. Maury rented a piano and hired a pianist to play the wedding march.

Before our ceremony began, both of my parents arrived at our wedding feigning illness. I did not know why, but I was just so disappointed, I could not bring myself to worry; instead we carried on with the ceremony.

The rabbi who married us had excused me for not converting to Judaism. Maury and his parents did not hold that against me either. My own parents did not hold it against Maury that he was Jewish, not Chinese.

In marrying Maury, I was lucky to have an instant family with his two daughters. Maury and I were surprised as they both cried and cried, even though Maury and I had been dating and going on vacation with them for several years. Years earlier, their mom had married right after Maury's divorce, so we thought maybe the reality of both Mom and Dad being married to other people was a jolt. Years later, I asked them why they had been overcome with tears, but neither remembered crying.

Both Maury and I tried not to think about my parents' meshuggaas and our daughters' sadness. During the ceremony, Maury and I had our backs to those gathered—we were looking out a bay window. In the apartment across the street was a dog running from one window to another. We could tell he was barking at the traffic below. Before the rabbi got to the wedding vows, we were mesmerized by the dog. Neither of us heard a word the rabbi said.

When the time for toasts came, my father suddenly perked up and gave his toast with no signs of a health issue. He said with a smile, "My job is finally over." And during our reception, Maury and I went to his parents. Maury said, "Connie would like to call you Mom and Dad." With wide smiles, they both said, "Yes! Of course." We approached my parents, too, and asked them what they'd like their new son-in-law to call them. My mother's response, "I prefer you call me Mrs. Chung." For the rest of their lives, Maury called them Mr. and Mrs. Chung.

Maury and I have been married since December 2, 1984. As of this writing, that's almost forty years. I love Maury with all my heart, and I know he loves me deeply, but sometimes, you know, I don't necessarily like him. My guess is that the feeling is mutual.

\* \* \*

Maury moved from news and talk to three back-to-back-to-back successful syndicated programs. He was not embarrassed about his tabloid program, *A Current Affair*, or the talk shows the critics called trashy. That did not bother him in the least. He has that rare capability to not give a damn what people think. I always fret about what people think. He refuses to give his critics power over him. He knows who he is and what his intentions are.

The Maury I know is not limited to the priceless words he utters on television. His vocabulary is impressively extensive, probably because he has a voracious appetite for reading—history, politics, biographies, novels, literature of all kinds. He has a thirst for knowledge and retains what he reads. If you ask him anything about politics, history, or geography, he knows the answer—or he declares the answer with such confidence, I am loath to question him.

Maury

I've long asked him, "Why don't you do a serious interview program?" He could run circles around those insufferable self-described intellectuals. "You are so smart, so well read, such a history buff and political buff," I tell him. Without fail he responds, "As long as you know that, I'm fine."

Maury is a serious person. I am the wacky partner. I'd come up with harebrained ideas which I'd share with Maury. I'd add, "You would do it." His reply: "Yes, but you have a reputation to uphold."

If I am to tell all my secrets about Maury, I must reveal something that is no secret to those who know him. The man is a golf addict.

Unwittingly, I contributed to my own golf widowhood. For his fiftieth birthday, I bought the ultimate gift: a lesson with the professional golf teacher Peter Kostis. In doing so, I created a golf monster. I curse myself for what I did.

Every year, Maury used to play golf with a disparate group of miscreants, as he liked to describe them—one of them being George W. Bush. This was when "W" was a Texas wildcatter, before he became governor of Texas and then President of the United States. Fast-forward to the White House, where Bush was hosting Maury at a special screening of Maury's 2003 Academy Award winner for Best Documentary Short Film, *Twin Towers*, on the 9/11 tragedy.

"Po," Bush said, "I was on the elliptical and I'm watching your show. How do you do that with a straight face?"

Maury replied, "Think about what you do, Mr. President, think of all the things you do every day with a straight face."

Maury's straight face has earned him a Lifetime Achievement Emmy award for being the longest-running daytime talk show host in the history of broadcast television. I am proud to say that makes him the GOAT (Greatest of All Time).

However, I am most proud that in 2007, Maury created the *Flathead Beacon*, a weekly newspaper in the Flathead Valley of Montana, where we have had a home for twenty-five years. Its publication is a tribute to his father, a master of the written word. From the year it was launched, the *Beacon* has swept statewide competitions for best newspaper, best website, best investigative reporting, best spot news coverage, best political coverage, best, best, best. Editor in Chief Kellyn Brown, a University of Montana graduate, has been at the helm since the newspaper's birth. He has hired a band of mighty reporters who break stories and show what unbiased, solid, credible journalism was and can be again.

Were it not for Maury, I could never have had the career I had. He has been my foundation, my support beam, my love, my partner in every way, for decades. He helped me navigate my treacherous path up the ladder. I used to think I could survive without him. The guy in me told me I was not dependent on anyone. I was just another white guy, just like him. Now I know I could not live without Maury.

# CHAPTER 18

# NBC: Nobody But Connie

T o recap where we were, before I interrupted myself to talk about Maury...

It was 1983 and my second contract with Channel 2 in Los Angeles had a year to go, but I had an out. If I had another offer, I could leave. After seven years in Hollywood, I was tired of being three hours behind the East Coast news cycle. National network news in New York was beckoning, and so were my closest friends. An added bonus on the personal front was that Maury had moved back to Washington.

Journalists who covered the media knew about my "out" clause and went crazy with speculation. Is she going back to the big leagues? It was as if I were a free agent about to be plucked from the farm team. Would I go to the Yankees, the Dodgers, or the Chicago White Sox? Could I hit?

They made much ado about my future because TV news was at

the peak of its popularity. In those days before the internet, it was prime time for television news. The competition in the business was stiff, and the climate was brutal. I knew it was no place for the weak. If I jumped in and couldn't measure up, I'd be toast. I was up for the challenge.

Allow me to further paint the television news landscape.

Seven years earlier, the *Today* show's morning star, Barbara Walters, had left NBC for ABC to crash the male bastion as the first woman to coanchor an evening newscast in broadcast history. That made huge headlines, but coanchor Harry Reasoner despised her, and two years later, she lost her pioneering job. She stayed at ABC (Reasoner left) and carved her successful legacy there.

Once again, women took a back seat, watching three white men deliver the news to millions of viewers: NBC's Tom Brokaw, ABC's Peter Jennings, and CBS's Dan Rather (who had taken the job from Walter Cronkite). Those three anchormen were battling to dominate the way Cronkite had. Why did they aim to be top dog? The highest-rated news program could command the highest advertising rates, which equaled more profits.

Then it dawned on the three networks that they could make *more* money during the morning programs because of all the commercials that could be sold for a two-hour program. (The nightly news was only a half hour long.) Mornings, where on-air women were welcome, became the networks' new cash cow.

ABC's *Good Morning America* with David Hartman and Joan Lunden had stolen NBC's thunder, overtaking *Today*'s Bryant Gumbel and Jane Pauley, who had dominated the airwaves after Barbara left. NBC desperately wanted to rectify that.

I entered the Art Deco NBC building at Rockefeller Plaza in New York, where the Christmas tree towers over the skating rink every year. Nervous but confident, I met with NBC News President Reuven Frank, a tall, thin, serious-looking older man with white hair, a long nose, and dark-framed glasses. He was the same man who'd told *Newsweek* in 1971, "I have a strong feeling...that audiences are less prepared to accept news from a woman's voice than from a man's." By the time I met him in 1983, more than a decade later, women had come a long way and so had he.

I pitched him an ambitious six-day workweek anchoring a morning news program called *Early Today* that aired at 6:00 a.m., right before *Today*; substituting for Tom Brokaw on *NBC Nightly News*; anchoring the Saturday *Nightly News*; doing political reporting for Brokaw's news, including taking a prominent role in the 1984 elections; and anchoring one-minute news updates in prime time two nights a week.

NBC News offered me everything I wanted, except the salary. Media writers claimed I was the highest-paid local anchor in the country. I don't know if that was true, but I took a pay cut because I felt the NBC job (or what some would call three jobs) had the most promise.

Also, I was terribly flattered—in fact, floored—when NBC Chairman and CEO Grant Tinker personally called, urging me to join his network. I was ready to say yes anyway, but this gesture tipped the balance for me and proved that NBC would be a welcoming home.

Before NBC, Tinker had started MTM Enterprises, those being the initials of his wife, the one and only multitalented Mary Tyler Moore. I suppose I thought he might help boost my career too. I saw him as an authority figure I could trust, one who would have my back.

Tinker was a charming man with an easygoing manner and

dynamic mind. He had gradually transformed NBC from a last-place network into a profitable ratings winner, with popular shows such as *Family Ties*, *Cheers*, and *Hill Street Blues*. This was also thanks to NBC's brilliant young programmer Brandon Tartikoff.

My goal with the workload I had proposed was to saturate the airwaves to show the national audience that I was back on the grid, appearing on the news at the crack of dawn as their coffee was brewing, then being part of their dinner hour on the *Nightly News*, and later delivering updates at nine and ten, smack in the middle of prime time and on Saturdays before they went out on the town.

The media frenzy was dizzying but glowing—and speculation was swirling.

*Newsweek* magazine called me "NBC's Early Morning Star" and said, "The ferociously indefatigable Chung began carrying the most grueling workload in the electronic press." It even predicted I would become a coanchor with Brokaw on *Nightly News*.

*New York* magazine: "Connie Chung is one of the hottest names in TV news."

*People* magazine, noting that the *Today* show with Bryant Gumbel and Jane Pauley had dropped to a distant second behind ABC's *Good Morning America*: "Some media mavens believe Chung is in fact being groomed as their *Today* successor."

Those predictions came out of thin air. My plate was full, and the truth was, I was not angling for any of those jobs. Yet the ascent of anchorwomen was the talk of the industry, especially after Barbara Walters's groundbreaking moment in the spotlight, even though it lasted only two years. *Glamour* magazine wondered if Barbara's achievement was an aberration: "The mid-seventies hiring surge is over and some real progress has been made. But still, there are no women in the top anchor slots—how long will it take?" Often asked if another woman would anchor or coanchor on weekdays again, I always said, "No, not in my lifetime." I hated to be so pessimistic, but I had been in the business long enough to know that was a tough ceiling to crack.

To publicize my newly named program, *NBC News at Sunrise* (which had been known as *Early Today*), the network held an early-morning breakfast news conference with never-shy New York media reporters.

The first question: "Are you replacing Jane Pauley on *Today?*"

Having covered some of the wiliest politicians, I'd picked up the art of deflecting a question.

"Did everyone hear the question?" I asked. I followed that with, "He said, 'What are you wearing your first day on the air?'"

Thank goodness, I got a laugh. The media boys were angling for a good ol' catfight. Nice try.

The early-morning program I was hired to anchor preceded *Today*. Its third-place ranking was dragging down the ratings of the once-dominant *Today*. I was hired on the gamble that I could bring new viewers to the network. *Today* Executive Producer Steve Friedman told every media reporter who called him, "Connie Chung's career is going to rise or fall depending on how this program does." Oh, thanks for the pressure, buddy.

NBC, as well as other networks, was convinced that I was the magic elixir because of my top secret "Q score." "Q" stood for quotient, a cockamamie formula that calculated a person's familiarity and likability. My score was supposedly one of the highest among television newswomen. (I assumed I had high familiarity simply because I was the only Asian female anchoring news on national television. Would I really be confused with Tom Brokaw?)

At the time, television networks hired "news doctors" to evaluate Q scores and conduct ludicrous surveys evaluating on-air newspeople. It was a shameful period when news executives replaced their journalistic judgment with advice from consultants.

On top of all this hoo-ha were unscientific polls like one conducted by *USA Today* asking readers which of the television anchors they would most like to have dinner with. My name was first, over those of the big three male evening anchors, Brokaw, Jennings, and Rather. Very nice!

Did I believe all this hype? I must confess it made the popular song "New York, New York" by John Kander and Fred Ebb ring in my ears: "If I can make it there, I'll make it anywhere." Yet guilt was my favorite emotion. (Hanging around Maury taught me that Chinese guilt is identical to Jewish guilt.) Feeling perpetually guilt ridden, I could not bring myself to indulge in the glory. I could not behave poorly and let it go to my head. That would be unseemly. I had to remain my humble self.

Besides, I knew I had to prove myself at NBC because that's what women do. We constantly feel we must give 200 percent, lest anyone doubt our competency, lest we be tagged imposters posing as professionals. I was quite familiar with the old bromide for swelled heads: "Do not believe your own press." Maury's mantra was the most apropos: "Don't take *yourself* seriously, take your *work* seriously." If I did a good story, that was great, but it would never be enough. I was only as good as my last story.

Despite the punishing hours, or perhaps because of them, the staff at *NBC News at Sunrise* made working a joy. We were all perennially sleep-deprived zombies trying to think and write, though we felt as if we were all suffering from perpetual jet lag.

It was quite a schedule I carved out for myself.

Up at 2:00 a.m., I'd shower, put on my makeup, hot-roll my hair, then dress in something I had carefully laid out the night before so as never to waste precious time in the morning.

When 3:00 a.m. rolled around, an NBC car picked me up at the hotel where I was staying until I found an apartment. It wasn't just a car; the network (insanely) sent a stretch limo for all on-air people, no doubt to be sure we'd show up.

Leaving the hotel, I always smiled and greeted the overnight hotel bellmen, doormen, housekeepers, and desk clerks with a hearty "Good morning!" I think they thought I was a hooker, all dressed up and made up in the middle of the night, heading off to work in a limo. *Today* weatherman Willard Scott told me, "We are like hookers. They pick us up—but we have to find our own way home." That was true. I always caught a cab home.

Three thirty in the morning. I'd arrive at the *NBC News at Sunrise* studio at 30 Rockefeller Plaza after reading the *Wall Street Journal* on the way. Walking into the studio, I was camera ready. (Others who did the early-morning gig sneaked into the studio incognito. A team of makeup, hair, and wardrobe people would whip them together. I couldn't do that. I was too insecure to allow anybody to see me sans makeup.)

I'd down a can of Coke for caffeine (coffee makes me jumpy) while writing the broadcast with the senior producer and a writer, the executive producer lending a helping hand.

Fifteen minutes to air. I never gave makeup maven Bobbie Armstrong much time to slap heavier TV makeup on me. She was a legendary NBC makeup artist for *Today* and *Saturday Night Live* who had made up every president, world leader, celebrity, and newsmaker you could name. Bobbie always managed to shadow the sides of my nose to make it more prominent and shadow the sides of my face to narrow it. What a touch she had. If I was tired, she could eliminate any trace of bags. She transformed me into a sunny, bright morning beacon.

I always did my hair myself. A little teasing here and there. Lots of hairspray. Helmet head was good to go.

Seconds before I greeted viewers with "Good morning" live on national television, *Sunrise* Executive Producer Gerry Solomon made sure I was on my toes. With his perpetual elfin smile, he'd look me in the eye and say with deadly seriousness, "Don't f*ck up." (Gerry was a dear friend and a superb, selfless producer who collaborated with me on many political assignments at NBC.)

At 7:00 a.m., when we were done, all of us on *Sunrise* had the same bodily reaction: hunger. Defying our craving for sleep, off we'd go to Hurley's, an NBC hangout bar, for pancakes, French toast, or eggs, bacon, home fries, and toast.

Sometimes, after that hearty meal, I'd head out into the field for *NBC Nightly News*. Running on fumes, I'd cover a story, write it, and put it together with a producer to air nationally on Tom Brokaw's *Nightly News*. It was on at six thirty, which made for a long working day.

That was not the norm. Most often, I could go home and flop to sleep for three hours. Two alarms jolted me awake at 5:30 p.m. After a quick bite of dinner, I'd cab it back to the studio and write a one-minute newsbreak to deliver live at 9:00 p.m. Another minute of news followed at 10:00 p.m. After that I'd hop in a taxi again, and it was back to the hotel for another three-hour nap before I began the cycle all over again.

Sleeping in two three-hour shifts was, to say the least, difficult. I had a few scares. In the dead of winter, five thirty in the late afternoon looks exactly like five thirty in the morning. I would panic and freak out. Was it a.m. or p.m.? If it was 5:30 a.m., I was cooked.

Each week, I felt the pressure when *Sunrise* ratings were left on my desk. We were stuck in third place. With networks obsessed with ratings, I knew I was judged by those numbers. Other than a good job, what could I do?

It turned out there was something unorthodox that I could do to pump up ratings. When I learned that not all NBC affiliates carried *Sunrise*, I revved into sales and PR mode.

Maury had long told me that local affiliate stations and the general managers who ran them were the backbone of the network. He was right.

I asked the head of NBC Affiliates to find out which big cities were *not* carrying my program. Target number one: Cecil Walker, the general manager of WXIA-TV, the NBC station in heavily populated Atlanta, Georgia. Cecil, a tall man with smiling eyes, was quite shocked to hear from me. It was highly unusual for an on-air anchor to call. It delighted Cecil to no end. I convinced him to carry *NBC News at Sunrise*.

Next I called Amy McCombs, the general manager at WDIV-TV in Detroit, Michigan. She, too, agreed to carry *Sunrise*. I worked the phone, gently encouraging other general managers in other cities to carry our program. When Boston started carrying *Sunrise*, I redoubled my effort by flying there to shoot a story for *Nightly News* and promote *Sunrise* at the same time. Then Tampa joined the early-morning gang, so I traveled there for promotion and a speech. Finally NBC's all-important New York station began broadcasting *Sunrise*, late in the game.

After two years, with more viewers in significant major cities watching *Sunrise*, our ratings shot up to number one. I became the NBC affiliates' new best friend, not to speak of the NBC executives, who gave me bragging rights for a mission accomplished. The icing on the cake was that *Sunrise*'s ratings delivered a bigger audience to the *Today* show, which boosted *Today*'s numbers, pushing CBS's morning program to the cellar.

*   *   *

In addition to anchoring *Sunrise*, I occasionally substituted for Jane Pauley on *Today* and enjoyed the two-hour program even though it was double duty. When Jane went on her first pregnancy leave for three months, I became her primary substitute. That's when I got a front row seat to what her life was like.

While women dominated the ranks of those who got *Today* on the air each day, the executives who ran the show were members of the boys' club. Females were the primary workhorses who booked the guests, preinterviewed them, and crafted suggested questions for Bryant and Jane. Without them, there would be no two-hour program. Barbara Walters had worked behind the camera before she busted the barriers and fought to an on-air position on *Today*, paving the way for all of us.

Jane Pauley's coanchor, Bryant Gumbel, set the macho tone. Steve Friedman, *Today* executive producer, was the cocaptain of the male brigade. Before the program started, the guys joked and talked among themselves. Even though I was sitting right next to Bryant, I was invisible. Quietly reviewing my material, I went about my business. Bryant would not talk to me until the red light went on and we were on the air. I wondered if they treated Jane Pauley the same way. Sometimes the boys tossed a baseball around the studio, even proudly pulling out what may have been their high school

NBC's "Fastest Four on the Floor" reporters at the DNC in San Francisco. From left to right: Ken Bode, Connie, Chris Wallace, and Don Oliver. This image was released to promote network coverage of the RNC in Dallas. July 1984. *(© 2024 NBCUniversal Media, LLC.)*

Getting strapped into my headset, battery pack, and microphone to cover the 1984 conventions for NBC. *(Author's personal collection.)*

Maury and Connie's wedding day. December 2, 1984. *(Photograph by Dennis Brack.)*

With Roger Mudd for the NBC magazine program *American Almanac*, later retitled *1986*. *(NBC via Getty Images.)*

Profile of Israeli Ambassador to the United Nations Benjamin Netanyahu as he was angling to become Israel's leader, for NBC's *1986* magazine. *(© 2024 NBCUniversal Media, LLC.)*

Receiving honorary doctorate from Brown University. May 1987. left: Stevie Wonder. Fa right: Joan Ganz Coon *(Author's personal collect*

Daughter Susan's graduation from Harvard Law School in 1988. Left to right: Connie, Amy, Susan, and Maury. *(Author's personal collection.)*

A publicity still promoting election coverage with anchor Tom Brokaw and John Chancellor in 1988. *(NBC via Getty Images.)*

Maury and Connie outside Madison Square Garden, where New York Knicks were playing then Washington Bullets (now Wizards). February 1989. *(Photograph by Nicole Bengiveno.)*

Reporting and anchoring the CBS News magazine *Saturday Night with Connie Chung*. 1989. *(Photograph by Tony Esparza. Photo Still from CBS Photo—Courtesy of CBS Broadcasting Inc.)*

Exclusive interview with the legendary, elusive actor Marlon Brando. Aired October 7, 1989, on *Saturday Night with Connie Chung*. *(Photo Still from CBS Photo—Courtesy of CBS Broadcasting Inc.)*

Maury and Connie. *(Author's personal collection.)*

Anchoring the Sunday *CBS Evening News* in 1989. *(Photo © Joe McNally. Photo Still from CBS Photo—Courtesy of CBS Broadcasting Inc.)*

Seated beside President George H. W. Bush at state dinner for Italian President Francesco Cossiga. October 11, 1989. *(White House Photograph by Susan Biddle. Image Courtesy George H. W. Bush Presidential Library and Museum.)*

Exclusive interview with Captain Joseph Hazelwood of the *Exxon Valdez*, which caused the worst oil spill of its time, on *Saturday Night with Connie Chung.* 1990. *(Photo Still from CBS Photo—Courtesy of CBS Broadcasting Inc.)*

Carefully signing the underwear of an oil rigger in Alaska while working on the *Exxon Valdez* oil spill story. 1990. *(Photo Still from CBS Photo—Courtesy of CBS Broadcasting Inc.)*

Emmy-winning *Face to Face* interview with Paul Newman and Joanne Woodward, with producer Hal Gessner. The actor gifted me some of "Newman's Own" sauce just in time for our Thanksgiving Day broadcast. 1990. *(Photo Still from CBS Photo—Courtesy of CBS Broadcasting Inc.)*

Exclusive interview with Earvin "Magic" Johnson, his first interview after announcing he was HIV positive. Inscribed: "Love you forever / stay sweet." December 1991. *(Photo Still from CBS Photo—Courtesy of CBS Broadcasting Inc.)*

Interviewing Maine Senator William Cohen on floor of Republican convention. 1992. Note: headphones with skinny white antenna protruding from my hair. *(Photo Still from CBS Photo—Courtesy of CBS Broadcasting Inc.)*

Anchoring on election night. Left: Dan Rather. Right: Bob Schieffer. 1992. *(© Patrick D. Pagnano Estate/ Patrick D. Pagnano Photographic Archive/The Dolph Briscoe Center for American History/The University of Texas at Austin.)*

With Dan Rather at teleconference announcement of the *CBS Evening News with Dan Rather and Connie Chung.* May 17, 1993. *(© Patrick D. Pagnano Estate/Patrick D. Pagnano Photographic Archive/ The Dolph Briscoe Center for American History/The University of Texas at Austin.)*

The *CBS Evening News with Dan Rather and Connie Chung* launched on June 1, 1993. *(Photograph by Tony Esparza. Photo Still from CBS Photo—Courtesy of CBS Broadcasting Inc.)*

Barbara Walters interviewed me for her *10 Most Fascinating People* special after I was named CBS coanchor. 1993. *(ABC Photo Archives.)*

Coanchoring with Dan Rather live coverage of Israeli-PLO Peace agreement at the Clinton White House. September 13, 1993. *(Photo Still from CBS Photo—Courtesy of CBS Broadcasting Inc.)*

mitts. How many times did I want to stick my hand out like a pro ball player and shortstop the ball that Gumbel was about to catch. I wanted to hear that nice pop when it landed in my hand instead of his. Rather than blow it, I chickened out.

When Jane went on her second three-month maternity leave, I discovered she was not allowed to say, "Good morning" *first* when the program opened, nor could she be the first to say, "Have a good day" at 9:00 a.m. to close the *Today* show. Contractually, those were privileges reserved for Bryant alone. I was astonished. Jane had coanchored *Today* with Tom Brokaw *before* Bryant was hired. She had seniority, and the pecking order should have been the exact opposite.

All of that reminded me of the antiquated restrictions Barbara Walters had had to abide by when she was climbing her way to the top on *Today*. Barbara was allowed to question an interviewee only after the male anchor Frank McGee had asked three questions first. Had women not advanced beyond that?

Jane did not take this subjugation to her male cohost lightly. Unbeknownst to me, she fought for her fair share. Apparently she had corporate meetings where she made her case that she and Bryant should be presented as equals, but she lost.

Not knowing about Jane's battle at the time, I told NBC I wanted equality. In many ways, it seemed like petty bargaining, but I asked, how about alternating who uttered, "Good morning" first? The answer was no. I sought the counsel of Grant Tinker, who suggested that I "not fight this one." I took his advice. I was powerless to create new rules for Jane or me or anyone else. When I first came to NBC, *Today* Executive Producer Steve Friedman, referring to me in *TV-Cable Week*, had said, "You need somebody we call in the trade—and I am using it in the best sense of the term—a ball-buster." I was a ball-buster, so I tucked my mitts away for another day.

Despite his pervasive boys' club mentality, Steve Friedman surprised me by offering to help me during my *Today* show stint. He told me he would come in very early every morning, before the program started, to meet with me about my interviews.

I had done interviews live and taped interviews for more than a dozen years, but a four- or five-minute live morning show interview, often about a lightweight subject, was a different animal from hard news interviews. There is a method to creating a beginning, middle, and end in those short interviews with time for only three or four short questions, depending on how verbose the interviewees are. The timing and pacing are important. Steve and I met after each program too. He was good, and I truly appreciated his help.

On mornings when Jane called in sick, I was an easy choice to call at 2:00 a.m. for double duty since I was anchoring *Sunrise* anyway. Each time, I'd ask for Jane's research so I could study and prepare in advance for my live interviews on *Today*. But at times, I did not receive the research either at home or at the *Sunrise* studio before *Today* began. So while Bryant was on air and during commercials, I'd have to skim the research and cram, minutes before my interviews. It was nerve-racking, forcing me to wing some segments. Was I being paranoid in thinking the boys "forgot" to send me the research on purpose? I dared not go there. Hoping no one would see the smoke coming out of my ears, I did not want to complain.

On one occasion, the *Today* folks called me on a Sunday night to tell me that Jane had called in sick, so I was subbing on *Today* after I finished *Sunrise*. I happily coanchored *Today*, and after Bryant said goodbye at 9:00 a.m., I stepped off the set.

To my shock, I found someone had forgotten to mention that I should remain in place, alongside Bryant, to coanchor a live special report on President Ronald Reagan's speech to the United Nations. Blindsided, I stood on the sidelines, annoyed that I had not been warned, which would have allowed me to properly prepare. Being neurotic, paranoid, and just insecure enough, I fumed inside. Maybe the *Today* executives had intentionally kept me in the dark?

Defiant and rebellious, I did something terribly unprofessional, and in the process, I cooked my own goose. As Bryant waved his arm, like, "Come on the field and take your position," I shook my head at him, stubbornly refusing to join him at the anchor desk. Knowing he had big-shot-itis, I thought he would hog the airtime anyway, and I walked out of the studio. Not good. Bryant was determined to make me pay.

From that incident on, when I introduced Bryant on *Sunrise* so he could promote *Today*, he would not acknowledge me by name. He would simply recite the "tease" of what was coming up on the show, then he would stop talking. Normally, if Jane was doing the *Today* tease, she would throw it back to me: "Connie?" And I would reply, "Thank you, Jane," and move on.

After a week or two of this nonsense, Tinker called me to ask, "Why doesn't Bryant say your name?" I told him about the drama. Tinker urged me to apologize. I went to Bryant's office and apologized, extending my right hand to shake his. Bryant gave me his left.

He appeared to hold grudges. Once David Letterman interrupted a live outdoor program Bryant was doing on Rockefeller Plaza. Using a bullhorn, Letterman shouted out a window, "My name is Larry Grossman, and I am wearing no pants!" (Grossman was president of NBC News.) Anybody who saw it laughed hysterically, except Bryant. Bryant refused to speak to Letterman (or me, for my transgression) for years.

When Maury and I ran into Bryant at sports events, he would look past me, as if I were not there. Years later, with the good sense of his wife Hilary, Bryant and I got over our tit-for-tat feud. She was a gem. I'm glad for Bryant (and me) that he found her.

The *Today* men had a nickname for Jane Pauley, "Lady Jane." I admired how kind, professional, and gracious she was with the boys. I shudder to think what they called me. Despite being so helpful when I was substituting for Jane, Steve Friedman turned the tables and began to denigrate me for reasons I do not know. Was he siding with Bryant to put me in my place? Was I too ballsy? Media reporters could depend on Steve for a juicy negative quote about anybody and everybody, and I was no exception. He told one reporter, "In all my years here, she proved beyond a shadow of a doubt she could read the news, but she never proved she could do anything else." Finding it difficult to either confront him or ignore him, I was just insecure enough to question my abilities.

Fortunately, I had allies at the network. It made such a difference to me that executives saw me as someone who had journalistic bona fides. When I was named one of four floor reporters (and the only female) at the 1984 Democratic convention in San Francisco, I was thrilled at this plum assignment.

The other three were Chris Wallace, Ken Bode, and Don Oliver. Chris Wallace, son of the legendary *60 Minutes* bulldog Mike Wallace, was a colleague I adored. He was smart and a superb reporter, and he had a delightful laugh. The best part of Chris was that he never seemed to have an overblown opinion of himself. Like me, he felt free to engage in self-deprecating humor. When a young intern recklessly drove the four of us through the bowels of the Moscone Convention Center, we thought we were not long for this world.

Chris quipped, "I can see the headline now. 'Connie Chung and three others were killed today...'"

Somehow Chris and I convinced the higher-ups to let us co-anchor one weekend night. We thought we would impress the bosses so much they would make us the new young anchor team of the *NBC Nightly News*. I really wanted us to knock our half hour out of the ballpark, thinking how great it would be to work with a man who would treat me as an equal. We were so nervous, we were dreadful. Afterward, we laughed about how far we'd let our minds fantasize.

As a floor reporter, I was outfitted with a six-pound battery pack strapped to a military belt that had a cluster of wires attached to a headset equipped with headphones, a protruding ten-inch antenna, and a microphone that curled around my face. For interviews, I was armed with a large handheld microphone.

I felt as if I were suited for outer space when I approached former astronaut and Ohio Senator John Glenn, a political star and potential challenger to the likely Democratic nominee, Vice President Walter Mondale. Glenn's campaign effort had faltered, but he was still worthy of an interview. I was about to question him on the convention floor, which was littered with papers and confetti, when a woman screamed, pointing and wiggling her finger at my rear. I looked behind me and saw smoke. When I moved away from the smoke, the billowing dark cloud moved *with* me. I realized my battery pack was on fire. I tried to unfasten the belt but couldn't remove it. While the people around me scattered, John Glenn—who said he smelled smoke like insulation burning—grabbed the red-hot wires, yanked them out of my battery pack, and smothered the fire. Glenn said, "I grabbed the belt to pull it away from her dress so that she wouldn't get burned, and then the two of us struggled to get it [the belt] off."

Senator Glenn shrugged modestly, saying, "It was no big deal." His aide added, proudly, "He saves lives all the time." Fortunately for me, my hero senator was made of the right stuff!

When I experienced another mishap one night while anchoring the Saturday *Nightly News*, I began to think I was accident-prone. NBC had recently installed robotic cameras in the studio to cut the cost of a live operator. I was delivering a story about the Middle East when my camera suddenly went rogue and took off, wandering to the left on its own. Where the heck was it going? I continued reading the news, slowly gliding to my right along with the camera, keeping my head in frame so as not to alarm the viewer. However, I knew my rolling desk chair was reaching the edge of the platform where my anchor desk was perched. Just before I would have fallen off the platform, I was relieved to see the camera jostle to a stop. Phew. Had the camera failed to stop moving, I would have disappeared out of sight, as if I'd dropped through a trapdoor.

NBC's publicity people actively booked the network's news anchors and beat reporters to cross-promote our special events and reports on Johnny Carson's *Tonight Show* and David Letterman's *Late Night*, following Carson. Since Brokaw appeared frequently on all those entertainment shows, I thought it was acceptable for me to follow suit when the publicity folks asked. I, too, was on Carson and Jay Leno a few times to promote programs I was doing, but I became a more frequent guest on Letterman. It was a wildly popular show for younger night owls, and we had a rollicking good time playing cat and mouse, a bit flirtatious, a bit combative, and mostly unpredictable. I'm not sure why our relationship was so watchable. He and his producers must have thought I was a good straight man, given Dave's incorrigible behavior and quick wit.

Many of my guest appearances were scheduled in advance, but

often this is how they came about. A Letterman producer would call me and ask if I was doing anything other than working. If I said, for example, "I have a dentist appointment," Dave would come along with a camera crew and turn it into a skit.

Another time, Dave wanted to spend the day with me. I had planned to buy shoe trees for Maury during my lunch break, so I invited him to come along. A camera crew started rolling as Dave and I boarded a van. We passed some construction workers eating their lunches.

Dave shouted out the window, "It's Connie Chung!"

One of the construction workers pointed to his crotch. I looked at Dave and said, "Did you see that?"

Dave always took great pains to feign jealousy of Maury. He'd purposely mispronounce his name, calling him Murray, Morley, or some such. Still in the van, we passed a New York City bus with a huge photo of Maury on the entire side of it. It was an ad for his program *A Current Affair.*

Dave shouted, "There's Murray on a bus! Oh brother." Then he muttered, "I'm spending the day with this guy's wife, and he rolls by on a bus."

When we picked up those shoe trees, I made a reference to the sizes of Maury's feet and Dave's feet and what they might be indicative of. Dave claimed he didn't know what I was talking about.

Once Dave taped a promotional announcement in which he said I was going to be on his show and would "crack walnuts with her bare hands." The NBC Standards and Practices stiffs asked the *Late Night* staff if I was actually doing that.

"No," they replied, honestly.

The stiffs declared, "Well then, Letterman cannot say that."

Dave's producer called me. "To spite them, would you come on the show and crack walnuts with your bare hands? We will show you how to do it." I showed up, taped the show, and—drum roll—after many tries—succeeded! The audience went nuts.

\* \* \*

As you know, Maury and I got married in my apartment on December 2, 1984, even though we were living in separate cities. We'd rendezvous every weekend, alternating between Washington and New York. When Maury approached the front desk of my apartment building, he was stopped as all guests were. Maury would say, "I'm Connie's husband." The man at the front desk would ring me on my landline: "Mr. Chung is here." It's one of Maury's favorite stories.

NBC asked me to take a two-month leave from *Sunrise* to join Roger Mudd as a correspondent on his new magazine program, *American Almanac*. It was a golden opportunity for Maury and me to see each other more often because Roger's program was based in Washington. How perfect that I had to tape introductions to my stories in DC, which enabled us to be together an extra day or two during the week.

For Roger's magazine program, I flew internationally for a number of interviews. To Tel Aviv for a profile on Benjamin Netanyahu, who at the time was Israel's ambassador to the United Nations and had been poised for decades to seize the leadership of the country; to Islamabad, Pakistan, for another profile of Prime Minister Benazir Bhutto, the first woman to be elected to lead a Muslim-dominated democratic country; and to Managua to interview Rosario Murillo, the powerful first lady of Nicaragua, married to President Daniel Ortega. I had been flying so much for *American Almanac* that when Maury and I went to see a movie, I sat down in the theater and tried to put on my seat belt.

Unfortunately, the ratings for *American Almanac* were abysmal, and media critics called the program underwhelming, dull, and stodgy. Changing the name of the program to *1986*, NBC placed me with Roger to coanchor, hoping I could magically boost the ratings. I knew it was an impossibly heavy lift. Nonetheless, I felt lucky because even though Roger preferred anchoring alone, he did not suffer from big-shot-itis. He was still gracious and respectful to me.

The title *1986* did not bode well. When the year ended, so did our program.

\* \* \*

When Maury moved to New York for work, it was a frightening change in our seven-year commuter relationship, for it was the first time we would live together, day in and day out—disconcerting for a forty-year-old single woman who was obsessively, compulsively neat and a forty-seven-year-old bachelor who'd spent his single years leaving everything in his kitchen sink.

But miraculously, it worked out. Our daughters came to visit and stayed with us from time to time. Susan, the brainiac in our family, went to college at the University of Michigan in Ann Arbor, then her smarts led to Harvard Law School. Amy went to Connecticut College and her acting talent got her into the Yale School of Drama for her graduate degree.

Maury was responsible for the girls' expenses—including college and graduate school for both. One night, I heard him on the telephone, needing to pay their tuitions but not having the money. It reminded me so vividly of my father on the phone, pleading with a bank to loan him some money. I could not bear it. Since I was making a higher salary than Maury at the time, I told him I *had* the money to pay the girls' tuitions. I was happy to help. The scene was much too painful, and I could not stand to see my husband stressed.

\* \* \*

At one point Maury gently made an important suggestion to me.

"You are forty. I know you want to have a baby sometime. I think this is the time."

"No, no," I replied, "I have another convention and election coming up. No, I have too much to do." Maury tried to muscle my birth control pills away from me. I clutched them in my hand. "Oh no, not yet. It's OK. We have time."

We did *not* have time. Maury was right. I had always envisioned having a baby, but I was so wrapped up in my career, I never had "time" to carve out a personal life. Time got away from me. First I forgot to get married, and then I forgot to have a baby. Now my biological clock was clanging loudly, even though my brain didn't listen. Having had control over my personal choices for so long, I did not understand how my body had a say in the matter. It never occurred to me that I could not have a baby whenever I wanted. I gave up my birth control pills and went to see my ob-gyn. The baby journey I was about to embark on was long and not what I expected. More on that later.

I had signed a new contract with NBC, dropping *NBC News at Sunrise* but still anchoring the Saturday *Nightly News* and continuing to do news updates in prime time, and I was the only woman on the short list of substitutes for Tom Brokaw on the weekday *NBC Nightly News*.

Since NBC had a history of fourteen failed magazine programs, the news division created a documentary unit instead. Happy to be assigned to that staff, I thought I would be creating solid hours of serious journalism, but Executive Producer Paul Greenberg and Senior Producer Sid Feders had other ideas for me.

I wanted to do a documentary about security breaches at the US embassy in the Soviet Union. Greenberg adamantly refused, knocking down the idea despite a well-researched pitch from a female producer and me. Nothing she or I said would convince him.

Instead, Feders suggested doing what I would not call a documentary. It was called *Scared Sexless* and was about sex and AIDS, a blatant ratings grabber. I vehemently resisted. I tried to fight in a civilized manner, but I could not find a way to buck the system. I lost, and it was a significant loss.

Just as I had known all those years before that the miniskirt special I'd been assigned at Channel 5 was not dignified, serious journalism, I knew this kind of tawdry play for ratings would hurt my career. My inability to extricate myself from the sex blather set in motion a perception that tarnished my reputation for all the years that followed. Much to my dismay, the curse was that it was a ratings hit—garnering the highest ratings for an NBC News documentary in ten years.

Another Sid Feders extravaganza followed, called *Life in the Fat Lane*, about weight loss. Yet again, I succumbed to the wishes of the men in charge, even though I was embarrassed by this hour of infotainment. Again, the ratings came in just short of the top ten of the week—it ended up eleventh. After each of those hours, I was skewered by media critics, especially the *Washington Post*'s Tom Shales, who called me "Connie Funn" and the programs "popumentaries." The insults were awful to read, yet frankly, I agreed with Shales. I earnestly traveled to do all the interviews, but it was my worst series of programs ever.

Later Shales, in a column about other documentaries by NBC

women, called *Real Life with Jane Pauley* "superficial friffle" and *Cutting Edge with Maria Shriver* "another exercise in thumb-twiddling anti-journalism from a news division that seems to be steadily losing interest in the news." Shales went on, "*Cutting Edge* was produced by Sid Feders, the man who perpetrated many of the mockumentaries and schlockumentaries that starred Connie Chung."

That story by Shales highlighted what I already knew. The men in the documentary unit, such as Tom Brokaw, would never touch the schlock and were never put in a position where they had to refuse to do celebrity-tainted superficial subjects. Three women were. We did not wiggle out of it. Why? I don't think it ruined Jane Pauley and Maria Shriver's reputations, yet I know it ruined mine. Unfortunately, I did not know how to fight it.

Another harebrained "documentary" idea, *Stressed to Kill*, about how to deal with stress, wound up making headlines I never anticipated. I interviewed the legendary Indiana University basketball coach Bobby Knight. Knight had trouble controlling his temper during practices and games. In an iconic video, he had thrown a folding chair across the court, almost into spectators. Knight was also seen on tape appearing to choke a player during practice.

In our interview, I asked Bobby Knight how he handled stress. On tape, Knight said, "I think that if rape is inevitable, relax and enjoy it..." Obviously, I was taken aback. Knight realized what he had just said and followed with, "That's just an old term that you're going to use. The plane's down so you have no control over it. I'm not talking about the act of rape. Don't misinterpret me there. But what I'm talking about is, something happened to you, so you have to handle it." Knight asked me if we were going to use what he'd just said. I told him I did not know. We'd have to see. I would let him know.

We did run it, making sure to include his explanation and the context in which he was speaking. A firestorm followed. Indiana's president released a statement, deploring Knight's "coarse language," saying it "was in very poor taste." Student protesters demanded a national apology from Knight, carrying signs that read, "Rape Is Every Woman's Knightmare" and "Rape Is No Game."

Years later, sports reporter Roy Firestone asked Knight, "What do you think of Connie Chung?" Knight said, "If Connie Chung was on fire, I wouldn't even piss on her."

\* \* \*

The upcoming 1988 presidential election gave me a way to escape from those horrible popumentaries.

I was assigned to cover various candidates. Colorado Senator Gary Hart was leading the pack of Democratic hopefuls in the run-up to the convention in 1987. I had known him well when he was George McGovern's campaign manager in 1972. But his campaign was derailed when he taunted reporters, daring them to follow him because of rumors he was a philanderer. The *Miami Herald* had started to do just that even before Hart's dare. The *Herald* caught Hart with a young blond named Donna Rice at his Washington town house. Then a photograph surfaced of Rice sitting on Hart's lap on a boat appropriately named *Monkey Business*. Hart withdrew from the race. His political career was over.

Years later, Maury and I were in the Bahamas on vacation, having dinner at a restaurant. A boat captain told us he had been docked right next to the *Monkey Business*, where he had seen Gary Hart and Donna Rice. The captain said, "I thought about calling Connie Chung" to spill the sordid but juicy beans. It would have been quite a scoop.

That revelation changed how reporters dealt with dalliances by public figures. For years, White House reporters had kept quiet about presidents who cheated on their first ladies. After the Hart revelation, all bets were off.

\* \* \*

By the time the Democratic convention was held, in July 1988, Jesse Jackson had mounted an impressive run for the presidential nomination. When I covered him on the campaign trail, he'd spot me among the press corps and enthusiastically shout, "Hi, Chonnie!" (a combo platter of Connie Chung). The looming question was, Would Jackson, who was second in the delegate count behind Massachusetts Governor Michael Dukakis, challenge him for the nomination? Or would Jackson use his power to squeeze concessions from Dukakis in exchange for an endorsement?

When the convention began, I had lined up an exclusive interview with Jackson, so I was in the catbird seat, in his trailer with my big coup. From his anchor booth, high above the convention hall, Tom Brokaw asked Jackson the first couple of questions as I patiently waited. I had purposely asked the cameraperson to let me sit very close to Jackson because he had a habit of answering his questions in long speechifying sentences. I knew that if I put my hand on his arm, he might get the cue to cut! When I took the baton from Brokaw, I asked Jackson pointed questions about what he got in exchange for backing down, which impressed the NBC brass. I proved I knew what I was talking about when it came to politics. And by the way, the hand-on-the-arm trick worked. I had to use my method a couple of times to force Jackson to wrap it up.

I interviewed Jackson again after his momentous floor speech and got the only interview with John F. Kennedy Jr. after he spoke at the convention podium, his maiden voyage in the Democratic limelight. It was a successful week for me.

But after the political year ended, my fortunes at NBC were beginning to feel bleak. I could not stomach returning to the documentary unit and sharing offices with Greenberg and Feders, so I asked to move my office to another area.

At about that time, NBC News President Larry Grossman asked me to come to his office. He told me something that took me completely by surprise. He said no executive producers wanted to work with me. Even more humiliating, disconcerting, and demeaning was his request. Grossman asked me to meet with each to ask them why—especially since it was I who did not want to work with Greenberg and Feders. I felt as if I were inviting each into a boxing ring: "Hit me with a right or a left or an uppercut." I don't remember exactly what happened in any of the conversations, but the men were loath to tell me to my face why I was so reprehensible. I knew that when my contract was up, I had best move on.

Right about that time, an earthquake shift occurred in broadcast news. No longer news friendly, the big three networks joined the age of eighties greed. The three companies cared only about the bottom line. At CBS, William Paley relinquished power to Larry Tisch; ABC had merged with Capital Cities Communications; and RCA, NBC's parent company, had merged with General Electric. Larry Grossman had been replaced as news president with a newspaper editor from the Louisville *Courier-Journal*, Michael Gartner, who had no experience in television. Gartner's mandate was to slash budgets, cut all fat, and offer buyouts to those who had earned seniority and high salaries.

Two of my fellow floor reporters at the 1984 convention left

NBC News—Chris Wallace fled to ABC News, and Ken Bode accepted a position in academia. I would be the third, with one foot out the door.

Bob Wright, NBC president and CEO and an incredibly kind man, threw a Hail Mary. He spent hours talking to me and made a follow-up call asking what it would take to keep me at NBC. He even called me at home on a weekend to talk again, but I moved swiftly, accepting an offer from CBS News. When I saw Bob at television industry events after that, I felt bad for having been rude, wanting him to know how deeply I appreciated his graciousness.

I was looking forward to my future with CBS News. I had no inkling that CBS would give me my highest high and my lowest low.

CHAPTER 19

# CBS: Connie's Big Shot

L ong before my contract was up at NBC in 1989, CBS Broadcast Group President Howard Stringer had begun trying to woo me back to where I had started my network career. For me, no persuasion was necessary. CBS was the home of news giants Edward R. Murrow and Walter Cronkite. I had long wanted CBS to be my home again too.

Howard was smart, genial, and charming—a people pleaser. Born in Wales, he spoke with an elegant accent, greeting me with a smile and a sigh: "Ah, Coh-nie." Howard had moved up the ranks at CBS, starting as a talented producer, then becoming head of the documentary unit, executive producer of the *CBS Evening News with Walter Cronkite*, CBS News president, and finally president of the CBS Broadcast Group—successful on each rung of the ladder. I adored him and assumed he would always have my back or at least have me on his radar.

Just below Stringer was the new CBS News President David Burke, who had been vice president at ABC News, helping build that network from an also-ran to a strong competitor. I had not known him before but soon discovered he was a refined and proper gentleman whom I liked and respected.

Next was Andy Lack, the man who had been named executive producer of a new CBS magazine I would anchor. Andy was a talented, creative producer who I thought yearned to be in Hollywood, directing and producing for the big screen, but settled for the small one.

My agent, Alfred, and I had negotiated my usual six-day workweek anchoring a CBS hour-long weekly magazine and the Sunday *CBS Evening News*, substituting for Dan Rather on the weekday *CBS Evening News*, and reporting stories as well.

It was April, and I felt the warmth of spring and the glow of a fresh start. My first week on the job, I flew to Sparta, Tennessee, for a story that aired on the *Evening News* and substituted for Rather on another night.

About a month into my new job, Maury and I received a welcome surprise. I was pregnant for the first time at forty-three. Because of my age, my doctor strongly recommended bed rest until we knew the pregnancy was progressing normally.

I asked Howard Stringer, David Burke, and Andy Lack to meet individually with me. There had been a lot of media hoopla about my arrival at CBS, so when I told them about my need to take it easy because of my pregnancy, I knew it would be disconcerting. All three assured me they understood. Howard was especially empathetic because he and his wife were also an older couple trying to have children.

In June 1989, the international story of the decade broke—

protests at Tiananmen Square. Dan Rather flew to China. I watched history in the making on television with my feet up. Of course, I wanted to be there covering the story, and at the same time I felt pangs on a personal level. Long ago in China, my parents had marched in the streets against oppression, but it seemed unfathomable that the undercurrent of unrest decades later could explode in such a dramatic manner. I had an inner feeling of pride that the Chinese protesters were fighting for democracy. The government crackdown was horrific to watch.

Yet I was happy to be an observer. It seemed a worthy trade-off to stay home if it meant we were on the road to having a baby.

All that bed rest turned out to be for naught. I had a miscarriage, the first of many. After a dilation and curettage procedure in the hospital, I plunged back to work immediately. The distraction helped me get past the disappointment, but Maury and I were undaunted. I approached having a baby the same way I did investigating a story. I tried to find out what might be wrong, consulting multiple doctors and experts.

But it was time to launch Andy Lack's brainchild, the prime-time program I had come to CBS News to do.

Andy was fascinated with the innovative Warren Beatty movie *Reds* about John Reed, the American radical socialist. Beatty interviewed real-life witnesses with knowledge of Reed's story and intercut those interviews with dramatizations of events.

"We could build a program with you as anchor and correspondent around that technique," Andy explained. "We'd make short movies about an important historical event or current news figures. Then we would follow the movie with a panel discussion, led by you." If anyone disagreed with what the depiction portrayed, they would be encouraged to say so.

Besides the Beatty movie, Andy had been inspired by Walter Cronkite's 1950s CBS program *You Are There*, in which historical events were dramatized by actors in period costume and interviewed by CBS News reporters. I remembered watching that program as a kid. One episode depicted the signing of the Declaration of Independence, and real-life reporters "interviewed" "Benjamin Franklin" and "Thomas Jefferson." Other episodes featured dramatizations about Joan of Arc, the Salem witch trials, and even the death of Socrates. Despite being hokey, the program had run for several years.

If it had been good enough for Walter Cronkite, I thought, it surely was good enough for me.

My program was called *Saturday Night with Connie Chung*, to air at 10:00 in the evening. Saturday was hardly a night for serious historical subject matter. I rationalized that if it was well done, it could work. Maybe viewers—even on Saturdays, traditionally date nights—would tune in for a quality depiction of an event (clearly labeled a dramatization) and gain thought-provoking knowledge from the panel discussion.

The first program, airing on September 23, 1989, told the story of Vernon Johns, who preceded Martin Luther King as the pastor of the Dexter Avenue Baptist Church in Montgomery, Alabama. Johns's story is described in the first chapter of the Pulitzer Prize–winning book *Parting the Waters* by Taylor Branch about Martin Luther King. Although Johns was a pioneer of the Civil Rights Movement, he had been overlooked and relegated to a footnote in history. We were thrilled when the acclaimed, respected actor James Earl Jones agreed to portray him in our dramatization.

The short movie was professional and well done. Afterward, I conducted a half-hour discussion with the Reverend Jesse Jackson,

Montgomery Mayor Emory Folmar, and Johns's daughter Toni Johns Anderson.

No sooner had the program aired than we were met with a firestorm of negative criticism. Print television critics excoriated the "re-creations." I was surprised that the vitriol was ubiquitous. Everyone at CBS News jumped into bunkers, disavowing any part of the program.

Not President David Burke. He eloquently reminded news purists of Walter Cronkite's *You Are There*. "There is nothing wrong with re-creation of news events unless you purposefully wish to deceive and you're not clear and concise about what you're doing." When a reporter asked if there was a risk that viewers would be confused, Burke said viewers are "intelligent people…rather wise….I'm not sure they have to be protected from some nefarious act on my part." I agreed with Burke and said so publicly.

But the critics were not swayed, and nothing would stop them from attacking the program. Re-creating historical events on a news program, they charged, was highly inappropriate and breached the line between entertainment and news.

A *TV Guide* writer, Robert MacKenzie, even took aim at me— making a gross error about my background. "Chung came to CBS with a credibility gap. Much of her career has been spent as an anchorwoman in Los Angeles." He continued, "But she hasn't spent those long, honing years in the trenches as a network correspondent, as Rather, Jennings, Brokaw and other heavyweights have. She doesn't swing the weight of authority that is earned that way, there is no substitute for it." That infuriated me. Had MacKenzie done his homework, he would have known he was dead wrong.

Just before our program, NBC News had also used re-creations in its new magazine program with Maria Shriver and Mary Alice Williams, the one I had been asked to anchor if I stayed at NBC. And ABC News' *World News Tonight* anchor, Peter Jennings, even used a re-creation in his hard news broadcast, for which he later delivered an on-air apology. The combination of all three networks engaging in the practice gave television critics a cause célèbre.

On top of that, viewers rejected *Saturday Night with Connie Chung*. The program ranked close to the bottom of the Nielsen ratings. CBS naturally took ratings seriously since high ratings translated to higher advertising rates, which equaled higher profits. The media reporters who had built me up to be a news star used my flop of a program to question my value to the network. I was numb. It was a disastrous start to what I had hoped would be a glorious career at CBS.

We eventually abandoned ship and morphed into the typical formulaic magazine, along the lines of *60 Minutes*: a serious story, then a profile and a human-interest feature.

The difference with our magazine program was that whereas similar programs had a fleet of reporters, I was our only one. That meant I was living on the road again, flying from city to city to meet producers and crews for interviews, extending my six-day week to seven. I was grateful that I had to be back in New York to tape the program and anchor the Sunday edition of the *CBS Evening News* live. At least I could be home with Maury once a week. Ratings rose a bit, so the media scrutiny dialed down a bit too.

I was so bushed, Michelle Cutler, who did my studio makeup at CBS, would hold my head up to keep it from bobbing as I'd doze off in her comfortable chair that had a relaxing footrest.

A refuge was substituting for Dan Rather on the *CBS Evening*

*News* when he was off on assignment or vacation. It was a pleasure when I got to work on a daily hard news broadcast again.

I did not think about it at the time, but substituting for Rather was a way for executives to see if I could handle network anchoring at CBS. It also meant that when there was breaking news, regardless of the time of day, I would jump into the anchor chair and break into regular programming to ad-lib a CBS Special Report on live television. Ad-libbing had always caused heart-thumping moments for me with the pressure to speak spontaneously, smoothly, and with authority before millions of people about complex, unfolding news events. I lived in fear the microphone on my lapel might pick up the beat of my heart, which I could hear thumping loudly in my own ears. Even though I had ad-libbed many times, I was always nervous and relieved when it was over.

Meanwhile, *Saturday Night with Connie Chung* remained a ratings cellar dweller no matter what we did.

Then one day, I got a call from Marlon Brando, the Hollywood uber legend, who had won wide acclaim portraying Stanley Kowalski in Tennessee Williams's *A Streetcar Named Desire*, Colonel Kurtz in *Apocalypse Now*, and of course Don Vito Corleone in *The Godfather*.

He called to grouse about a film in which he appeared, *A Dry White Season*, about apartheid in South Africa. He accused the director of watering down the antiapartheid theme and ruining the film in editing.

This was not the first time he had called me.

As you know, I had anchored local news at the CBS station in Los Angeles. One evening, I'd stepped off the set after *The 6 O'Clock News* when someone told me I had a call.

"Connie, this is Marlon Brando."

"Sure, right," I said, certain it was a joke. "Why don't you continue talking? I'll decide if you are Marlon Brando."

He started to ramble about Indigenous Americans. While listening to him, I remembered that he had refused to accept an Oscar, his second, for his role in *The Godfather*. In his place, Brando had sent a woman named Sacheen Littlefeather to read a statement he had written. Littlefeather claimed to be an Apache, though after her death in 2022 her sisters disputed this. Brando was protesting the portrayal of Indigenous people in movies and on television.

The voice sounded just like Brando's. And he was speaking as if he had a few marbles in his mouth. Could it really be?

Indeed, it was.

The calls at work kept coming until I finally agreed to meet him for a drink after work. Brando was rumored to have an Asian fetish, which gave me pause. But I was much too curious.

"Meet me at Le Dome on Sunset," I said. "After I get off *The 11 O'Clock News*. I'll be there around midnight."

As I entered the restaurant, I didn't need to look around much—I couldn't miss him. Marlon Brando was no longer the irresistible young man with piercing eyes, full lips, and a brooding, sexy look. He was a round-faced, terribly overweight man who was poured onto a velvet banquette. I said hello with a hesitant smile on my face, not knowing what to expect.

What did we talk about? Damned if I remember. He probably did most of the talking. After about an hour, I said goodbye and drove home.

As the years passed, I had given him my home phone number (never my home address), hoping to cajole him into doing an interview. He left interminable messages on my old-fashioned answering machine. Sometimes he would use up the entire cassette. I kept one cassette, which I cannot find now, in which he mumbled forever about taking me down the Nile. He also asked what I wear to bed at night. I told him flannel pajamas with feet.

When Maury and I started dating, Brando was still calling. Once, Maury picked up the phone, but that did not prove to be a deterrent to Marlon the Persistent.

After years of phone games and me coaxing him to sit down for an interview, Brando finally said yes, provided he could vent about *A Dry White Season*. It was to be his first interview in sixteen years.

When our ten-person team—including two camera crews, CBS still photographer Tony Esparza, producer Chris Dalrymple, and me—arrived at his home in the Hollywood Hills, Brando's assistant, an Asian woman, had laid out quite a spread of food for us. Brando insisted we eat before we set up.

We chose his beautiful patio for the interview. We settled into garden chairs, and for the next six-plus hours, while we rolled many tapes, he toyed with me and never gave me a serious answer to any of my serious questions.

Brando denigrated his craft as if his work had been frivolous. He was evasive as I asked him to acknowledge and discuss his successes. He had been trained by the masters of Method acting, Stella Adler and Stanislavski. He was idolized, even worshipped, by other actors.

I pressed him, but he waved off his whole career and the entire industry as superficial, refusing to respect his profession.

He said, "It's a waste of time. I don't find it stimulating or interesting. It's not a consuming passion."

Brando continued to scoff.

"I find it odious, unpleasant. I don't find acting satisfying. I'm much more interested in writing...focusing on other things."

"Such as?" I asked.

"I'm interested in everything. I've spent hours and hours watching ants go up and down my sink. Picking up crumbs and finding out where they come from." What the heck was he talking about? He went off on wacky tangents. I tried to remain composed, despite his bizarre behavior.

We had talked for so long, the sun had set—the light dropping dramatically to darkness. The crew had to set up lights on the patio. I kept at it, even though I was at my wit's end, trying over and over to squeeze some substance out of him. But I never did.

While writing this book, I discovered on YouTube an interview Brando did with talk show host Dick Cavett on June 12, 1973. Brando played cat and mouse with him too. Like me, Cavett gave Brando a forum for his favorite cause: how Indigenous people were shown in movies. Cavett even invited several tribal leaders on his talk show, no doubt quid pro quo for the actor. But Brando did not reciprocate. When Cavett asked him about *The Godfather*, the recalcitrant Brando responded, "I don't want to talk about movies."

Had I seen Cavett's interview before I sat down with Brando, I would have been forewarned. Too bad YouTube wasn't invented then.

Thanks to the internet and my researcher John Yuro, I was able to read a transcript of Brando's interview with Edward R. Murrow on *Person to Person* on April 1, 1955. Brando was only thirty at the time. The interview was as inane and mortifying as mine.

Murrow asked, "You heard any good stories lately?"

To which Brando replied, "...What time is it when the Chinaman goes to the dentist?"

Murrow played straight man. "What time is it when the Chinaman goes to the dentist?"

Brando delivered the punch line. "...Well, it's tooth dirty. You know? Two thirty."

Frankly, I was not at ease interviewing Brando because he was looking at me as if I were a nice cut of Asian meat. He had several children with an Asian woman. It was not hard to see he had a fetish.

Asian women have long been perceived as submissive, exotic, and hypersexual. It goes back as far as the 1800s but came into greater focus during World War II, the Korean War, and the Vietnam War, during which Asian sex workers serviced white soldiers. During those times, Asian women recoiled if mistaken for one of "those women"—streetwalkers. The way in which we are sexualized is something I find unbearable.

Unfortunately, this was not the first time I had encountered an Asian fetish.

The salacious look that some men had when they stared at me was repulsive. Some of them would invariably reveal their thoughts: "I spent a lot of time in China and Japan, and I just think you people are so pretty."

Maury and I were once invited by a couple to a small dinner party that included two other couples: actor Michael Douglas and his wife and Helen Gurley Brown, editor in chief of the magazine *Cosmopolitan*, and her husband, producer David Brown. Helen's book *Sex and the Single Girl* had created a climate of free discussion about women and sex, previously too touchy a subject for magazines.

As the three of us sat around a coffee table having cocktails, Michael Douglas asked Helen Gurley Brown, "Why do you think Connie is so appealing on the news?"

Brown quickly replied, "It's the Asian thing."

I was speechless. I let it pass after an awkward silence.

It's difficult to describe the feeling we get when we hear comments like these. It's a dirty, alienating jab, as if nothing else about us matters. It's also hard to know how to combat such rude statements from otherwise intelligent people. Is there a way to confront their deeply ingrained prejudice? I empathize greatly with other minorities who face reprehensible bias, often far worse.

When the Brando interview aired, it proved to be a ratings bonanza, even on a Saturday night. I was surprised that the actor touched a nerve with a cross section of people—Hollywood actors, neighbors, people I had not heard from in years, people on the street. Warren Beatty begged me to give him a copy of the raw tapes. I never did.

Although I won an Emmy for Best Interview, I thought it was an awful encounter, and it soured me on the idea of interviewing actors. Barbara Walters once said she liked doing celebrity interviews because they are both entertaining and informational. I did not see the purpose. I preferred serious news. Actors and actresses typically agreed to interviews to promote their movies. They usually didn't want to reveal their innermost thoughts, and why would we want to pry anyway?

Shortly after the Brando interview aired, Maury and I were invited to a White House State Dinner for President of Italy Francesco Cossiga. Out of more than a hundred guests, I was honored and flattered to be seated next to President George H. W. Bush.

I had covered him when he was a member of Congress, chairman of the Republican National Committee, and head of the Central Intelligence Agency. When he was chief of the liaison office in China, he wrote me lovely letters. His first was just a week after arriving in Beijing.

*Dear Connie,*

*It is 8:04 pm on Friday. Barbara and I have just bid "farewell" to a visiting group of Philadelphians and to a visiting group of US Linguists. I flicked on the shortwave VOA and who should we hear—you guessed it—Connie Chung, CBS News. We felt close to home, warm and comfortable.*

He added, "I don't miss Watergate. I do miss politics."

At the state dinner, I engaged in small talk with President Bush. No doubt he had been briefed about my interview with Marlon Brando.

"So, Connie," he said, "I hear you had a big interview. What was Yul Brynner really like?"

I didn't want to embarrass the president, so I answered with a straight face, "He was not what I expected."

Someone at our table must have overheard it and reported our conversation to the *Washington Post*. The next morning a *Post* columnist called me. "Is it true that Bush asked you how your interview with Yul Brynner went...but it was Marlon Brando you interviewed?"

"No, that's not correct," I replied with no hesitation.

I could not throw President Bush under the bus. After all, it wasn't Iran-Contra.

CHAPTER 20

# Getting the Get

In the late 1980s and early 1990s, the television news industry devolved from the straight, "Just the facts, ma'am" approach that was the hallmark of its beginnings. Reporting the news accurately wasn't enough. There was a new paradigm.

First, competition had been amped up by the birth of twenty-four-hour cable news—first CNN in 1980 and later MSNBC and Fox. Expanded news or news-like programs saturated the airwaves—morning wake-up shows, daytime talk shows, noon newscasts, afternoon chat fests, tabloid shows, prime-time magazines, and, of course, network news. Such fierce competition caused some outlets to not only oversaturate viewers with a story but, in a mad scramble to be first, fail to verify all the facts.

Second, name-brand reporters were locked in a battle for "gets," newsroom parlance for the big interviews du jour with newsmakers, hot celebrities, and tell-all tattlers. It was an unbecoming footrace for an exclusive to draw viewers or sell newspapers.

I was caught up in that maelstrom, as were other women at the networks—Barbara Walters, Diane Sawyer, Katie Couric, and the like. The potential interviewee was in the driver's seat, compelling us to make pilgrimages to ingratiate ourselves. Male anchors did not want to dirty their hands with such obsequious behavior.

I was able to snare a few worthwhile gets of which I was proud. One was an exclusive with Joseph Hazelwood, the captain of the *Exxon Valdez*, the tanker that had run aground on a reef in Alaska's Prince William Sound on March 24, 1989, resulting in the worst oil spill in the history of the United States. Almost eleven million gallons of black, sticky crude oil covered miles of the Alaska coastline, killing seals, sea otters, whales, and bald eagles—an environmental disaster.

*Saturday Night* Senior Producer Michael Rubin and producer Doug Hamilton created a detailed "tick-tock," a minute-by-minute report explaining just how the disaster had unfolded. It was impressive. Television news organizations rarely spent the time and money to produce such a thorough piece.

No one had pinned down Captain Hazelwood on what had occurred. Why wasn't he on the bridge at the time of the disaster? Was he in his cabin, drunk? Hazelwood was ridiculed and demonized, even called the most hated man in America.

After the tick-tock segment aired, we pitched an interview with the elusive Captain Hazelwood, who faced felony charges, accused of being inebriated at the time of the accident. He had refused all interviews.

So Michael, Doug, and I met with Hazelwood's lawyer, Michael Chalos.

No doubt the lawyer had not seen our tick-tock. He said, "I guess I better tell you what happened."

We replied, "Why don't we tell you what happened?"

The three of us recited chapter and verse from Michael and Doug's exhaustive narrative, interjecting questions that still lingered.

"Yes, that's right," the lawyer said. Michael and Doug's deep understanding of the facts clinched it. Nothing substitutes for factual knowledge.

We three had quite an adventure in Alaska. We happened upon some oil rigging guys at a dock, one of whom asked me to sign his backside. I agreed. He pulled down his pants and mooned me. Taking a moment to think about the task at hand, I asked him if he'd be OK if I signed his underwear instead. He happily agreed. I took a Magic Marker and gingerly signed my name. I have quite a snapshot of this once-in-a-lifetime moment. It's one of my favorite photos.

Michael, Doug, our crew, and I also went to a bar the night before our interview. It was the same bar that Hazelwood had frequented, including on the night before he ran the *Exxon Valdez* aground. We asked around, and every person we talked to, including the bartender, said Hazelwood had not been drunk.

Hazelwood turned out to be a thoughtful, intelligent, well-read man. He was brimming with literary references. He had been the youngest captain, working for Exxon at thirty-two. After the spill, with no investigation, Exxon had hung Hazelwood out to dry, pronouncing him drunk and guilty—and then unceremoniously fired him by telegram.

"Were you drinking just before you got on board the *Exxon Valdez*?" I asked.

Even though his lawyers had warned him to avoid my queries

about his sobriety, Hazelwood replied, "Yeah. I consumed some alcohol that afternoon. Late in the afternoon."

He admitted to having three vodkas but added, "I wasn't drunk. I can say that. I wasn't intoxicated. I wasn't impaired or whatever... the other plethora of words have been used to describe my condition."

Hazelwood uttered the perfect closer to the interview. (Producers and reporters always know it when we hear it.) Hazelwood said he was not the villain he had been portrayed as.

Hazelwood: "Well, I think it'll fade from memory in time. How many people remember Captain Smith?"

I fell into his clever trap. "Who?" I asked.

Hazelwood wryly replied, "He was the captain of the *Titanic.*"

Hazelwood was ultimately found *not* guilty of operating a vessel while intoxicated and convicted of a misdemeanor for negligently discharging oil. For that he was fined $50,000 and sentenced to a thousand hours of community service. A jury ordered Exxon to pay $5 billion, but the US Supreme Court ultimately whittled that figure down to $500 million, still a hefty fine for an environmental crime but hardly a dent in Exxon's profits.

\* \* \*

Another gem of a get was Bill Gates. Have you ever seen the Microsoft cofounder and billionaire jump over a chair from a standing position? You must see it. I'll wait here while you go to YouTube and watch it.

Astounding, right? Somehow, I found out he could accomplish that feat and asked him to show me before the interview. He obliged. He succeeded in just one take. After that icebreaker, I grilled him about his efforts to overtake small companies by battling them in court with all his money and might. He was so angry with my questions that he walked out on my interview.

\* \* \*

One of the most delightful gets was with the ultimate heartthrob actor, Paul Newman, and actress Joanne Woodward. It was a coup that *Saturday Night* arts producer Vicki Gordon nurtured and snagged for me. She had extraordinary connections and sources in the book world, Hollywood, television, and every corner of media.

The Newman and Woodward interviews were unique because the actors did not want to be interviewed together, but producer Hal Gessner put a microphone and camera on Woodward while I was interviewing Newman. She was in a devilish mood, making comments about his answers. Thanks to Woodward's charming hijinks, I won an Emmy for Best Interview.

Another heartthrob get Vicki arranged for me was with Kevin Costner when he was about to release *Dances with Wolves*, a movie he produced, directed, and starred in and that later won seven Oscars, including Best Picture and Best Director.

The executive producer of the magazine program I did at the time, who happened to be single, had dated women in Hollywood. One of those women told him Costner was well-endowed.

Need I say more? As I interviewed Costner, though very handsome, I had a heck of a time concentrating on his face.

\* \* \*

Here's a blockbuster get that you may remember.

On Thursday, November 7, 1991, at the height of the AIDS epidemic, Earvin "Magic" Johnson shocked America when he announced he was retiring from the Los Angeles Lakers because he had tested positive for HIV. Magic Johnson was the masterful point guard who had led the Lakers—with the great Kareem Abdul-Jabbar—to five National Basketball Association championships. He was beloved by his fans (including me).

As soon as I saw the news, I told my bosses at CBS, "I've booked a flight to LA—I think I can get Magic to do an exclusive interview with me."

They were skeptical. "What makes you think he will talk with you?"

I answered confidently, "When I did the news in Los Angeles for seven years, I sort of knew Magic—we were friends."

Back then, our Channel 2 sportscaster, Jim Hill, had often interviewed Magic live on the news. Magic never missed a chance during his interviews to flash his unforgettable warm smile: "Say hi to Connie!" It was beyond endearing.

I don't remember how it came about, but Magic had invited me to join him for dinner with his very tall friends at Maurice's Snack and Chat on Pico Boulevard. Magic suggested I order his favorite: chicken and waffles with lots of gravy. A cheerful mommy type emerged from the kitchen with piping hot monster-size meals she had cooked for Magic and his guests. We all wolfed down our hearty dinners.

I was sure Magic would choose me for this important interview. But when I called a few friends in the news business in LA, every one of them said the same thing: "Magic and I are friends." I soon realized that Magic made everyone he knew feel special.

When I called Magic's agent to ask for a meeting, his assistant firmly replied, "He cannot meet with you."

I quickly noted, "But I'm Magic's friend."

She shot back, "Yeah, yeah, everybody is."

After landing in LA, I drove directly to the agent's office and plopped myself down on the couch outside his closed door, telling his assistant that I would wait until he came out. I became a squatter who would not leave. Wanting to go home at the end of the day, the agent gave up and allowed me to make my pitch.

A few days later, I was on my way to Magic's spacious house in Los Angeles. While the camera crew set up two chairs and two cameras near his pool, he invited me into his living room to chat. It was impossible not to notice that the furniture in his house was extremely large. When I sat on the sofa, it swallowed me. My feet could not touch the floor. I felt like Lily Tomlin's character Edith Ann in her oversize chair.

Magic had learned that he was HIV positive from a blood test he had done for insurance purposes. To be clear, he had not been diagnosed with AIDS and had no symptoms of the disease.

During the interview, I had to ask many awkward, personal questions that were intrusive. The burning question was how he had become HIV positive. Magic was honest and open, answering every uncomfortable question: how he'd told his wife, Cookie, who was pregnant with their first child; how did he think he had been infected; if he was having sex with a woman other than his wife; whether he could have become HIV positive from sex with a man. His answers were direct and straightforward.

It was a woman who was not his wife.

He did not know who, but he was contacting possible women.

No, he had never had sex with a man.

At one point I was struggling with how to phrase more delicate questions. It was as if he could see my heart wrestling with my brain.

"You know it's funny," he said, as he read my mind. "'How do

I ask him that? Am I a reporter now or am I his friend? You know, how am I gonna approach him with these questions?'"

Magic paused and said to the camera and me, "You just come on with it. Don't you worry about it. I still love you no matter what happens here. You know that."

What a gentle soul he was! What a relief.

It was highly unusual for me to interview someone I'd been friendly with. But the story of one of the greatest athletes of the era facing one of the greatest health crises of the era was too important for me to bow out.

\* \* \*

In 1993, I nailed another bigger-than-life athlete when I interviewed the phenomenal Michael Jordan, the GOAT (Greatest of All Time). News and sports reporters were clamoring to talk to Jordan when, in midcareer, he was mired in a gambling scandal. He needed to put questions and rumors to rest. I had met him before at celebrity golf tournaments when I tagged along with Maury.

And one of those celebrity golf tournaments in Lake Tahoe was the setting for our exclusive. In a relaxed sit-down interview, I asked Jordan the critical question: "Do you have a gambling problem?"

"No," he answered, "because I can stop gambling. I have a competition problem, a competitive problem."

The gambling issue did not affect his jump shot nor tarnish his well-deserved glory. By the time Jordan retired, he had won six NBA championships for the Chicago Bulls.

\* \* \*

The story that had a surprising impact on thousands of women was my report that prompted one critically important man to contact me.

For twenty years, women had been undergoing breast augmentation at the astounding average of 250 implant operations a day in the US. What came as a shock to these women and me was that the most common implant used for the procedure had never been approved by the federal government.

Producer Valerie Cummings found multiple women who had experienced unexplained illnesses after their operations. One woman who got implants after a double mastectomy had begun suffering from swollen glands, fevers, chills, sore throats. She discovered her body had been poisoned by leaking silicone that spread to her lymph glands, profoundly affecting her immune system over five years.

Another woman even developed the debilitating autoimmune disease lupus. We found doctors who were trying desperately to warn women about the alarming problem.

Remarkably, David Kessler, commissioner of the Food and Drug Administration, happened to be watching our program and called me for more information about our report. He was so disturbed that he acted quickly and decisively, launching an investigation. Ultimately Kessler banned silicone breast implants, which were primarily produced by Dow Chemical. Eventually Dow had to declare bankruptcy.

This was the type of story I found most worthwhile—the kind that spurred a change in government policy or enlightened society about a wrong that required correction.

Fourteen years later, the FDA allowed silicone breast implants back on the market, under more stringent regulations that included a requirement for long-term studies.

While *Saturday Night with Connie Chung* was still limping along, no one could figure out why viewers were not tuning in. I would meet with CBS News President David Burke often, looking for guidance. One day, David called me to his office to tell me that Don Hewitt, executive producer of *60 Minutes*, wanted to produce a new program for me. That was an extraordinary offer. Any reporter would have jumped at the opportunity to work with Hewitt.

After all, he was a living legend—the most creative producer at CBS News ever. In 1952, Hewitt had given birth to the first coast-to-coast news broadcast, *Douglas Edwards with the News*. He was the man behind Walter Cronkite's *CBS Evening News*, and the one who'd directed and produced the first presidential debate between John F. Kennedy and Richard M. Nixon.

The *New York Times* declared that Hewitt had "changed the course of broadcast history" with *60 Minutes*, a top-ten program for decades, "fusing journalism and show business."

Hewitt wanted to do a personality interview program with me, reviving Edward R. Murrow's *Person to Person*. For that program, Murrow had interviewed notables live as they sat in their living rooms or gave him a mini tour of their homes. When I was told of Hewitt's modern take on the program, I winced. He envisioned a celebrity-oriented interview program.

I did not want to be CBS's version of Robin Leach, the celebrity-worshipping Brit whose show, *Lifestyles of the Rich and Famous*, was popular at that time. Surely this kind of fluff would revive *Washington Post* TV writer Tom Shales's declaration that I was "Connie Funn" who did "schlockumentaries." I had already spent a long time on a spit, getting skewered by critics, when I was at NBC. I did not want to be a razzle-dazzle newswoman chasing Hollywood stars. I would not let a producer, no matter who he was, take me down that road again.

Plus, I was loyal. I thought it would be wrong to abandon Andy

Lack, the executive producer with whom I was working. I told Burke, "Please tell Don thank you, but I'll stick with what I am doing."

Big mistake. I'd dared to reject the thousand-pound gorilla at CBS, who enjoyed throwing his weight around. Even Maury asked me if I was sure. I don't know why I didn't pursue it. I should have.

Now I had offended Hewitt, and I was persona non grata. I vividly remember him saying to me later, "I don't know why people like you."

His negative opinion did not bode well for me. There was no way I could change his mind.

# CHAPTER 21

# Baby Track

C BS was in ratings hell.
With no prime-time hit dramas, entertainment executives asked Andy Lack and me to produce two special May editions of our program for Mondays at 10:00 p.m. (in addition to our regular *Saturday Night* program). Even though it doubled our workload, we were excited to seize the opportunity to reach new viewers. We named our specials *Face to Face with Connie Chung*. News programs often rescued a network with holes in its schedule for the simple reason that they were cheap to produce—less than half a million dollars per episode, compared to entertainment shows' budgets that ran into the millions.

At the annual meeting with advertisers, CBS announced that my program would air on Mondays, the strongest night on the network. I would follow two back-to-back hit sitcoms produced by and starring women: at nine o'clock, *Murphy Brown*, created by Diane

English, a show about a newswoman with a cutting, biting attitude, masterfully played by star Candice Bergen; and at nine thirty, *Designing Women*, created by Linda Bloodworth-Thomason, a show about an interior decorating firm in the South.

With the only two winning half hours running before us, we were ensured a captive audience at 10:00 p.m. In television land, that's known as a strong "lead-in." *Murphy Brown* and *Designing Women* were guaranteed to deliver our specials a hefty audience.

When the *Face to Face* specials posted better ratings than even the blockbuster sitcoms, we became the toast of the town. CBS Entertainment rewarded us by placing us on the coveted Monday schedule for the fall. After being buried in the Saturday-night dungeon, we could now shine. I was overwhelmed by that huge vote of confidence.

All that happened in May. As spring became summer, I was terribly anxious, knowing that in the fall I'd be the *only* correspondent on *Face to Face*, which meant traveling all week long to shoot interviews and stories, then heading back to New York so I could anchor *Face to Face* and the Sunday *CBS Evening News*. I knew it would be a brutal schedule, but I was thrilled to have a hit and was eager to make it last.

Faced with that load, I knew the only way to get ahead of the game was to use June, July, and August to bank stories for the fall. Having a bushel of reports including investigations and exclusive interviews shot and in the can would help me breathe a bit more easily. Yet we were *not* doing that. Our offices were not buzzing with activity. Andy Lack retreated to the Hamptons for long weekends.

Why? I could not figure it out. I kept pressing Andy about the need to work every day throughout the summer.

By August, I was beginning to truly panic. Then Howard

Stringer called me at home. What he said on the telephone took me completely by surprise. Howard announced *Face to Face with Connie Chung* would *not* be on the CBS schedule after all—we were canceled before we even premiered. No explanation as to why. He had simply decided to try a new drama, *The Trials of Rosie O'Neill*, in our time slot. The show's producers had been campaigning for Monday nights at ten. (Actress Sharon Gless, of *Cagney & Lacey*, was the star.) Even though I was crestfallen, I knew this kind of last-minute switcheroo was part of the business, so I reluctantly accepted the decision.

What followed was shocking. Howard knew I'd had a few miscarriages and that we were still trying to have a baby. He suggested I use my efforts to start a family as the excuse for the sudden disappearance of my new program. In other words, he wanted me to use my personal situation and take the fall for the cancellation of my program. I was so surprised I did not ask why.

I discussed Howard's proposal with my husband. I had to think clearly.

Here is one of the reasons I thought I should agree. Since I was in my late forties, Maury and I had privately turned to fertility doctors for artificial insemination and in vitro fertilization (IVF). Daily injections and the extraction of my eggs under anesthesia on a strict schedule made traveling for stories a logistical nightmare. My age and workload were working against me. I knew I could not do it all.

Was Howard's proposal my saving grace? Was it a way out of my conundrum? He insisted I give him an answer quickly so that he could announce the new fall schedule the following week. Since Howard was the boss, I had always thought he had my best interests in mind and would never let me hang out to dry. So I agreed to the party line—like the obedient, dutiful employee in the face of power.

I should *not* have agreed to Howard's subterfuge. I should *not* have taken the blame for the cancellation of my program. What a gigantic mistake. I had not anticipated what was to come.

That weekend Maury helped me compose a statement to release to the news media. With my draft in hand, I met CBS News Vice President Joe Peyronnin in his office to thrash out the final wording.

One phrase in the statement became the punch line of comedians' jokes—that we were "aggressively" pursuing having a baby. What we meant was that we were seeking extraordinary measures such as in vitro fertilization and artificial insemination. We did not spell it all out in the announcement, thinking we could at least keep those details private. We foolishly did not realize that using the word "aggressive" was an invitation to mockery.

When I broke the news to our magazine staff (just before the statement was released), I abided by the party line—the baby excuse. It was a difficult announcement to say the least. Everyone on the staff was gracious, but I knew it was crushing news. I was also taking the blame for their uncertain futures.

With the baby announcement out, I unwittingly became the poster child for the story of the older career woman who wants to have a baby.

*People* magazine called for an interview, but I would not answer any questions. Instead, I begged and pleaded with *People* to kill the story, explaining I had not intended for this to be a big deal. *People* purchased a photo from a photographer and slapped my face on the cover with the headline "I Want a Child." Truly mortified, I wanted to hide.

While I talked to no reporters, the media had a field day. One writer was particularly snarky—Elinor J. Brecher of the *Miami Herald*, who said I was being paid to "roll around in the sack, take her temperature and run to the doctor. She's welcome back when she gets pregnant or bored, whichever comes first."

Any couple who has undergone IVF or even artificial insemination knows the process is anything but a roll in the hay. I don't remember all the details, but I can't forget giving myself daily subcutaneous shots in my stomach and injections of Pergonal with a long syringe in my buttocks. Some women ask their husbands to administer the shots, but Maury was too freaked out by it. I was told to practice on a banana and found it to be easy. The shots helped to stimulate more eggs to develop in my ovaries. Bottom line: the process is about as unromantic as anyone can imagine.

Nurses drew my blood daily to determine when my estrogen was at its peak, which was when the doctor would extract my eggs, of which I produced several. Just before I underwent general anesthesia to remove the eggs—how can I put this?—Maury would "submit" his sperm. If I may add, the nurses would put his collection up on monitors and marvel at how his sample swam furiously, filling every inch of the TV screens. "Oh, Mr. Povich," the nurses exclaimed, "what motility!" Walking tall, Mighty Maury strutted out of the doctor's office.

After extracting my eggs, the doctor fertilized all of them in a petri dish and waited for viable embryos.

A few days later, the fertilized embryo or embryos would be implanted in my uterus. I had several biochemical pregnancies, as they are called. We would get a positive result on a pregnancy test, but in a few short weeks, we would learn that the embryo had not attached to my uterus. So the embryo would be expelled. That's when I would ride the emotional roller coaster. Knowing it was not normal for me to cry uncontrollably, I sought advice from my doctor, who told me it was simply the dramatic loss of estrogen. Once I learned that, I felt comforted, knowing my emotional state was purely hormonal and I was still in control. That fact was important to me.

Those were the ups and downs of the baby game. I don't envy any couples who must try this process. After several years of IVF, I figured out why I could conceive yet kept having early miscarriages. I have autoimmune issues, which caused my body to reject any embryo we created. I was incredibly annoyed when news reports stated I could not conceive. Wrong. I could not hold on to our embryo. Since IVF was still new and information lacking, it took good old-fashioned investigative reporting for me to come to my own conclusion—working the phone and talking to experts, doctors, and scientists to figure out my problem. Today science is closer to uncovering the details of my problem and perhaps those of other women.

Since it was not advisable to undergo IVF *every* month, I was able to travel to cover and shoot stories. I substituted for Dan Rather and on the *CBS Morning Program*, anchored my news on Sundays, and much more. Anybody who thought I was lollygagging was dead wrong.

Later, women friends in the news business confided that watching my quest to have a baby was a wake-up call for them. Just like me, they'd allowed their careers to swallow their personal lives. Those friends began getting married and having babies (or vice versa) at late ages. I witnessed a mini baby boom. It was the one part of this horrible episode that gratified me. At least others had learned from my experience.

The jokes on comedy shows would not stop, especially from Letterman, who refused to let up. After several years of endless jokes, I wrote him a note that basically said, "Come on, can you cool it? Please?" He did not.

* * *

The 1992 presidential election was a welcome news story I was happy to dive into, away from all the baby drama. I was surprised to be the only woman joining the male anchors on election night. Dan Rather was the lead anchor, joined by Ed Bradley, Mike Wallace, Bob Schieffer, Charles Kuralt, and me. My job was to report the results of governors' races.

* * *

Despite my rocky three years at CBS, I still felt it was where I wanted to be. ABC's Roone Arledge had asked me to lunch to lure me to his network, but in the end, I wanted to negotiate a new CBS contract. My lawyer/agent, Alfred, thought to include a clause specifying that if anyone is named the coanchor of the *CBS Evening News with Dan Rather*, that person would be me. I never thought it was a remote possibility. I told Alfred, "Sure, I doubt they will agree to it—but go ahead and try." CBS agreed to the stipulation. I did not think it mattered. These corporations had a way of weaseling out of promises anyway. I wasn't holding my breath.

CHAPTER 22

# Dream Job

T hursday, May 14, 1993, was the best day of my professional life. On this warm spring morning, I was heading to CBS corporate headquarters on the fancy East Side of midtown Manhattan. The austere black limestone skyscraper was known as "Black Rock," an iconic landmark created by CBS Chairman William Paley. I had been there before, but as I entered Howard Stringer's corporate office bright and early, at eight, I had no idea what was about to happen.

Howard was sitting on a sofa beside CBS News President Eric Ober. I was biting into a Danish when Howard broke the wonderful news. He was naming me coanchor of the *CBS Evening News with Dan Rather.* I was stunned! I'd never imagined I would ever hear those words save in fantasy.

After a few minutes, Alfred was invited to join us in Howard's office to enjoy the moment. It had been his idea to write into my contract that if anyone was named coanchor, it would be me.

This wasn't just a personal milestone but one for women and minorities, as I would be the first of both groups to coanchor the CBS News flagship broadcast. I felt incredibly lucky to be the one riding the crest.

In 1976, Barbara Walters had become the first woman to co-anchor the evening news at ABC, but after that, we women sat in the desert for seventeen long years. This morning, my hopes were soaring. I had my dream job.

Although Howard and Eric expected me to drop my new magazine program, *Eye to Eye with Connie Chung*, I did not want to give it up. What would happen to the correspondents and staff? Would they suddenly lose their jobs? Many were the same friends with whom I'd worked when my previous magazine was canceled. No, I could not let that happen. I would work twice as hard and do both programs to make sure their jobs were secure.

Despite my shock at being chosen, it wasn't a surprise to anyone at CBS that something would change on the *Evening News* as ratings slid downhill. After Rather replaced Walter Cronkite in 1981, he had held his own for about five years. Then he'd tumbled to third place. When a new ratings system took effect, he appeared to be back on top. But gradually he slipped to number two behind number one Peter Jennings at ABC. And he was fighting to stay number two against number three, NBC's Tom Brokaw.

Rather tried everything he could think of to make himself more appealing to viewers: wearing a sweater vest; anchoring while standing up, then sitting down again; changing his sign-off from a simple "Good night" to "Courage."

More troubling, Rather had engaged in several peculiar, highly publicized incidents that tarnished his sterling career.

The first occurred in March 1974 during Watergate as President

Richard Nixon was answering questions before a large audience at the National Association of Broadcasters. Rather stood up to ask a question, introducing himself.

"Thank you, Mr. President, Dan Rather with CBS News." Inexplicably, he was met with a chorus of boos and jeers with only a sprinkling of claps.

Nixon said to Rather, "Are you running for something?"

To which Rather replied, "No, sir, Mr. President. Are you?" Media critics perceived his quip as disrespectful.

Six years later, Rather accused a Chicago taxi driver of "kidnapping" him, holding him captive on a wild, high-speed ride from the Chicago airport. A woman driver saw Rather "gesticulating rather madly in the back seat of a taxi cab," according to United Press International. She helped pull the taxi over. Rather filed police charges. The driver said Rather was trying to stiff him out of his cab fare. Rather dropped the charges. CBS paid the bill.

Seven years after that, Rather was about to go on the air to anchor the *CBS Evening News* when CBS Sports notified the network that the US Open tennis tournament was running long and might delay the beginning of his program. I had anchored the news on Saturdays and Sundays for years at NBC and CBS—and so had Rather at CBS. Sports events (including tennis matches) frequently ran longer than expected. It was common for us to wait until sports wrapped up its program to begin our news. It was not a big deal.

Rather, in a fit of anchor pique, took off his microphone and walked off the set. What was the control room to do? They could not show an empty chair. Instead, for almost seven minutes, viewers saw a blank black screen of dead air, all because of Rather's hissy fit.

The head of the all-important CBS Affiliates Board said Rather "blew it" and demanded an apology from him.

Walter Cronkite said that if he were in charge, "I would have fired him."

The *Washington Post*'s Tom Shales wrote a scathing article referring to "rampant rumors suggesting Rather was losing his emotional balance."

CBS affiliates were clamoring for a change that could lead to better ratings on the *Evening News* and in prime time too. The pressure on CBS News executives was intense.

With that backdrop, I was added to right the sinking ship.

Howard and Eric wanted to make the new coanchor team public as quickly as possible. We would keep the news under wraps over the weekend.

On Monday, May 17, CBS held a news conference to announce the renamed *CBS Evening News with Dan Rather and Connie Chung*.

Each of us spoke at the teleconference. I thanked the wives of CBS executives for "raising their husbands' consciousness," noting men had realized that the time had come for a woman to sit in the top newscaster chair.

The reporters covering the media directed the bulk of their questions to Rather. They were openly skeptical about whether he had amicably agreed to the dual anchorship or if a gun had been held to his head. (Frankly, I did not know either and was curious to hear what he'd say.) The reporters and critics had their antennae out for any hint of friction between the two of us.

Cynical as reporters are, they doubted Rather's protestations when he declared, "I hope you will report accurately that what you're looking at is a *very* happy and very excited Dan Rather." His explanation for my sharing the broadcast was that it would allow him to get out in the field as a reporter, leaving the confines of the studio to me. The dual anchor team would succeed, he continued, "You can take it to the bank."

Cameras captured Rather hugging me and kissing me on the cheek. I thought it was cheesy, like when an icky uncle hugs and kisses a female relative.

After the news conference, Rather asked me to join him at the corner dive for a cup of coffee. I did not know what to expect. Did I believe Rather's public comments? I wanted to, but I had known him for twenty-two years, especially when we worked together in Washington. He was wound tight and had no sense of humor. I could not figure out his true persona. Taking him at face value, I was nonetheless cautious and always on guard.

He stared into my eyes and said, "Now you are going to have to start reading the newspaper." I swallowed hard. Was this his idea of how to start a partnership? I was forty-seven and had spent half my life in the news business—did he think I had been reading the comics? We were just out of the gate in what I hoped would be a long run. My response: silence.

But I could hear Bette Davis in the classic motion picture *All About Eve*, saying, "Fasten your seat belts, it's going to be a bumpy night."

The next day I received a handwritten letter from Rather.

*Just a note to say that it is the day after, and I am still absolutely convinced—convinced more than ever—that we are going to be a great team. I believe in you, Connie, and your talent. Depend on me to be at your back and side, always looking out for you as we meet this challenge together.*

Having grown up the daughter of an intelligence officer, I had trouble trusting people. And being a cynical reporter, I felt always that I should watch my back.

I received hundreds of notes, letters, emails, and bunches of flowers congratulating me for invading the white male triumvirate of nightly news anchors, Rather, Brokaw, and Jennings.

Tom Shales called me "Little Miss Fix-it." I had moved *NBC News at Sunrise* from number three to number one. Then I had been plopped next to Roger Mudd on his magazine program to boost ratings. Now, once again, I was to be the magic elixir that would bring viewers in droves. And just like the other jobs, I knew it would be a heavy lift.

Other media critics pummeled me, questioning my qualifications. *TV Guide* splashed my photo on the cover with the headline, "Connie Chung: Dan Rather Has a New Partner—Does She Have the Stuff?"

Other television columnists chimed in, accusing me of lacking gravitas. Ed Siegel of the *Boston Globe*: "Chung has not proven herself in the Washington trenches as have Andrea Mitchell, Carole Simpson and Lesley Stahl."

He went on to say I had not made "a name for [myself] covering a beat."

Infuriated by those two articles, I showed them to Maury. Without even knowing why I was steaming, he'd said with a smile, "Do I have to remove all the sharp objects from the kitchen?" Then came Maury's wisdom about "bad press."

"You know you covered important beats. You know you were in the trenches. You know who you are. Don't take them seriously." Still, the feeling of always having to prove myself weighed heavily on my mind.

I wanted to believe I had been chosen because I deserved the job. I must have been dreaming. They wanted me to put a bow around Dan Rather's neck that would make him appear friendly and cuddly and normal. But instead, it was I who ended up in a noose.

My belief is that viewers choose an anchor they trust and with whom they feel a personal connection—someone who is credible, honest, and objective. That was the perfect description of Walter Cronkite. No matter how awful the news, if Uncle Walter told us about it, it was palatable. He was kindly and comforting, as well as authoritative.

When I was named coanchor, Walter called to congratulate me—and gave me one important bit of advice: "Be yourself." Perfect. I could not be anything but myself. Certainly I needed to prove that I could handle the rigors of the job and deliver quality work. So I set about to show I could carry the mantle. I dove into hard news stories to deliver my half of the anchor bargain.

Roxanne Russell, a superb *CBS Evening News* producer, suggested a great story about secret back-channel negotiations between Israel and the Palestine Liberation Organization that would lead to a historic peace agreement when Bill Clinton was president.

After the *Evening News* one night, I flew to Norway to interview the key figures who had brought the warring sides together for what was called the Oslo Accords. It was an intriguing drama of high-stakes negotiations between Israel and the PLO, who had been enemies to the death for decades. The participants shared a house in the countryside and talked intensely into the early-morning hours. They also gathered for informal drinks and meals, achieving what front-channel diplomats in Washington could not. Norway proved to be the bridge to peace.

On September 13, 1993, when Rather and I coanchored the

momentous signing of an Israeli–PLO peace agreement at the Clinton White House, my work in Norway provided me with a wealth of knowledge to share with viewers. I had also interviewed Israeli Foreign Minister Shimon Peres after the signing ceremony.

With the solid stories I was racking up on the *Evening News*, who could doubt my credentials?

As I settled into working with Rather daily, I began to develop an impression of who he was behind the persona he presented to the public. In my experience, he was the ultimate gentleman, treating women delicately, as if we were porcelain teacups that might break. We women know that kind of old-fashioned guy who feels women should not get their hands soiled, lest dirt end up under their manicured fingernails—the kind who never says a swear word in the presence of a woman, and blanches when a woman says one. My potty mouth made him supremely uncomfortable.

After we began coanchoring together, it seemed to me as if he had an inherent bias regarding women. I felt he perceived women journalists as competitors against one another, like cats scratching each other's eyes out.

Once, minutes before we were about to anchor the news, he asked me if I had seen a big article in the *Washington Post* about television journalist Judy Woodruff.

He sniffed, "The only reason she is anything is because of her husband." (Judy was married to Al Hunt, a *Wall Street Journal* reporter.)

How rude. Judy was a superb journalist, not to mention a dear friend who deserved every accolade. What he said insulted Judy— *and* me.

Another time, just minutes to air, he commented, "You know, Christiane Amanpour is not as good looking in person as she is on television." What was that all about? Christiane was CNN's premier international war correspondent, whom I admired greatly.

I felt as if Rather despised my presence. On the surface, he appeared to be fine, but I can only imagine how much he was seething inside. I tried not to worry about him. I would worry only about my work.

I interviewed President Clinton about NAFTA, the North American Free Trade Agreement involving the United States, Mexico, and Canada. Afterward, White House advisor David Gergen called me to complain bitterly about how tough I had been in my questioning of the president. That kind of critique is a badge of honor for reporters. It means we did our jobs.

On a Thursday in October, after coanchoring the news, I flew to the US military hospital in Germany to pitch an interview with Michael Durant, the Black Hawk helicopter pilot who had been shot down in the Battle of Mogadishu and held captive in Somalia. He was released from the hospital eleven days later. After many phone calls, I got the "get" with Durant for *Eye to Eye*. His story was later made into a motion picture, *Black Hawk Down*.

After the NAFTA story and the Durant interviews aired, I received a note from *60 Minutes'* Mike Wallace, who I thought was the best interviewer in television news. Mike must have known I was feeling the heat and pressure and could use an attaboy. He complimented me on the Durant interview and said the NAFTA story was "first rate." He closed his note with "Hang in there."

I did hang in, but the job of a lifetime was beginning to be quite a challenge. What came next were assignments that took me down a road of no return.

## CHAPTER 23

# I'd Rather Not

W hy, why, why?" Olympic figure skater Nancy Kerrigan screamed and cried after a burly thug whacked her in the knee with a metal bar.

"Why, why?" is what I exclaimed when CBS News executives told me I had to cover the sordid soap opera starring Olympic archrivals Tonya Harding and Nancy Kerrigan. I had been co-anchoring the *CBS Evening News* for six months. Would either Walter Cronkite or Dan Rather ever have been dispatched to chase after two women who twirled, jumped, and glided to the delight of audiences? Absolutely not. Then why would CBS ask me to do that?

CBS had bought the rights to televise the 1994 Olympics for a reported $300 million, and since figure skating was typically the most watched sport, the suits were salivating at a potential ratings bonanza in prime time. CBS had a vested interest in covering and hyping the rivalry between the competitors.

In this era of feeding frenzies, the media happily fueled the fairy tale. Nancy Kerrigan was the beautiful Snow White in Vera Wang tutus. Tonya Harding was an ugly duckling from the wrong side of the tracks. She had lived a rough life, claiming that both her estranged husband and her mother, a night shift waitress, had physically abused her. Yet she had remarkable athletic talent and was a feisty, driven toughie, fueled by guts, not grace. As Tonya's story unfolded, authorities uncovered evidence that her ex-husband had hatched the attack on Nancy.

What emerged from the Tonya-Nancy saga was a drama that played out like a made-for-TV movie rife with Shakespearean themes:

**Love:** Both loved and lived to skate.
**Hate:** Tonya hated Nancy.
**Lust:** For fame and fortune.
**Betrayal:** Of fair competition; of the spirit of the Olympics.

I ferociously fought covering the skaters, but the pressure was intense.

CBS brass told me, "You must do this for the network." I had no choice.

Soon I was on a plane to Portland, Oregon, to dog Tonya. I was not alone. Media from all over the world had descended on the Clackamas Town Center, a shopping complex near Happy Valley, a suburb of Portland. Jammed into the mall's public skating rink were cameras and crews from as far away as Japan and Australia, including reporters from British tabloids, the *National Enquirer*, and even the venerable *New York Times*.

I found myself staring down a steep eight-foot wall to a large rink below me, dangling my microphone for a word with skating's "bad girl" as she circled the rink.

"Tonya, Tonya!" I beckoned her to come to my camera. But what swirled in my head was: would Walter Cronkite, in his deep, serious voice, be shouting, "Tonya, Tonya. Come over here, Tonya!"? Not a chance. Oh, how I wanted to leave and defy my bosses.

I had thought my days of covering unworthy stories were over. Yet, knowing I had to deliver, I persuaded Tonya to do an interview for my magazine program, *Eye to Eye*. The curse, once again, was that the interview resulted in record-high ratings. I could not have been more disappointed.

How embarrassed I was, toddling along with Tonya to the Olympics in Norway, not only to coanchor the *CBS Evening News* from Lillehammer but also to get yet another interview with Tonya. She agreed to a one-on-one before the Olympic competition. Tonya handled the questions like a seasoned politician, refusing to discuss the dastardly act against Nancy. Then, fed up with my repeated attempts to get her to talk about the attack, she suddenly yanked off her microphone and walked out, just like a petulant Capitol Hill insider. I was criticized for pressing her, which any good reporter would have done. It was not until later that she pleaded guilty to complicity in the cover-up.

Here I thought I had shed the taint I had acquired at NBC with those frivolous specials. But now I found myself chasing a worthless story again, reviving that tabloid perception.

Frustrated and unhappy, I attempted to take control of my career and suggested my next story.

Violence had erupted in Haiti as a military coup overturned Jean-Bertrand Aristide, the first popularly elected president in Haitian history. The US intervened, sending troops in 1994. Even former

President Jimmy Carter offered to broker a peace for the troubled country. Dan Rather flew to Haiti and got an exclusive interview with Haiti's Military General Raoul Cédras, who had led the coup. I pitched an interview with Haiti's President Aristide.

"It would be a great one-two punch," I told my bosses. "Dan and I would *own* the Haiti conflict story." The CBS executives flatly turned me down. Instead, they insisted I pursue the O. J. Simpson story.

I was livid. We had all agreed the Simpson murder case had no place on the *CBS Evening News*. It was a tabloid story that none of us wanted anything to do with. But the news executives told me, "We need you to get an interview with one of the characters in the O. J. Simpson story for your magazine."

Their rationale was even worse.

Barbara Walters and Diane Sawyer were getting O. J. "gets," and they were scoring big ratings.

They explained, "*60 Minutes* will not touch the O. J. story, and neither will Dan Rather."

Again I pushed back. Why put this on me? The reply was direct.

"We have no one else who will do this, and we know you can."

Could I outright refuse? I was fit to be tied. How could I allow myself to be a chump again? What was becoming clear to me was that the demands of my magazine were conflicting with my need to be credible on the news. Honestly, looking back, I shake my head. I should have stood up to them and said no. I knew that the story would further damage my reputation.

How could I object without being called that dreaded name, "bitch"? I had always taken it upon myself to be the easy child growing up, the one who did the right thing for my parents. Now I was the easy employee, the one who was not difficult, who did not make trouble, the one who would not act like a diva, the peerless good girl who was self-effacing, always the reasonable, calm anchor. When hot tempers flared, I stayed cool, no BS. The last thing I wanted was to emulate those pompous, self-absorbed anchormen who had hissy fits.

Grudgingly, I worked the phones and scheduled an interview with O. J. Simpson's mother. I flew to her home in California and discovered she had no teeth. I called my husband to tell him. Maury, who was hosting his own talk show at the time, told me, "If we have guests who have no teeth, we send them to the dentist."

I did the interview anyway and sat down with O. J.'s lawyer, Johnnie Cochran. I thought the story was now behind me. But CBS insisted I get an interview that Diane Sawyer had already done, with a girlfriend of Simpson's murdered wife. I was widely criticized for all the O. J. Simpson interviews, again being portrayed as someone who was too lightweight to do anything but sensational blather. It was madness.

In between, I doubled down to produce serious stories, hoping that if I just worked harder, I could get notches on the positive side of my ledger.

But when O. J. and his friend Al Cowlings played games with authorities in the infamous slow Bronco chase, CBS followed the media herd and went live with Rather and me anchoring.

Rather, who had been vehement about eschewing the murder case, suddenly changed his mind. The O. J. story was no longer beneath his journalistic standards. While we were on the air live and the chase was on the screen, Rather excitedly wrote me a note: "THIS IS GREAT!" I gave him a blank look.

All three networks aired the Bronco chase live, a low moment for television news. But it had made a convert out of Rather—he was happy to anchor O. J. trial coverage live. The other two networks' anchors did the same. Not one of them suffered from the taint or received any blowback.

Meanwhile, I kept trying to dig out of the snake pit I found myself in. Each time I covered a story, it seemed that Rather was unhappy. He quietly made it clear that he thought the story should be his. Rather was in South Africa for an interview with Nelson Mandela at his swearing in as the first Black president when President Richard Nixon suffered a stroke and suddenly died. I was asked to anchor the Nixon funeral solo. Rather was not happy that he could not be in two places at one time.

A month later, I worked hard to get a brief interview with Chinese Premier Li Peng on the fifth anniversary of Tiananmen Square. I happened to speak the same Chinese dialect as Li. Since President Clinton was trying to tie human rights to trade sanctions, it was an important time for a reporter to question Chinese leaders. My impression was that since Rather had covered the Tiananmen Square demonstrations, once again I crossed his line in the sand.

Five months later, when Israel and Jordan were to sign a new historic peace treaty, I was thrilled to fly to Amman to anchor CBS coverage live. I figured Rather was offered that trip but turned it down because it would not occur in prime time. Because of the time difference, it would take place during the *CBS Morning News*, which had no ratings.

When I followed President Clinton as he visited troops in Kuwait, Rather made a point of complaining to the executive producer about why I was assigned, not him.

With all these stories under my belt, Rather asked me to meet him at the coffee shop near CBS—just the two of us. We were not ones who frequently broke bread together, so I was braced for what was on his mind. What he said completely shocked me.

He told me I should confine myself to the studio every night. "Just read the news on the teleprompter," he said. I should leave reporting or anchoring from the field to him. He was instructing me to stay put in New York. I should stay home, where I belonged.

I repeated Rather's audacious demand to CBS News President Eric Ober. Eric said he knew—Rather had told him the same. In so many words, Eric told me to carry on. I was not sure what that meant.

In a private phone conversation with me, a news executive confided that Dan thought of me as his rival. The executive put it this way: we were two powerful people fighting for our professional lives, both thinking our reputations and credibility were at stake.

As time marched on, matters got much worse.

# CHAPTER 24

# The Art of the Spin

When Georgia Congressman Newt Gingrich led Republicans to an astounding midterm landslide in Congress, he left President Clinton and Democrats in the dust, running off with more than fifty seats in the House and eight in the Senate. The upset was known as the "Republican Revolution" because Newt was the architect of a unified message for congressional candidates that won the GOP control of both houses. With that, he ripped the coveted job of speaker of the House of Representatives from the Democrats, who had held it for almost half a century. With that crown, Gingrich was second in the line of presidential succession. Whatever came out of the mouth of this sharp-tongued, opinionated, abrasive Republican was guaranteed to make headlines. He was the most powerful Republican and a brilliant politician who was happy to butt heads with the Democratic President Bill Clinton.

The night before Gingrich was to be sworn in as speaker, CBS, in a blatant attempt to drum up ratings for my magazine, *Eye to Eye*, put out a press release promoting my interview with his mother, Kathleen Gingrich, including a transcript of a thirty-second excerpt. In it, Mrs. Gingrich revealed that her son, Newt, had called First Lady Hillary Clinton "a bitch."

How I elicited her eye-popping answer unleashed a wildfire known as "Bitchgate" that just about incinerated my career.

Gingrich handled Bitchgate the way any skilled politico would—he flipped the blame to me for the incendiary word his mother used. Political reporters are all too familiar with the art of the spin. When a politician makes a gaffe, he and his aides descend on reporters to spin the remark and deflect it. With Bitchgate, I found myself in the bull's-eye of the spin, thanks to Newt, the spinmeister par excellence.

Allow me to roll back the videotape to unpeel the layers of his clever strategy.

When I had requested an interview with Gingrich, he had declined but sanctioned interviews with his mother, father, and three sisters.

Our team arrived at his parents' home in Dauphin, Pennsylvania. It was unusual to devote three camera crews to any interview, but this wasn't just *any* interview, given Gingrich's new status in the country. The crews dragged dollies full of equipment along with a labyrinth of wires, lights, and tripods, creating quite a mess throughout their living room and dining room, while the Gingriches and I ducked into the kitchen to chat, with a camera rolling tape.

His father, a friendly tobacco-chewing gentleman, had baked me a cake! It was delicious. Mrs. Gingrich struck me as a feisty, fearless woman who was ready and willing to enjoy her moment before the cameras. I thought to myself, "Now I know where her son got his chutzpah." (He was known to shoot from the lip.) I loved meeting women who were strong, not shy—who appeared proud to have been around the block. That was the joy of my job. I could meet real people and relish their takes on life.

Mrs. Gingrich said of her husband, "He sits right there and does his crossword puzzles, and I watch TV and drink my coffee and have my cigarettes." She smoked during our interview—and since I was an occasional smoker, I craved one too, but I dared not bum one off her.

When our crews were all set up, they helped the couple duck under the lights and navigate the tangle of wires so they could sit in their dining room chairs for the interview. Our audio men wired them with microphones.

With lights flipped on, audio checked, and cameras rolling, I asked them if Newt was a true southerner.

Mr. Gingrich said Newt, a staunch conservative and proud southern Republican congressman from Georgia, had, in fact, been born north of the Mason-Dixon Line, in Harrisburg, Pennsylvania. He had spent his first ten years in Pennsylvania.

> **Connie:** So he's kind of a Yankee. He's a Yankee?
>
> **Mrs. Gingrich** *(whispering, establishing a playful atmosphere):* I think so.
>
> **Connie** *(mimicking her whisper):* But we won't tell anybody.
>
> **Mrs. Gingrich** *(continuing in a whisper):* OK, it's better. *(then, starting off in a whisper and gradually resuming her normal voice)* 'Cause he has enough Democrats against him.

That set the stage for the tone of our interview—the Gingrich parents kibitzing with me around the dining room table.

On Wednesday, January 4, 1995, the morning of Newt Gingrich's history-making day, *CBS Morning* anchors Harry Smith and Paula Zahn were joined in their studio for live interviews with the two most powerful Republicans in the country, Senate Majority Leader Bob Dole and Gingrich. The four of them sat at a table as if they were playing a card game.

Paula introduced a thirty-second clip from my interview, which, because of the CBS press release, had blanketed newspapers, radio, and television all morning.

What Gingrich and the viewers saw was the following:

**Connie:** Mrs. Gingrich, what has Newt told you about President Clinton?

**Mrs. Gingrich:** Nothing. And I can't tell you what he's said about Hillary.

**Connie:** You can't?

**Mrs. Gingrich:** I can't.

**Connie** *(playing off the previous whispering game):* Why don't you just whisper it to me, just between you and me?

**Mrs. Gingrich** *(leaning forward and in a stage whisper):* She's a bitch. *(returning to her normal voice)* About the only thing he ever said about her. I think they had some meeting, you know, and she takes over.

**Connie:** She does?

**Mrs. Gingrich:** Oh yeah, but with Newty there, she can't.

What the viewers did *not* see in the clip was the coy whispering game that Mrs. Gingrich had established herself.

Immediately after the excerpt was aired, Gingrich, appearing angry, reacted quickly and decisively. "She says to my mother, who spent eight hours with her, my dad baked her a cake. She says, 'Whisper it to me.' My mother's not a professional politician. She's not a national figure. She's not a millionaire television correspondent. My mother's a simple woman who loves her son and who wants this to be a nice day. And I think it is disreputable for a national correspondent to say, 'Whisper it to me' and then put it on the air."

He ended his planned response with a peculiar comment: "I'm not going to argue with my mother today."

*Morning* anchor Paula Zahn followed up, "Did you tell your mother that?"

He offered no answer to her question. "I would not comment to you anything I would ever say to my mother, and I think it is a disreputable act."

Gingrich had apparently crafted his response, based on the CBS transcript released the night before, and had successfully deflected attention *away* from himself for calling Hillary Clinton an unbecoming name. In doing so, he'd shifted attention to me as the unscrupulous interviewer who had tricked his politically naive mother into whispering a secret "between you and me."

*Eye to Eye* Executive Producer Susan Zirinsky had approved releasing the clip to CBS' morning news program. Ah, if only it had included the entire exchange. That publicity stunt by CBS—taking my interview out of context and merely releasing the truncated, sexy sound bite—ignited a media feeding frenzy over journalistic ethics.

Suddenly I found myself facing a firing squad of critics who decried me as a "liar" for "betraying" Mrs. Gingrich's confidence and "deceiving" her. I was extremely upset by the unthinkable words the press used to describe me: "irresponsible," "unethical," "misleading," "predator," "sneaky," "smarmy," "cheesy," "reprehensible," "nefarious." I received phone calls and faxes calling me a "c***" and "motherf*cker." Adding to the drubbing, my "pal" David Letterman ripped me in a Top Ten List, and I became a running joke on *Saturday Night Live*.

What stung the most was that fellow journalists ridiculed me. Whatever credibility I'd had left, after being assigned to chase two ice skaters and O. J., was shattered.

Departing the White House, Gingrich stood before a herd of reporters and said, "I told him [Clinton] I was very sorry what Connie Chung had done and he agreed with me. I don't want to comment on Connie Chung's total collapse of the Edward R. Murrow tradition, but I cannot imagine that Edward R. Murrow would ever have lied to somebody's mother in order to get the story."

A reporter yelled, "Did you say it?"

Gingrich: "You have no idea what I called Mrs. Clinton because I have never commented on any of those things, and I won't."

Another question: "Is your mother a liar?"

To which Gingrich slammed the door of his Chevy Suburban.

CBS News President Eric Ober tried to rescue me from the withering onslaught and admitted it was the network's fault for releasing an excerpt out of context. Had the entire twelve-minute story aired, he said, viewers could have seen for themselves Mrs. Gingrich's stage-whispering game.

Ober also explained my use of the phrase "between you and me."

"That's the standard Mike Wallace *60 Minutes* technique," he said. "Mike always says 'between you and me,' and that's when the guy he's interviewing comes clean with the cameras rolling." (*Between You and Me* was the title of Mike's 2005 memoir.)

Mike called me with his support, as did many other journalists, including Walter Cronkite, Barbara Walters, Helen Thomas, Lesley Stahl, Diane Sawyer, and even *60 Minutes* Executive Producer Don Hewitt.

Ober told me the controversy would likely die down when *Eye to Eye* aired the full interview the next day. But the uproar did not subside—not even when Cronkite weighed in publicly. "I don't think Connie did a damn thing wrong," he said. And he told another reporter, "It clearly was an unfortunate remark by Mrs. Gingrich, but that could hardly be laid at Connie's feet. She was practicing perfectly sound journalism in asking the question with cameras and microphones present in a situation which obviously was to be televised."

Two female writers lambasted Speaker Gingrich for throwing his own mother under the bus. One wrote, "If Kathleen Gingrich chooses to say on national television that her son called Hillary Clinton a bitch, why is his only out to claim that his mother was duped? Frankly, I resent his patronizing tone. Just because your mom is not a professional politician…doesn't mean she's an idiot!"

The other asked, "Why do people assume that women over sixty-five are helpless and sort of stupid?"

By coincidence, three days after the ruckus started, Eric Ober and Howard Stringer had to face the Television Critics Association forum in Pasadena, California. Eric took the heat. Yes, we at CBS had "shot ourselves in the foot" and had "only ourselves to blame."

"Did we cause it ourselves?" he asked out loud. "Absolutely," Ober concluded.

When Howard Stringer faced the same forum, a television critic noted that my news magazine was putting me in "harm's way," and asked if I would continue to anchor both the news and *Eye to Eye.*

Howard said he would not make any changes but conceded that the dichotomy between "credibility" on the *Evening News* and the intense battle for magazine ratings was "our fault, that's not Connie's fault."

"We've demanded a lot of her, and I think it's time that we were fair to her." Stringer told the critics he was going to call me and tell me it was time for me to "throttle back" so that I wouldn't be "permanently poised at the end of the plank with the sharks snapping in the water below."

There was no throttling back for me. I was already in fifth gear, on edge and furious. In separate conversations, I angrily told Eric and Howard their poor decisions had led to my systematic public dismemberment. I told them to stop assigning me to cover stories that they knew would hurt whatever decent reputation I had left.

Yet the damage had been done. I was sinking in quicksand.

Later, as if to rub my nose in Bitchgate, and perhaps to absolve the network, Rather scheduled a one-on-one live interview with Newt Gingrich on our *CBS Evening News* program. How incredibly humiliating for me as I sat silently, not allowed to participate.

How about this for an ironic coincidence? That week, *Seinfeld* (*Eye to Eye*'s direct competition on NBC) aired a highly promoted episode in which Kramer's mom reveals a secret: that his first name is "Cosmo."

Kramer's mom beat Newt's mom two to one in the ratings.

\* \* \*

Many years later, I ran into Gingrich on an Acela train from New York to DC. He was looking for a seat. I initiated a greeting: "Hi, Mr. Gingrich. Connie Chung." I extended my hand. But he was schlepping many bags and had only one appendage available. He looked at me, expressionless, muttered, "Oh," and extended one of his left fingers. I gladly shook the finger. He quickly settled into the seat in front of me.

By this point, he had been driven out of the speakership because of Republican losses in the 1998 election and a controversial political contribution that led to a two-year House ethics committee investigation. The full House reprimanded Gingrich and fined him $300,000. He did not run again for Congress and had a failed presidential bid in 2012.

Later, when I went to the restroom, I saw him snoozing. The devil in me wanted to wake him up and ask him to whisper something to me.

Upon arriving in DC, I loaded my luggage in a mobile cart and hopped in. As I waited while others piled their luggage in the cart too, Gingrich, carrying a load of bags, walked by. He turned his head, looking back at me, and with a big smile waved goodbye. As the redcap started up the cart, I asked him to stop when we were alongside Gingrich and shouted, "Do you want a ride?"

"No thanks," he said with a smile, continuing to walk. "This is good for me."

I thought the Gingrich controversy was the worst incident I would face while coanchoring the *CBS Evening News*, but what was to come made Bitchgate pale in comparison.

# CHAPTER 25

# Oklahoma Explosion

O n April 19, 1995, a massive explosion killed 168 innocent people, including nineteen children, at the Alfred P. Murrah Federal Building in Oklahoma City. It was, at the time, the deadliest domestic terrorist bomb attack in US history. Two culprits, Timothy McVeigh and Terry Nichols, had planted the bombs in a rental truck parked right in front of the nine-story building. The children had just been dropped off by their parents to spend the day at a day care center on the second floor. I will never forget the gruesome sight of the aftermath. It was like a war zone.

I was in Sacramento, working on a story for *Eye to Eye*. As soon as I heard about the explosion, I called New York and asked if CBS wanted me to drop everything and head to Oklahoma City. That's what reporters do—when news breaks, we run to it.

While I flew there from the West Coast, CBS correspondent Scott Pelley flew from New York. We were the first reporters on the ground from the three networks. That night, I anchored the *CBS Evening News* live from the site and afterward, at eight, did a special hour-long report. Because of our speedy reaction, I was the only anchor from the three networks on the scene.

Dan Rather was on vacation. I don't know when he learned about the events of the day. (This was before smartphones, so it was actually possible to be out of touch with the news.) *CBS Evening News* Executive Producer Andrew Heyward, responding to television critics who noticed Rather's absence, said, "I made a split-second decision to send her. By the time I tracked Dan down later, he and I agreed that we were covered." Even though I was a coanchor, Rather was still perceived as the top choice to cover such a major event. But the fact that Andrew chose his words carefully to explain why Rather was not in Oklahoma City meant something was abuzz in the media world.

For the next couple of nights, I anchored the news and special reports, and in between I interviewed survivors and victims' families. It was a sad, wrenching experience.

When I returned to New York, I walked into a tornado. It turned out that Dan Rather was extremely upset that I had been covering the tragedy, not he. Management had instructed him to join me in Oklahoma City, where he could also anchor his magazine program, *48 Hours.* Furious, he had refused both assignments.

Now Rather decided he would travel to Oklahoma City to anchor from there and follow up, along with other CBS reporters, while I did my part of the news from New York.

While he was on the ground there, Rather reportedly did something despicable that put me in the eye of a new media feeding frenzy.

According to CBS correspondent Bernard Goldberg, "Dan was so incensed that Connie was on the air first and getting all the airtime that when he finally arrived in Oklahoma City, he spent hours and hours on the phone with TV writers, blasting Connie Chung as a second-rate journalist."

In his 2001 book, *Bias* (about liberal bias in the media), Bernie continued, "Several CBS News people heard him do it. Dan was behind a curtain in a makeshift CBS newsroom in Oklahoma City...ripping her. Of course he wasn't speaking 'on the record,' so you couldn't find his name in any of the stories."

Bernie had been at CBS News for twenty-four years and knew Dan well, and he describes the "ugly, take-no-prisoners side of Dan that comes out when he feels threatened."

Soon after, local radio talk show hosts began to berate my coverage. A whisper campaign spread like wildfire from Oklahoma City to TV critics in New York, Washington, and all over the country. One absurd rumor claimed that I had reported that crime in Oklahoma City had become rampant in the aftermath of the bombing because police were focused on the bombing scene to the exclusion of all else. That was an outright lie. I never reported anything of the kind.

More rumors were flying through Oklahoma: that I had worn a nurse's uniform to sneak into a hospital for an interview with a survivor; that I had dressed up as a nun to attend a victim's funeral; that I had been handcuffed for crossing a perimeter line; and, ultimately, that I had been ordered out of the state by the governor. All scurrilous and unfounded.

Locals printed T-shirts that read, "Who the hell is Connie Chung?" The back read, "Bite me Connie Chung." High school students wrote me letters saying they were offended by my reporting, tone of voice, and facial expressions.

A Tulsa newspaper published a letter from a reader who told me to go home and not come back.

"Her insensitive remarks and condescending attitude toward

Okies is outrageous. Texan Dan Rather would have been the appropriate journalist to let cover the entire ordeal."

The worst dagger came when I was also accused of denigrating the city's fire department as incapable of dealing with the crisis. As we discussed the difficulty of recovering bodies while protecting evidence, I had asked Assistant Fire Chief Jon Hansen, "Can you handle this? I know you're doing a great job, but it's extraordinarily difficult."

CBS News President Eric Ober once again leaped to my defense.

> Connie Chung was sympathetically questioning Assistant Fire Chief Hansen and in no way denigrating either the Oklahoma City Fire Department or the people of Oklahoma City. Her reporting and anchoring were outstanding and extremely sensitive under very difficult circumstances.

Despite that, CBS insisted I apologize on air to Chief Hansen. I set up a follow-up interview with him on the *CBS Evening News* to say I was sorry. He did not want to do the interview, even defending me, declaring all my questions had been "fair." Hansen told me that there was nothing to apologize for. But he kindly talked to me anyway so I could apologize and hopefully move past the insanity.

Writing this chapter, I did my due diligence and called Bernie Goldberg to ask who had told him that Rather was the source of the false rumors. Reporters never reveal their sources, so Bernie refused to give their names, even to me, a colleague, despite my promise that I would protect their identities. I wanted to know for the sake of accuracy.

But he did say, "They are people you know and people I know. They had no reason to lie to me. Why would they lie to me about that?" He added, "Several people heard it, and Rather never denied it."

The walls were closing in on me, with media critics openly speculating about my future. I could hear the steady drumbeat of calls to kick me out the door.

A CBS executive called me to negotiate a peace agreement between Rather and me. I took notes.

First, he told me Rather was always the reluctant groom.

The executive was direct and blunt as he relayed Rather's feelings: "He thinks you are out to take anything he has."

"He has drawn a line in the sand."

"He's in a fight for his life."

"There is no room for compromise."

"What you feel you need," the executive added, "Dan isn't willing to give."

This executive warned me, "We are headed for a showdown."

It appeared there was no way to salvage this contentious relationship. Had we hammered out our roles and duties when we first started, the coanchor arrangement might have worked, but now it was too late.

Even though it had been only two years since I started coanchoring with Rather, it felt like a lifetime. By then Howard Stringer, the one who had chosen me for my dream job, had left CBS for a new position.

Desperate to save myself, I requested separate meetings with Eric Ober; Howard's successor, Peter Lund; and CBS owner Larry Tisch. I urged each to avoid taking precipitous action and to give the *Evening News* dual anchor team more time.

But Rather had met with CBS Broadcast Group President Peter Lund, too, and this time he did not mince words. Rather said he "could not go on like this." Then came the ultimatum—her or me.

I knew my days were numbered.

# CHAPTER 26

# The Ax

A month later, my world collapsed.
It was just before six thirty on a Thursday in April 1995. Time for the *CBS Evening News with Dan Rather and Connie Chung*.

I was just about to take my place on the news set when the phone rang in my office. My longtime lawyer/agent and dear friend, Alfred, was on the other end with the bombshell I dreaded.

My dream job was over. I had been removed from the *CBS Evening News*.

I knew I had been hanging by my fingernails, but the finality of the news devastated me. Here I had reached the pinnacle of television news, and suddenly I was out. I was offered a consolation prize, but I could not think about that. I was angry.

Thank goodness Alfred did not hold back and told me. I was shocked that my bosses, CBS President Eric Ober and CBS Broadcast Group President Peter Lund, hadn't fired me from the *Evening*

*News* themselves. I'd thought I had open, honest relationships with both men, yet neither had the grace, gumption, or decency to tell me in a face-to-face meeting. If I were the boss, I would be man enough to look my employee in the eye and tell her myself.

Frankly, that infuriated me more than the fact that—unthinkably—I was to anchor my last *CBS Evening News* in minutes. I made a quick call to Maury, but there was no time to talk. We would do that when we both got home.

I wondered if those executives were beset with fear that I might say something untoward about my dismissal on *live* television on my last night. Perhaps they knew me too well. It never occurred to me to announce that I'd gotten the boot on live television. I was still the loyal soldier doing my regular duty, showing no inkling I had lost all I had worked so hard to achieve. I would bite my tongue and anchor the news the way I always did.

Sitting down beside Rather, I took a deep breath and glanced over at him. Would his demeanor tell me that he knew what had happened to me? I saw nothing written on his face.

And I telegraphed nothing as well. I proceeded to do the job I had so happily and proudly done for two short years—deliver the news to America. When I walked off the set for the last time, I felt as if I had left my life behind.

On the cab ride home, I mulled over what Alfred had told me CBS had offered: substituting for Dan Rather on the *CBS Evening News*, which he would anchor solo going forward; anchoring the *CBS Evening News* both Saturdays and Sundays; and also anchoring and reporting a few news specials. Since I was still under contract with the network, I had time to think about what I wanted to do.

I went home mad as hell. No tears.

Maury was not back at our apartment when I got there. But

Liane Ramirez, whom I had hired as my "wife"—a home assistant to help me keep up with my off-air life—was. Liane and I had become close when we first met at CBS. By now, she was a dear, lifelong friend. When I told her I had been dumped from the *CBS Evening News*, she burst into tears. That's when I finally broke down from the stress and anger.

That night Maury and I each had a stiff scotch on the rocks. By now, Maury was an old hand at talking me off the ledge. This time he walked me through the day he had been fired and his tussles with executives in our brutal world of news. Although I took losing my coanchor job personally, I knew he was right when he said it was strictly business.

I spent Friday on the phone with Alfred, weighing my options. Could I walk away from what CBS was offering me? If I did, I would desperately miss my job. Yet continuing to work at the same network as Dan Rather was unthinkable.

My very Chinese reaction was to feel I had lost face. All the joy of reaching my ultimate goal had evaporated in an instant. And in that moment, I also recognized that my entire life had been wrapped up in my work and how much it was a part of me—despite the difficulties and impossible personalities along the way.

I loved being present when history was made. I loved digging for the truth. I loved conveying accurate information to viewers who trusted me. I loved being able to uncover information that could change the course of history.

Coanchoring the news meant power to me. Power I otherwise could not command. Power to be *heard*. When the anchors spoke, everyone listened. And *leadership* power. Anchors were the ones who carried the flag for their network. For two years, I had held what I'd thought was an equal seat at the table with three white men. But now

Interviewing Israeli Foreign Minister Shimon Peres for the *CBS Evening News* at the Mayflower Hotel. September 1993. *(Photo Still from CBS Photo—Courtesy of CBS Broadcasting Inc.)*

Interviewing President Bill Clinton at the White House about NAFTA for *Eye to Eye with Connie Chung.* November 9, 1993. *(White House Photo by Sharon Farmer, who later became the first female White House photo director. Image courtesy William J. Clinton Presidential Library.)*

Exclusive interview with the basketball great, the GOAT Michael Jordan about his gambling controversy. 1993. *(Photo Still from CBS Photo—Courtesy of CBS Broadcasting Inc.)*

On set in Poland with Steven Spielberg for *Schindler's List.* Far right: CBS producer Patrick Weiland. Aired December 1993 on *Eye to Eye with Connie Chung.* The segment also included interviews with Holocaust survivors and the actors who portrayed them in the film. *(Photo Still from CBS Photo— Courtesy of CBS Broadcasting Inc.*

Interviewing Tonya Harding in Oregon, just before the start of the 1994 Winter Olympics in Norway. Aired February 10, 1994, on *Eye to Eye with Connie Chung. (Photo Still from CBS Photo—Courtesy of CBS Broadcasting Inc.)*

Solo anchoring Israeli-Jordan peace agreement in Amman for CBS. Right: Peter Jennings anchoring for ABC. Left: CBS producer Al Berman. *(Photo Still from CBS Photo— Courtesy of CBS Broadcasting Inc.)*

With US troops at Camp Doha, Kuwait, in October 1994. *LA Times*: "Clinton seemed a lesser source of excitement than CBS news anchor Connie Chung, who autographed helmets and regimental colors for the troops…" *(Photo Still from CBS Photo— Courtesy of CBS Broadcasting Inc.)*

Collaborating with CBS editor in makeshift workspace for CBS report on Clinton's Middle East trip. October 1994. *(Photo Still from CBS Photo—Courtesy of CBS Broadcasting Inc.)*

With Maury attending a black-tie event. 1995. *(Ron Galella / Getty Images.)*

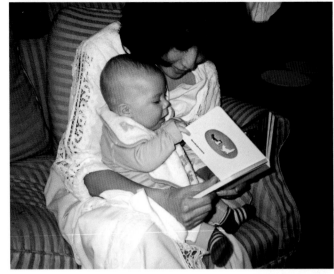

Matthew brilliantly turning a page of *Goodnight Moon* at only three months. *(Author's personal collection.)*

Daddy, Mommy, and Matthew. 1995. *(Author's personal collection.)*

My one and only dear Matthew with Mommy. 1996. *(Photograph by Tony Esparza.)*

ABC News magazine anchors, left to right: Charles Gibson, Sam Donaldson, Diane Sawyer, Barbara Walters, Hugh Downs, and Connie. *(ABC Photo Archives.)*

Interviewing Ernest Avants, a hate-crime murderer, reviving a cold 1960s civil rights case. *(ABC Photo Archives.)*

Exclusive interview with California Congressman Gary Condit about the disappearance of intern Chandra Levy. August 2001. *(ABC Photo Archives.)*

Maury, Connie, and Matthew.
*(Photo by Bryan Blanken for Freed
Photography.)*

Our family at Matthew's bar mitzvah. Front row,
left to right: Susan Povich, Connie, Amy Povich
Agus, Charley Gorham, Jesse Gorham. Back
row, left to right: David Agus (Amy's husband),
Matthew Povich, Sydney Agus, Maury, Ralph
Gorham (Susan's husband), Miles Agus. 2008.
*(Photo by Bryan Blanken for Freed Photography.)*

Maury, Connie, and Matthew.
*(Photograph by Izzy Povich.)*

Presenting Maury with the National Academy of Television Arts and Sciences Lifetime Achievement Emmy. 2023. *(JC Olivera / Getty Images)*

Rewinding back to 1984, when gaining equality felt like the dinosaur days (just ask this triceratops named "Uncle Beazley"). We've come a long way but we still aren't there yet. *(© by Marianne Barcellona.)*

Matthew and his fiancée, Hunter
*(Author's personal collection.)*

Connies at *New York Times*
photo shoot. Left insert:
Photographer Connie
Chung Aramaki. Right
insert: Writer of "Generation
Connie" for NYT Sunday
Opinion, Connie Wang.
*(Group photograph and portrait
of Connie Aramaki courtesy of
Connie Aramaki / Coco Foto.
Connie Wang portrait by Chris
Buck, courtesy of Connie Wang.)*

I saw clearly that was never true. Losing all that was gut-wrenching, breaking my rock-solid confidence.

On Saturday morning, barely two days after I was fired from the news, I heard the sweetest words I could ever have imagined.

Our adoption lawyer was calling.

"Your son will be born in the next couple of weeks."

It was serendipitous!

Allow me to backtrack to explain.

On the baby front, my body had been rejecting every embryo we conceived. Maury and I knew we would not give up. Maury had already experienced the joys of being a father with his two wonderful daughters, who became my daughters too. He didn't feel the need to reexperience that joy, but he knew that I would want to feel that unfathomable deep love for a child.

So he had suggested we adopt. The depth of his love for me was so extraordinary, he was willing to start from square one again at fifty-six. I was forty-nine, and I had been so hyperfocused on my work and all the drama that went with it, when Maury suggested adoption, I embraced it.

What helped me believe adoption was right for me was when a girlfriend of mine, Karen Danaher Dorr, shared her wisdom with me. She had adopted one son and had also given birth to another. "Wanting to preserve our gene pool is overrated," she declared. So nicely put, Karen. I realized that if I adopted a son, he would *not* be neurotic and paranoid like me, my parents, and the rest of my family! What a gift!

In 1993, we had started the process of adoption and hired a lawyer. It was right around the time I was named coanchor of the *CBS Evening News*.

Our intention was to adopt an American boy (a mini Maury)

and a Chinese girl (a mini me). For two long years, while I was consumed with staying alive at CBS, there had been no news on the baby front. We had kept our plans secret, just as I did not tell you a few chapters ago.

Then I was unceremoniously dumped, and two days later we received the incredible news that our son was about to be born. It was impeccable timing. I would never have quit my job, never have halted my career.

My sister Charlotte uttered the old adage "When one door closes, another opens." She was right. To me, losing my job and quickly being blessed with our son was meant to be.

Now you are caught up and no doubt understand that the decision about my professional future was obvious. My personal life would finally take priority.

I would not accept the offer of a consolation prize from CBS. Alfred and I would negotiate a separation from CBS. My future would be all about Matthew. No one knew of our impending good fortune. We kept our baby news under wraps.

My departure from the coanchor job made headlines from coast to coast.

I received an avalanche of emails, letters, notes, flowers, and cards from coworkers; on-air reporters; studio, field, technical, and cafeteria workers; print journalists; colleagues at other networks; and other people I knew and did not know.

They all put a wide smile on my face—some even made me laugh.

"To our favorite scapegoat!"

A male television critic sent flowers with the note "Screw the bastards."

Ruth Ashton Taylor, a close colleague who had blazed a trail in Los Angeles back in the 1940s, wrote, "I hope Dan's protestations of surprise, sorrow and friendship haven't made you too sick to your stomach." Ruth was fired up but said she was glad for my "mental health" that I would no longer be exposed "to your conceited, arrogant, two-faced coanchor."

Margaret Carlson, the first female columnist for *Time* magazine: "The bad guys in journalism win all too often. The good guys are all rooting for you. You will be happier than your tormentors and that's the best revenge."

Helen Thomas, the venerable White House correspondent for United Press International: "You have always had the right stuff. Those who were there know what you are going through."

Others used words I deeply appreciated: "heartbroken," "made my blood boil," "raw deal," "appalled," "treated shabbily," "devastated," "undeserved," "unfair," "one-sided," "mean-spirited," "awful injustice."

Marty Dick, the CBS lighting director, told me I had "widespread and deep support."

One letter in particular stood out. It was from my friend Richard Threlkeld, a veteran Vietnam War reporter at CBS and later ABC.

> You handled a terribly difficult situation with strength and courage and raw guts, and I have only everything to be proud of. I don't know anybody who could have gone thru the hail of slings and arrows of outrageous fortune (and some deliberate) with more dignity and class.
>
> What you have proved in this time of trial is what I guess I always knew...you are a superior person, a very special woman and an altogether class act.

As if those heartwarming words weren't enough, my dear friend Lesley Stahl, who by then was a CBS News *60 Minutes* correspondent, cooked up a magnificent occasion I will never forget.

She threw a lunch for me at Gabriel's, a west side New York restaurant not far from CBS. But it was not just *any* lunch. Lesley invited virtually every top woman in journalism for the express purpose of telling me, "You are not alone. We are with you."

I could not believe so many high-powered women I respected had taken precious time off from a working weekday to attend the occasion. Some even ventured from Washington, like Helen Thomas, *Newsweek*'s political journalist Eleanor Clift, CNN's Judy Woodruff, and Cokie Roberts of ABC and NPR.

Anyone stopping by Gabriel's that afternoon would have been treated to a who's who of female power players in news: CBS correspondents Edie Magnus, Roberta Baskin, and Erin Moriarty; executive producer Susan Zirinsky; NBC's Jane Pauley and Katie Couric; ABC's Sylvia Chase, Lynn Sherr, Renee Poussaint, and Catherine Crier; and of course the leader of the pack, Barbara Walters. ABC executives Patti Matson, Joanna Bistany, and Sherrie Rollins came, as did my dear sister-in-law Lynn Povich, editor in chief of *Working Woman.*

Even news pioneer Nancy Dickerson, the first female correspondent at CBS and later NBC and the person I had watched as a kid, attended. ABC's Diane Sawyer and producer Phyllis McGrady sent regrets from California but sweetened them with a bottle of tequila.

Almost everyone stood and spoke. Jane Pauley reminded me I had not lost my identity when she said, "You are still Connie Chung." I felt as if I were eavesdropping on my own funeral.

The first man to stop by the lunch was Maury. But I was shocked when Lesley's *60 Minutes* colleagues Mike Wallace, Morley Safer, and Executive Producer Don Hewitt walked into the restaurant to lend their support. (Their attendance insured that Lesley would not suffer any consequences for throwing me the party.) Bravo to Lesley for conquering the boys' club! That glorious, sunny day sent my heart sky high.

I had never enjoyed such camaraderie among fellow women journalists. I cherished it and will never forget it.

Now I was about to move into another world—a world of diapers, sleepless nights, and the unsurpassed joy of a new kind of love—love of my son.

CHAPTER 27

# Matthew

S uddenly my world shifted in every way imaginable.
Our son, Matthew, was about to enter our lives!

My first call went to our family lawyer and confidant, who had advised us during every step of our adoption process. Next the two couples who had kept our path to parenthood secret: my best friend, Andrea Reiter, and her husband, Allan; and Nancy and Alan Bubes, whom we knew even before they were married and who had three children. Alan and his three brothers were crazy golfers, just like Maury. None of them had said a word about our adoption for two years.

Nancy had prepared three large care packages filled with everything we would need for a newborn. She had sent them to our apartment in New York months before we needed them. Fortunately, no one was curious enough to ask what was inside those large boxes in our spare bedroom. No one knew it was a portable nursery: a big basket that would serve as a bassinet, a baby bottle sterilizer, bottles and nipples, sleepers, baby blankets, sheets, Pampers, wipes, undershirts, and cream for the tushy. You name it—Nancy thought of it all.

Our adoption lawyer told us we would meet our son in California. Andrea and her husband would put us up at their house. We could not stay in a hotel. The press would be tipped off immediately. We did not want to be hounded by inquiring reporters and paparazzi.

Our plans were in place. We were just waiting for the phone to ring to take the next step. That call came in the middle of the night. The adoption lawyer told us Matthew was going to be born in a matter of hours!

I quickly made reservations to fly from New York to California. We called Maury's extraordinary assistant, Amy, at her apartment in New York, woke her up, and asked her to pack a bag. She would be joining us on our most excellent adventure for the simple reason that Maury and I could not go out shopping for baby items—a dead giveaway if someone recognized us.

Despite being woken up at 2:00 a.m. and packing the rest of the night, we couldn't possibly sleep on the plane. We were much too anxious.

After arriving in LA, we rented a car, stacked our boxes of baby supplies in the back, and headed to Andrea and Allan's house. They happened to be in France visiting relatives, so Andrea had told me to look for a loose brick on the left side of the house, where I'd find the key to the front door.

The clock was ticking, and our nerves were shot. We had only two hours to unpack the boxes and wash everything in them before Matthew would be brought to Andrea's house. I needed to be ready.

Maury searched the side of the house. He panicked. "All the bricks are tight!" he said. "I can't find the loose one!!" Egad. Had I gotten it wrong? Had Andrea said she'd put the key in the begonia plant?

At last, Maury discovered the loose brick and opened the door. Thank goodness.

A couple of hours later, the doorbell rang. Standing at the front door was a woman with the adoption agency who put our precious baby in my arms. Oh, my heavens. Matthew was the most beautiful baby I had ever seen in my life, and he was *our* boy. He was only nineteen hours old—less than a day! I held him in my arms, and our eyes met and have never strayed.

We had spent only two sleepless nights with Matthew when a disruption shook our idyllic journey with our new son.

Liane, our assistant in New York, called to warn me she'd received a strange call—from someone who was fishing for information, hinting at the adoption. I had shared our secret with Liane earlier in the day and asked her to deflect any calls.

Soon thereafter, Andrea's home telephone rang. A woman asked for *me*, claiming to be from an adoption agency. Immediately, I could tell it was a tabloid leak. Why would anyone call me on my friend's home number?

Then we learned that tabloid reporters had called our relatives as well to find out what they knew. Fortunately, they could tell the truth. They knew nothing. (The tabloids pay retainers to people who work at hospitals, adoption agencies, and airports to get tips. We assumed there had been several leaks along the way.)

We were terrified because ours was a closed adoption. The identities of all the parties involved were unknown. We wanted to keep it that way. We wanted to protect and preserve confidentiality.

Out of necessity, we had to devise a way to skirt the paparazzi. Neither Maury nor I could be seen with Matthew. This was the plan we carried out.

It was simple. Maury, Matthew, and I would all take separate flights to different East Coast airports.

First Maury flew solo from California to DC, where he caught a shuttle flight to New York. After stopping at his office in the city, he drove to our weekend house in New Jersey.

Our family lawyer, who had hired a baby nurse to help, picked up Matthew at Andrea's house. I was a little nervous letting Matthew out of my arms, but I trusted our family lawyer with my life. They flew with Matthew from California to Newark Airport. During the flight, Matthew made sure to welcome our lawyer friend to the family properly, showering him with a spray while he changed our boy's diaper. After landing, the lawyer and the baby nurse drove to our home in New Jersey.

Right after Matthew was on his way, I closed up Andrea's house and took a plane solo from California to JFK Airport in New York and drove to our New Jersey place too.

The plan worked like a charm.

All these years later, I can still see our dear friend holding Matthew, walking from a back street behind our New Jersey house across our back lawn, emerging from the darkness onto our back porch, where Maury and I were waiting. It was just an incredible sight. I well up just thinking about it.

From the beginning, I'd boast, "Matthew looks exactly like me." (Matthew has blond hair and beautiful blue eyes.) When he was a newborn, his eyes were always incredibly expressive. He would stare at me. I was hooked.

This was not my first rodeo with a baby. My sister and I used to babysit all summer for our oldest niece and oldest nephew. I was an old hand at the baby routine. Matthew easily became a part of my cradling left arm. But he was also an extension of my heart and every part of me.

Maury was super about caring for Matthew, although he was not that good at diaper duty. Matthew had a habit of always giving Maury a good, healthy spritz.

We thought we could carry on, undetected, all summer, enjoying our new life, but we began to see stories in the press—not only in tabloids but also in legitimate outlets—spreading rumors about our adoption. We were mum, causing reporters and paparazzi to descend on our home in New Jersey.

As reporters ourselves, both Maury and I had in the past been sent by assignment editors to stake out newsmakers, hoping for a quote, a sound bite, or at least a photo. Knowing it was lousy duty to stand outside on the curb of someone's home all day, Maury went out to greet the reporters and photographers on our front yard, graciously telling them we weren't doing anything for the cameras. He gave them coffee, pizza, and bottled water since they were forced by their assignment editors to stay until dark.

Not long after, the *National Enquirer*, the grandfather of tabloid newspapers, contacted us about our son. The paper had numerous details of our story, but many of them were wrong. That's when we discovered the *Enquirer* was the one behind the nosy phone calls to us and our relatives.

Maury came up with the idea of allowing the tabloid to "break the story"—meaning we would confirm to the *Enquirer* that we had indeed adopted Matthew but with two conditions our trusted family lawyer negotiated.

One, we would control *when* the *Enquirer* could publish the story. (We wanted to be sure we were safely back at our New York apartment, where it was easier to control paparazzi traffic.)

Two, we'd have editorial control over what the paper wrote. In other words, the *Enquirer* had to show us a copy of the story, and we could correct any inaccuracies. (We would mask any *accurate* information and allow the tabloid to make mistakes, a clever way to protect everyone involved in our adoption.)

When our story became public, we were deluged with four hundred cards, letters, faxes, and gifts. How sweet!

Everyone involved in my dismissal from the CBS coanchor job sent presents. We even received a congratulatory note from President Bill Clinton and First Lady Hillary Clinton. A huge stuffed puppy arrived from "Auntie" Barbara (Walters); Lesley Stahl gave Matthew a washable rattle; and my favorite neighbors in New Jersey, Dot Bradley and her husband, Mike, who helped us gather baby necessities, hand-made and painted a classic rocking lamb (not horse). During Matthew's nap times, I handwrote heartfelt thank-you notes.

I wrote all of Matthew's milestones in a book: first word, first step, when he began to eat baby food, then solid food, and I took more photos than on all my worldwide trips combined.

When Matthew was only eight weeks old, Maury would hold him upright and he would strut, putting one foot in front of the other, as if he were marching. We wondered, "Is he walking at eight weeks?" Obviously our kid possessed out-of-this-world talents, as all parents boast.

Matthew was only three months when I read *Goodnight Moon* to him. I'd say, "Turn the page." (The book had heavy cardboard pages.) With his big hands (Maury called them "mitts") he would actually grasp the page to move it. True. I have photos to prove it. We declared our son was brilliant.

Matthew was a strong dude, walking on his own at ten months. His big blue eyes were expressive and curious. I was especially glad that he was an always-happy, easy boy—not a crybaby.

During his first year, I did not go out much. New York law dictated that adoptions could not be finalized for twelve months, and I lived with agonizing, nerve-racking fear that a change of heart could lead to our losing Matthew.

I was especially paranoid about being spotted by photographers. One time, Maury and I were taking Matthew to Washington, DC, to visit family. As we drove off from our apartment to the airport, we saw a car tailing us, obviously a photographer. As we walked to the shuttle terminal, I saw him following us. I decided to talk to him. Maury held Matthew while I walked toward him. He was backing up—no doubt wondering what I was about to do. I was amused by his slight fear of me.

I reasoned with him, explaining that our adoption would not be finalized for a year and I would very much appreciate it if he did not take a photo of us with Matthew. Thank goodness he had a soft spot. He agreed to leave. I was surprised and grateful.

After our adoption was finalized, I would take Matthew to Central Park. One of his first words besides "mama" and "dada" was "hi." In fact, it was his favorite word when we went for stroller walks. He'd say hi to everyone, including total strangers. We'd play in Central Park playgrounds, in the sandboxes and on the swings and jungle gyms. New York was a city filled with nannies at the park who would look at me and ask whom I worked for, no doubt because I am Chinese. I replied blandly, "*I* am the mommy." Chinese people are always reminded that we look like foreigners, lest we should forget.

Our family settled into a routine. After celebrating his birthday, the next day we'd celebrate Adoption Day. We brought Matthew up with Jewish traditions including Friday-night Shabbat; at thirteen, he had a Bar Mitzvah, and we celebrated the High Holidays. I never converted, but I am essentially Jewish by osmosis.

After Matthew started nursery school, Maury and I attended parents' night. Along the walls were drawings of faces made by the children. The teacher told us to look for ourselves, but we could not find ourselves, so we asked the teacher for help. Remarkably, Maury and I both had blond hair and blue eyes! Matthew decided we were reflections of him.

When it was time for Matthew to go to kindergarten, I was shocked to learn that a five-year-old had to apply to attend certain New York City schools. Ridiculous as it was, I, being a helicopter mom, just like many older parents, wanted the best for Matthew.

Matthew was shy. At an interview at one school, he would not leave my side. The teacher told me I could sit on the sidelines as the children played. The children were called one by one to meet with the interviewing teacher. I quietly watched as the interviewer asked a little girl to identify shapes—a circle, a square, a rectangle. Then she was asked to draw her own shape. "Good!" the teacher exclaimed, "and what is that?" The precocious little sweetheart replied, "A trapezoid." Oh dear. Competitive New Yorkers were obviously coaching their children.

We once asked Matthew his earliest memory. He remembered being in the back of our car, in his car seat, as Maury drove us to New Jersey. Maury cannot tolerate traffic jams. Frustrated, he let loose with the f-bomb.

"Don't say that word in front of Matthew," I growled at Maury.

Years later, as an adult, Matthew recalled, "Dad said, 'He's *never* going to f*cking remember it.'"

One of Matthew's middle school teachers told me, "Matthew

knows who he is." That was unusual for a kid his age. "He does?" I thought. The teacher continued, "Matthew will not allow himself to be bullied." How proud I was that my son knew how to survive in this world.

When he was growing up, we were stay-at-home parents, rarely going out on date nights. One night, when Matthew was still single digits old, we told him we were going to see a movie.

"Why?" he asked.

"Because we haven't seen a movie in a long time," I said.

"No," Matthew noted, "you went last year."

One of the best parts of that time was getting to know the mothers of Matthew's friends and classmates. They were all accomplished women. Some had stopped working; others still had their careers. Many of them were older (although I was the oldest—by then fiftysomething). One morning, when I saw one of my favorite moms as we were dropping our sons off for school, she noticed I was dressed up. "Did you go back to the dark side?" she wondered. No, I had not gone back to work.

About a dozen of us would meet for dinner around once a month, which I found helped me navigate parenthood. I'd learn that my experiences with my son were identical to theirs with their children. We were a diverse group—one was a member of the Council on Foreign Relations, another an avid ice hockey player.

One mother with twins would eavesdrop on her boys' conversations and surprised us with what one twin had told the other about the gym teacher's sex education classes. When I realized what the boys were learning at age twelve or thirteen, I alerted Maury that we had to have "the talk."

It was probably too late, but Maury and I huddled. "I need to read some articles and books to see how to approach this subject," Maury said. Okaaaay. I was resourceful, gathering numerous books and articles. I read them all and then called a meeting for Maury and me.

"Did you read what I gave you?" I asked. He had not. Annoyed, I suggested, "Let's practice what we are going to say to Matthew."

Maury, Mr. Avoidance, said, "What do you think we should say?" I proceeded to go through chapter and verse of everything I'd gleaned was important to pass along to our dear son.

The serious moment of truth arrived.

"Are you ready?" I asked Maury. He mumbled something. We asked Matthew to join us in the den. Maury shifted from his booming voice to his endearing "inside" voice (which I love), which he deploys when he's speaking to overweight babies on his show, as in, "Your mommy tells me that you eat three McDonald's Big Macs for breakfast?"

In his fatherly inside voice, as Matthew slumped in his chair because he knew something was up, Maury said, "Now, Matthew, Mom and I want to talk to you about something that my parents never talked to me about and Mom's parents never talked to her about. Now here's your mom…!"

"Really, Maury?" I thought. "You chicken."

I did not flinch, proceeding to give Matthew too much information—but just the facts. Matthew was sufficiently embarrassed not at the clinical details, but because I was so frank.

As he was growing up, I was glad he felt free to talk to me about anything. When he was in high school, he asked, "What do you think I could major in in college? And pursue as a career?"

"Identify your passion," I said. "Then you'll be happy to get up every morning, go to work, and enjoy your work because you are passionate about it. I loved my job," I told him.

That was the truth, yet raising a child was by far more challenging than even the hardest assignments during my career. There were no rule books for parents. We were committed to giving Matthew a normal life, out of the limelight, insulated from Maury's and my public lives. Avoiding public outings, we always ate dinner together every night at home. It's an important tradition we maintain when we spend summers with Matthew and his longtime girlfriend and now fiancée, Hunter. They are great cooks and can even make my mother's Chinese dumplings better than I can.

And now that he's an adult, we still carry on our tradition of keeping his life private. Just because we chose to live in the public eye doesn't mean he should have to.

Every day is all about my son. Even that silly Hallmark holiday, Mother's Day, is not *my* day. I see it as Matthew's day. Having a child is all about him, *not me.* And therein lies the reason I am filled with gratitude that Matthew is my son. I could finally get outside myself and my work. What a deep, worthwhile feeling of overwhelming love and sheer happiness to give and receive.

As for my son, Matthew, every day he displays unequivocal affection for me, with a smile, a hug, a gesture, and warm words I cherish. I am a very lucky mom. Thanks to Maury, who was willing to start all over for me, Matthew is the most precious being in my life.

\* \* \*

As I was writing my book, my seventy-seventh birthday hit me like a sledgehammer. I was not anxious to celebrate—the clock was ticking, and I was facing my publisher's deadline for the first draft of my manuscript. Matthew surprised me with a gift I cherish—he made an elegant desk nameplate.

On one side, the text reads, "Author at Work."

On the other side, "Coolest Mom Ever."

"Love, Matthew."

# CHAPTER 28

# Harvard

During Matthew's baby years, I was happy to immerse myself in his care and enjoy life out of the public eye.

Every morning, I'd peek in his crib. When he saw me, he'd lift his head and beam. I can picture it now. "Good morning, Matthew!" I'd say, smiling back at him. "Good morning, sunshine!" I cherished coddling my son in the peaceful quiet of our apartment.

It was a welcome respite from the madness of my last work experience. The truth is that my departure had shattered my confidence. I joked that I had become agoraphobic since I was trepidatious about coming out of my cocoon.

Yet I didn't consider myself retired, and neither did the television news industry. Comedy Central asked me to do a show. (I wish I had explored it.)

Then, after less than two years off the small screen, I was asked to narrate a four-part Public Broadcasting Service (PBS) series,

*Knife to the Heart*, about the legal and moral controversy over organ transplants. I agreed. It was easy work, a compelling subject, and best of all, it did not require my being away from Matthew for very long.

Shortly afterward, I received a call from Marvin Kalb, the distinguished chief diplomatic correspondent with whom I had worked at CBS and NBC. He had left news to become the founding director of Harvard University's Joan Shorenstein Center on the Press, Politics and Public Policy, part of the Kennedy School.

Back when Bitchgate was at fever pitch, a reporter had asked Marvin for a comment about my interview with Mrs. Gingrich. Just like the rest of the public, Marvin had not seen my full report. Based on what the reporter told him and pressed to react, he gave negative comments about me. A couple of days later, he took the time to watch the entire interview and wrote me a letter offering a profuse apology. He was adamant that I had been unfairly scorched.

Now Marvin was calling to offer me a fellowship at the center. I was surprised and honored. Fellowships were coveted breaks from the daily grind of the news business. A number of universities offered them, but this one at Harvard was one of the best. It felt as if Marvin knew I needed to be prodded and coaxed to emerge from hiding and join society again. Engaging in adult conversation again would be refreshing. Harvard would be a stimulating environment where I could read, think, write, and absorb—a sort of reboot.

Also, it was driving Maury nuts to come home from work each night to find me there. In the past, I was never home. He needed his alone *down*time, and I needed some *up*time.

So during the spring of 1998, I flew to Boston to spend two days a week on the Harvard campus. It was an exhilarating experience to dwell in the ivory tower of the Ivy League. The Shorenstein Center gave me the opportunity to research, discuss, and engage with students and faculty about the relationship between the press and politics—a subject I knew well from experience that was simultaneously symbiotic and adversarial. I made the most of every minute.

As a fellow, I could audit a few classes too. In one history class, an older woman kept asking the professor annoying questions. Afterward, I thanked the professor for allowing me to sit in and told him I was appalled at the impertinent questions the woman had been asking him. "Oh," the professor said, "that was my wife."

Each Shorenstein fellow was required to write a twelve-thousand-word final paper. Marvin encouraged me to write about the Gingrich matter, but I could not bring myself to relive that ugly experience. It was too painful.

Instead, I wrote about the phenomenon of "Getting the Get: Nailing an Exclusive Interview in Prime Time." Competing for high-profile interviews had been a thorn in my career, but I thought it was important to dissect the process from an insider's point of view. It turned into the perfect way to exercise my brain again.

Walking around campus one day, I passed a center that helped students with their study habits and psychological issues. I had always thought I had a reading disability because I was a slow reader and had trouble comprehending and retaining dense material. Through trial and error, I'd found the best way for me to absorb heavy information was to interview an expert on the phone while I took notes. That gave me a better foundational understanding when I read the material.

When I had covered Vice President Nelson Rockefeller, I'd discovered he had dyslexia and had found a way to overcome it. Maybe I had dyslexia too? I wandered into the Harvard building and asked to be tested.

The psychologist determined I was a visual, spatial person who benefited most from verbal and visual learning. And he added that I had chosen the exact *wrong* profession for someone with my particular wiring. A profession as an architect, he said, would have been easy sailing for me. Here I was, finding out in my fifties!

He did have some good news: my IQ was in the "genius" range. I grew twelve inches as I walked out of that office.

Coincidentally, during one of my days on campus, Barbara Walters came to Harvard to receive an award. One of the students at the Shorenstein Center was thrilled with the assignment to pick her up at the airport. "What's she like?" the student asked eagerly. I eased his nervousness, assuring him, "Barbara is warm and charming. You will love her!" He later told me that as she emerged from her gate at the airport, he extended his hand to shake hers. In response, she handed him her carry-on bag and purse. When he told me, I apologized on her behalf, explaining that she was probably tired from her flight.

When I was back in New York with Matthew, Barbara called to offer me a job. She was creating a program called *The View* in which four women of different generations would chat about their varying views. She would appear as the anchor two or three days a week. She asked me to serve as anchor when she was on her off days.

About the same time, former Walt Disney Studios Chief Jeffrey Katzenberg pitched Maury and me to coanchor a half-hour newsy program for DreamWorks, the company he had founded with music mogul David Geffen and the phenomenal director Steven Spielberg. I had met Spielberg before, in 1993, when I interviewed him in Poland for *Schindler's List*. Maury and I would model our program after ABC's *Nightline*, but it would air earlier, sometime between seven and eight on weeknights.

Maury and I had already agreed to pursue that opportunity, so I told Barbara that when it came to choosing between Maury and her, she knew which way I'd swing.

Unfortunately, our DreamWorks project never got off the ground.

The next offer came from CBS News President Andrew Heyward, who called me for a meeting. He graciously came to my apartment for lunch and popped the question: Would I come back to CBS? I was truly thrilled and sincerely grateful for the offer. But, still feeling too raw about my experience there, I said no precipitously, without even knowing what job he had in mind. What a mistake to fail to follow up.

Another option was waiting in the wings.

# CHAPTER 29

# ABC: Anybody but Connie

The brilliant television producer and ABC Sports President Roone Arledge was the mastermind behind *Wide World of Sports* and *Monday Night Football*. He dared to air the Olympics in prime time and created stars in Howard Cosell, Jim McKay, and Frank Gifford.

And when he was appointed president of ABC News in addition to ABC Sports, he collected stars like baseball cards. In addition to the heavy hitters he already had on his team—Peter Jennings, Ted Koppel, and Sam Donaldson—Roone raided other news networks for Barbara Walters, David Brinkley, Hugh Downs, and Diane Sawyer.

Roone had wooed me years earlier, but in 1997, after I had been away from television news for two years, he called to offer me a job at ABC News. After all his tremendous success, this latest overture felt like being anointed with his golden scepter. The great Roone Arledge wanted to hire me despite my rough ride at CBS.

Like all the others who leaped to the network, thinking Roone was a career savior, I, too, drank the Kool-Aid. I didn't know he had a habit of showering someone with attention during the hiring process but becoming unavailable once the deal was done. He was MIA.

My job was to coanchor a new edition of *20/20*. It would be a spin-off of Barbara Walters's and Hugh Downs's original, airing on a separate night, and coanchored by me and Charlie Gibson, a solid ABC correspondent I had known for years when we both covered stories in Washington. We were a good fit.

My contract also stipulated that I serve as a substitute anchor for Peter Jennings on *World News Tonight*. Peter was another thousand-pound gorilla, just like Rather and Brokaw, and I was sure Peter had the power to nix me, but he apparently did not perceive me as a threat, which was correct. I had no designs on his job. Whenever he was off and I sat in his chair, I felt no pressure. At ABC, it was a pleasure to be on the hard news side.

On the magazine side, I saw Barbara Walters, Diane Sawyer, and me as a powerful triumvirate. I envisioned we would be a sisterhood, taking on the boys' club. But television critics anticipated a rivalry. When asked whether three women could share the spotlight, I smiled and snapped, "If you're asking if I am going to compete with Barbara and Diane, I'll tell you I'm also going to compete with Peter and Ted [Koppel], you sexist pig!"

I had a unique personal bond with Barbara. Both of us needed our jobs because we were the breadwinners in our families. After her father's successful nightclubs had tanked, Barbara was forced to support her parents as well as her mentally disabled older sister. I, too, supported my parents after my father's heart attack and for the rest of their days. Since both Barbara and I depended on our salaries, we put up with the sexism. (In addition, I put up with the racism while she put up with the ageism.)

And we had both become parents through adoption.

In 1976, Barbara was the first woman to coanchor the network evening news when she did so at ABC. In 1993, I was the first to coanchor the network evening news at CBS, the second female in broadcast history behind Barbara. Both of our coanchors were men who abhorred us. Both Barbara and I were dumped after two years. After I got the ax, she called me and consoled me, as only she could.

Barbara loved to gossip. Maury and I were invited to the opening of Steve Wynn's hotel in Las Vegas, the Wynn. Maury had attended the University of Pennsylvania with Wynn. Barbara Walters was invited because she was Barbara Walters. At the hotel, I happened to be getting a manicure at the same time she was. We sat next to each other like neighbors leaning over our backyard fences.

"Any news, Barbara?" I asked.

She couldn't wait to tell me, "Have you heard about Walter Cronkite? You know his wife, Betsy, died. Well, Walter's neighbor invited him to her apartment for a drink. She is a widow. And he's already schtupping her!" That was Barbara.

I did not know Diane Sawyer as well. We barely crossed paths. When I was a CBS News reporter covering Watergate, she was working for President Nixon in the White House press office. When Nixon resigned, Diane followed him to California to help him with his memoirs. Years later, she had crossed the line from politics to television news at CBS in Washington.

She had arrived there several years after I departed, yet reporters in the media pitted us against each other when we were at competing networks, the same way they always did, just because we were women.

To welcome me to ABC, Diane generously threw a lunch at her apartment—round tables in the dining room with pretty tablecloths and lovely settings. She was incredibly kind and gracious. I marveled at how she could work 24-7, go to fancy social events, *and* entertain all of us for lunch. I gave dinner parties once a decade.

She thoughtfully combined the lunch as a goodbye to correspondent Judd Rose, who was leaving ABC News due to a serious illness. All the ABC News names were there: Barbara Walters; Hugh Downs; Sam Donaldson, who coanchored *PrimeTime* with Diane; Charlie Gibson; and many more on-air stars. Each spoke glowingly about my arrival—and regretfully about Judd's departure.

While we developed my edition of *20/20* with Charlie Gibson, I was expected to report stories for Barbara's *20/20* or Diane's *PrimeTime*.

That's when something odd happened. Diane called me to ask if I would like to try for an interview with Mary Kay Letourneau, a thirty-four-year-old teacher in Seattle who was accused of having a sexual relationship with her twelve-year-old student. It's highly unusual for an anchor to call another anchor or reporter to suggest—let alone "assign"—a story. An executive producer or senior producer typically does that. Instead of questioning it, I simply agreed.

Diane informed me I would be competing with Barbara for the one-on-one, along with anyone else at other news organizations. Being new to ABC, I found it particularly uncomfortable to be in direct competition with Barbara right out of the gate.

Producers booked separate lunches with Letourneau's public relations person for each of us. How absurd that the teacher had her own PR rep. Diane sent along one of her trusted producers to join me for my lunch. Fine. This is what I hated about trying to get one of these exclusive interviews, having to grovel for a seedy story. The whole thing made my skin crawl.

A few days later, Diane called me at home to say that Barbara had said disparaging things about me at her lunch with Letourneau's representative. According to Diane, Barbara had said I was not trustworthy, and she quoted Barbara as saying, "Look at what happened to Newt Gingrich's mother." Diane told me she was furious about that, saying, "Would you mind if I take over and go head-to-head with Barbara?"

"Please, be my guest," I quickly replied, delighted to duck out of the cross fire.

Later David Westin learned of the competition for the interview and ordered both Diane and Barbara to abandon the story. Fortunately, I had already left the playground.

What ensued after that incident was a game of Whac-A-Mole. Each time I'd pop my head up, Barbara or Diane would whack me with a spongy hammer. Or they'd try to recruit me to gang up on the "enemy." It was no longer one-on-one basketball, it was double-teaming, two on one.

I'd had no idea I had parachuted into a minefield. The ground was littered with land mines planted by Diane for Barbara—and by Barbara for Diane. The buried explosives were aimed at those two feuding females, but I found myself accidentally stepping on a few of them. Some of them may have had my name on them. I don't know.

Instead of battling men, I found myself squeezed between two people I thought should have been allies. I'd foolishly believed the women would be my comrades. After surviving the brutal news business for so many years, how could I be so naive as to think that they would part the waters for me?

Realizing I needed to find out the rules, I made the rounds of ABC executives. I was shocked when I was told I was not allowed to get my mitts on anyone Barbara or Diane pursued.

"Let me get this straight," I said, incredulous. "You are telling me that *only* Barbara and Diane can *compete against each other* for an interview or story, but I am barred?"

From the executive producer to the vice president to the president of ABC News, each one confirmed the edict. Had I known, I never would have taken the job.

Back when we were at competing networks, Barbara and I would vie for gets. When I got one she'd wanted, she would write me a beautiful note praising my interview. She mom-ed many of the women in the business. I loved it.

Barbara was most proud of one interview she'd snatched from right under the nose of none other than Walter Cronkite. Cronkite wrote in his memoir that in the late 1970s, he had arranged to fly Egyptian President Anwar Sadat from Cairo to Tel Aviv for a historic meeting with Israeli Prime Minister Menachem Begin.

"It looked like a clean beat. But we hadn't figured on Barbara Walters, a serious mistake," he admitted. "Just as we were boarding Sadat's plane, along she came, running across the field with hand upraised like a substitute entering a sporting contest. Sadat invited her aboard and her enterprise robbed us of our exclusive." Walter gave Barbara the respect most of her male colleagues did not.

Barbara's version of her coup was a bit different, but the end was the same. She always described it as her crowning achievement.

Now, years later, I was witnessing guerilla warfare between Diane and Barbara.

Some of their battles sank to sheer pettiness. When Barbara announced she would retire from regularly anchoring *20/20*, a girl-friend, former CBS News correspondent Edie Magnus, suggested we give Barbara a lunch to honor her. Fantastic! I had not hosted a meal at our apartment in years.

We invited every newsperson we felt was touched by Barbara's pioneering career—fifty plus women. I gave Barbara our list and told her it would be totally confidential. Though terribly torn about whether to include Diane, Barbara finally relented. When I called Diane's office, her assistant told me, "Diane has to do an interview. She will come for hors d'oeuvres but must leave and cannot be there for lunch."

The only problem was that the producer of Diane's story was someone I knew well. The producer told me Diane specifically asked her to schedule the interview at precisely the time of the lunch. The producer said, "it was the only time Diane could do the interview." At the time I laughed, but in my mind, I wanted to tell both Barbara and Diane to grow up.

I was happy to avoid engaging in their firefight but disappointed and perplexed by their same-sex battle. Honestly, I could see taking on the men who were denying us equality. But I could not see the value of Diane butting heads with the woman who had paved the way for all of us.

Frankly, I believed Barbara Walters had earned the right to be a diva, to push anybody off the cliff who tried to dethrone her. Barbara had stood alone fighting the all-boys network—busting down every obstacle in her way—so that all of us could have careers like hers. All women in the business owed her for her drive, her aggressiveness, and her success.

The only way I could rise above the fray was to find stories no one would think to do. Those were the kinds of stories that gave me the most satisfaction, anyway. I had been burned by those scalding-hot gets, so I decided I would pursue stories like the one I had done at CBS on breast implants that had changed government policy—the types of enterprising, worthy, and fulfilling investigations.

My first story for *20/20* turned out to be one of those stories. It was centered around a twenty-year-old Black gold miner in Colorado, Roy Smith. For years, he repeatedly had been attacked, brutalized, and terrorized. He was hanged by his feet, naked, from a beam in his cabin. His racist tormentors strung him up with rope and wire and mutilated his private parts. The local sheriff's department had done nothing about complaints he filed and even admitted to referring to him as "N*gger Roy" in the police department computer. Incredibly, all this happened in the 1990s. I was passionate about telling Roy Smith's story but anxious and nervous at the same time. I wanted my story about Roy Smith to be as dignified and respectful as he was.

I told the producer, Alan Goldberg, who had come to ABC from *60 Minutes*, "This is my first time back doing interviews, and I'm very nervous and unsure of myself." Roy Smith proceeded to tell me his gut-wrenching story with not a drop of hatred. After I completed the emotional interview, Alan said to me with a smile, "You are back."

The *Denver Post* reported the story first but gave us quite a tribute and, in doing so, described the value of television news: "The TV production exemplifies the medium at its best. It does more than evoke emotion. It opens us to understanding. It moves us to a higher place. With an amazing cast of real-life heroes and villains, videotaped testimony, spectacular scenery, and an awe-inspiring central character, this is riveting TV journalism."

In the end, a team of local lawyers won a $700,000 settlement for Smith and a written apology from the sheriff's department.

If I could continue that kind of gratifying work, I was happy to stay out of the sights of Barbara and Diane.

When an ABC suit flew from Los Angeles to meet with Barbara in a large room full of *20/20* staff, he was there to deliver bad news. ABC Entertainment was moving Barbara's *20/20* to a deadly time slot. I stuck my neck out and told the executive forcefully and bluntly that ABC was doing Barbara a great injustice. After all, she had contributed to the network's success, especially financially. Executives would come and go through the revolving door, but Barbara was consistently there, delivering the goods. Several *20/20* staffers sent me emails and notes, giving me props for saying out loud what they were thinking.

None was as precious as Barbara's note: "There are no words....I will never forget—neither will anyone else. Your dignity and class shine on us all. Thank you, dear Connie."

The executives did not change their minds. Her *20/20* was moved to a different night and still commanded decent ratings.

\* \* \*

No good deed goes unpunished. When ABC News decided to carry blanket worldwide coverage of the millennium, I was thrilled to be assigned to welcome in the year 2000 in Paris at the Eiffel Tower. Maury and I made plans to bring our entire family. Susan and her husband and son, Amy and her husband and daughter, and our son, Matthew. But one day, an ABC News vice president asked to come to my office.

He put it simply. "Barbara wants to go to Paris."

I asked, "Then where am I going?"

"Las Vegas."

I laughed and accepted it.

* * *

Over the years, I did my best magazine work at ABC News. I felt as if I had returned to my days at CBS News in Washington, when my reporting was important and worthwhile. And since I was not under the microscope, I was liberated from scrutiny and judgment.

I was most proud of a story about the 1966 murder of a Black Mississippi farmhand, Ben Chester White, who had been killed by suspected Ku Klux Klan members. His body was discovered face down in a creek near Natchez. He had been shot more than a dozen times with an assault rifle and once with a shotgun blast so powerful that it literally blew his brains out.

Producer Harry Phillips and I had read a newspaper article about the case, which had long been dormant. We hoped to uncover more information.

At the time, a man named Ernest Avants had been tried in Mississippi state court and found *not* guilty of killing White. But we found two critical pieces of new evidence that revived the case against Avants.

In a musty basement in a historic building, home of the Natchez Foundation, we uncovered a transcript of a confession by a KKK member who had implicated himself and two others, including Ernest Avants.

The other fact we discovered was that the murder occurred on *federal* land, not *state* land—making the crime a federal offense. And that meant Avants could face federal murder changes, even though he had already been found not guilty in state court.

We tracked down Avants at his trailer home. I knocked on the door, not knowing if he would greet me with a smile or a shotgun. Surprisingly, he agreed to an interview at his wooden picnic table just outside his trailer.

In a thick southern accent, he set the stage of those times, thirty-two years earlier.

"A white man has run this world. A white man has run this United States. That's why it's great like it is. The Jews own Adams County, and the Catholics run it. And the n*ggers enjoyed it."

I asked him if he'd killed Ben Chester White. He denied it with this reasoning: "Why, if this n*gger was killed like they said he was, why wouldn't the buzzards eat him? The buzzards won't eat nothing that dies of rabies or poison."

I asked him to clarify. "You are saying that because the buzzards didn't get at Ben Chester White's body that he had to have died of either rabies or poison?"

"Evidently," Avants replied.

I followed up, "Not gunshot wounds."

"Evidently."

The feds moved quickly on the case, thanks to us. When FBI agents went to Avants's trailer to arrest him, our camera crew and I were there. A woman emerged from the trailer shouting in my direction, "I'm going to blow her brains out."

The feds indicted, charged, and convicted Ernest Avants for murder. He died in prison.

Our report resulted in the first Civil Rights era murder prosecution by federal authorities. Other civil rights cases were revived in state courts. The feds determined that White's murder was part of a plot to lure Martin Luther King Jr. to Natchez, Mississippi, to kill him. King was assassinated two years after in Memphis, Tennessee. Our story brought closure to Ben Chester White's son, and I felt I had reclaimed my confidence and reputation.

I was feeling good about myself again and very proud when Matthew's lower school history teacher asked me to show my story to his class and lead a discussion afterward. That night at our regular family dinner, Maury said, "Mommy said she taught your history class today and the kids were very interested and asked good questions, right?"

Matthew replied, "The teacher said if we were good, he'd give us candy."

I was fortunate to create a blockbuster team: producer Teri Whitcraft and booker Santina Leuci. They had both worked with Maury on *A Current Affair.* He sang their praises, saying they were go-getters, aggressive, smart, excellent, dedicated journalists who knew a story and how to pursue it. Maury was spot on.

Teri Whitcraft, packed with her big Texas smile and boundless energy and enthusiasm, would produce the pants off anybody. She was, bar none, the very best producer I had ever been lucky enough to work with—organized, methodical, thorough, and a stickler for accuracy.

Santina Leuci, our indefatigable booker, was the daughter of famed New York Police Department's Narcotics Detective Robert Leuci, who had exposed police corruption in the criminal justice system. Her father's story was dramatized in the Sidney Lumet movie *Prince of the City* starring Treat Williams. Santina would stop at nothing to dig up whatever we were investigating. With sources all over the map, she knew how to sleuth out the best approach to investigating, uncovering, and capturing the story.

Thanks to Santina's doggedness (and mine!), we reported on

another Civil Rights era case—the grisly murders of two young Black men in Meadville, Mississippi, in 1964. A college student, Charles Moore, and his friend Henry Dee were ambushed and forced into a pickup truck by Ku Klux Klansmen. They were beaten and whipped, then tied to an engine block and dumped in the Mississippi River—alive.

Santina found a man who knew the identities of the alleged killers, two of whom were still alive. The man, Ernest Gilbert, had been an imperial wizard of the Klan and had become an FBI informant. Together, Santina and I convinced him to break his thirty-six-year silence, revealing his identity in an exclusive interview. He'd told the FBI the killers had confessed to him.

Choking up with tears, he told me, "I wish to God I had never known about this. I really do. I'm speaking because I'd like to clear my conscience."

We tracked down the two alleged killers. One of them denied killing anyone and added, "I have nothing to say to you. Life's been good. Had a job, raised five kids, and had the American dream."

This case was never revived. Sadly, we could not bring closure to the families of Charles Moore and Henry Dee.

Teri came up with a story that took us to Bangladesh. She discovered a teenage girl, Bina Akhter, who had spurned the advances of a man. In an act of revenge, he threw sulfuric acid in her face. It burned Bina's flesh and muscle away. Tragically, it was not a random incident. Every week, three to five women in Bangladesh—usually teenagers from poor families—were attacked in a similar way. Bina shed her veil when we sat down for an interview, revealing her horrible facial disfigurement. She was articulate and forceful in describing the emotional and social costs she and other young burn victims suffered. Some were ostracized by their communities, even by their own families.

Several men I interviewed in a Bangladesh prison had been convicted of such crimes. I asked the prime minister of Bangladesh what could be done about the horrid attacks. He offered no solutions for deterring such violence.

Then I got the interview that became the talk of the summer of 2001. It was the dog days of August, when Congress was out of session and news was sparse. A feeding frenzy erupted over the disappearance of a young woman, a summer intern from Ohio named Chandra Levy. Every reporter was trying to pierce the story by getting to the man at the center of the mystery.

He was married California Congressman Gary Condit, accused of having an affair with Chandra Levy, who had been working at the Federal Bureau of Prisons. She had disappeared in May. By summer, it had become the subject of conversation around every water cooler.

Santina started talking to Condit's lawyer, Abbe Lowell, and connected him with me. We appeared to be making headway after I wrote a note to Congressman Condit.

But ABC News Vice President Phyllis McGrady took me to lunch to tell me that I was forbidden from pursuing an interview with him. If anyone was to get the interview, she told me, it would be Barbara. I told Santina we had to stand down.

I called lawyer Lowell to tell him that our executives had decided ABC's designated hitter was Barbara, not me. Much to my surprise, Lowell called me back to say he had winnowed down interview requests and the choice was between me and someone at another network. If I was not the one to conduct the interview for ABC, he would give Condit to the competition.

I marched up to David Westin's office and told him, "I am the one or nobody at ABC. Do you really want to lose the Condit interview?" The answer was obvious.

The interview turned out to be quite an extravaganza, the event of the summer, at the home of a friend of Condit's in California. ABC News sent a caravan of remote trucks, which ultimately caused $50,000 in damages to the friend's property. CNN dispatched a helicopter to follow me from my hotel to the site of the interview, as if I were O. J. during the slow Bronco chase. A voice on CNN narrated, "Connie is leaving now, heading to the house where she will do the Condit interview." How ridiculous!

We fed the interview live from the remote truck to New York. Producers dropped in commercials in between parts of the interview and aired it on national television at 10:00 p.m.

From the moment the interview began to the end, the tension was palpable. It was Congressman Condit's chance to come clean about his relationship with Chandra Levy and tell the truth about what he knew. He denied he had anything to do with her disappearance, dodging and weaving and repeating himself like a record stuck in a groove, refusing to answer questions about their relationship.

When the interview was over, Condit was so anxious to leave that he got up out of his chair with his microphone still clipped to his clothes. He quickly thanked all the crew members but said to me, "I'm not sure if I should thank you or not. You look nice but you are not nice."

The president of ABC News, David Westin, called me after the interview and said enthusiastically, "You nailed it, didn't you think so?" Yes, I did.

Afterward, back in New York, the kudos poured in. Walter Cronkite, Ed Bradley, Tom Brokaw, Barbara and Diane, ABC's Martha Raddatz, even Roone Arledge. Bob Iger, president of ABC's parent company, Disney, emailed me: "You were sensational last night. Tough, focused, relentless, tenacious, and even charming!

It was the best interview I've seen in a very long time…compelling and riveting."

Almost twenty-four million viewers tuned in, making this the highest-rated news program on any network in that season. Condit lost his reelection bid and faded from public life. Who murdered Chandra Levy remains a mystery to this day.

\* \* \*

While still under my second contract with ABC News, I received a knock on my door.

CNN was interested in hiring me to anchor the 8:00 p.m. hour Monday to Friday. Having grown up with big three network news, I had never thought of joining cable television. Despite the Barbara-and-Diane insanity, after four years there, I had turned a corner. I was pleased with the niche of worthwhile stories I had carved out with Teri and Santina.

Still, it was flattering to know someone out there was inquiring. Why not listen?

My ABC News contract obligated me to notify executives if I merely talked to another prospective employer. I assured them I was not leaving—I was just checking out the offer.

Little did I know that would trigger an offer to Santina. An ABC executive offered her an impossible-to-beat senior position at *Good Morning America*. I had no choice but to hug my close friend and let her out of my clutches.

I am sure it was I who invited the poaching because I always touted the abilities of everyone with whom I worked. I like giving credit where credit is due. I find it is a female phenomenon. We avoid boasting about what a great job *we* did. We give credit to the "team." I always named everyone who had contributed to a story and would not claim personal victory. I could never bring myself to take all the credit, as I watched some men do effortlessly. Rarely did I hear women declare, "I successfully led the charge."

No one had asked me if I'd mind if Santina were offered a new job. And when they did not even tell me, I took it as a signal that ABC executives were a tad too happy to see me go.

What was appealing about my offer from CNN was Walter Isaacson. The highly respected journalist, former editor of *Time* magazine, and author had just been named chairman and chief executive officer of the CNN News Group.

I took the job to anchor an hour-long program and formed long-lasting relationships with the wonderful staff, but Isaacson left after only a year and a half for his dream job to head the Aspen Institute. The new management lacked confidence in me and fired me after I had been there less than a year. At least that executive was brave enough to tell me in person. I appreciated that.

My second firing was another blow, but I did not take it as hard as the one at CBS. Once again, my dismissal turned into a gift.

Matthew was still young, in lower school. While the hours at CNN allowed me to take him to school in the morning, the downside was that my CNN program didn't end until 9:00 p.m., which meant I was not at my front door until nine fifteen or nine thirty at night. Matthew wanted to stay up in time for me to put him to bed, as I always did. Maury would try to keep him up for me, but the little guy would be tired in the morning, which we feared affected him at school.

Once again, my losing my job was meant to be. Being cut loose from CNN meant I could focus again entirely on my son. I dearly wanted to get this part of my life correct.

# CHAPTER 30

# Catharsis

Finally! Maury and I would have another crack at working together. We had been asked many times in the past to give it a whirl. I was afraid it would alter our off-air relationship, which was more important to me than a television program.

But this time, we agreed. *Weekends with Maury and Connie* premiered on MSNBC in January 2006. It was our attempt at a week-in-review program. By then, I was incredibly rusty and unsure of myself. Our program was a dud, but, thankfully, no one watched, and we were off the air after six months.

Since I had embraced a very what-the-heck attitude, I decided to sing a parody for our last episode. Yes, a song on the news program.

It was not the first time I had sung off-key in public. I had a short history of lame comedic attempts using clever lyrics. On *The View*, I serenaded Barbara Walters on air to the tune of "You Made Me Love You (I Didn't Want to Do It)":

*You made me, Barbara,*
*And every time I'd see you,*
*I'd simply want to be you.*

Off air, I warbled parodies when CNN threw me a launch party—and again before a couple hundred TV women when I received an award from American Women in Radio and Television. Each time, I received a lot of hearty laughs and a standing ovation.

Here I was on MSNBC in an evening gown, like a torch song chanteuse on a grand piano, belting out an off-key parody of "Thanks for the Memory."

Well, my attempt at being a comedienne was promptly booed off the earth. Media critics and early internet denizens collectively declared me off my rocker. (Though a telephone repairman told me he thought my swan song was hysterical.)

Maury usually stopped me before I could make a fool of myself. He must have been tired of trying to knock the evil twin off my left shoulder—that baddy who was always after me with a dare. Dudley Do-Right on my right shoulder repeatedly countered the evil one: "You will destroy everything you've worked for. Do NOT do it."

Not this time. The good guy must have been taking a nap, asleep at the wheel.

Jay Leno gave me a chance to explain my insane behavior on *The Tonight Show*. His first question was the same one he'd asked Hugh Grant after Grant had been caught soliciting a sex worker on Sunset Boulevard.

After playing a clip of my infamous "song," Jay asked, "What were you thinking?"

My answer was simple: "It was just a joke for the two viewers who watched *Weekends with Maury and Connie*."

"It was probably the first time an anchorwoman had her feet in the air," Jay quipped.

To which I deadpanned, "I seriously doubt that." (Spontaneous laughter.)

Please don't ask me why I did it. Maybe it was cathartic to wrap myself in a swan song. Of course I regret it.

Someone asked me if I have found the process of writing my memoir cathartic. According to Merriam-Webster, "catharsis" comes from the Greek word *kathairein*, meaning "to cleanse, purge." It entered the English language as "a medical term having to do with purging the body—especially the '*bowels*'—of unwanted material." In later years, the definition of "catharsis" morphed into "a release of repressed emotions that results in renewal and restoration." That sounds like shrink mumbo jumbo. But given the original definition, I would answer yes, writing this book has been medically cathartic!

Expunging unwanted waste, especially painful old memories, has been excruciating, particularly when my editor—who is no novice at this ball game—repeatedly advised me to stop "reporting" just facts. A memoir, she patiently explained, is much more intimate. Dozens of times, she prodded me with "But how did you feel?"

For decades, as a reporter, I was trained to suppress how I felt. Yesterday's journalism was the perfect fit for me. I preferred to keep my innermost thoughts to myself, where they belonged, in the name of objectivity and integrity. Unlike in news today, during my working years, personal feelings were verboten.

Now, with each sentence I have written in my book, I've tried to flesh out my feelings, as if performing sleight-of-hand surgery on myself.

Ah, what to do?

Needing a guiding light, I asked my husband to recommend the best memoir he had ever read. He named *Personal History* by Katharine Graham, the first female publisher of a major newspaper in her era, who had led the *Washington Post* during the tumultuous times of the Pentagon Papers and Watergate. In it, Graham described her most anguishing moments in a dignified manner, never crying, "Woe is me." I was rooting for her all the way to her last page.

And now I have reached the eighth inning of my book, having rewound my life as the first Chinese woman in television news. My story was both a woman's tale and a Chinese one. They were separate issues.

First the woman part. With the benefit of years behind me, I can safely say I moved the needle a bit for women.

Today, in 2024, Norah O'Donnell solo-anchors the *CBS Evening News*, and women in sports television are doing play-by-play and analysis.

And every time a female achieves a first, I am immensely proud and cheer her on. In 2024, Iowa Hawkeye superstar Caitlin Clark topped Hall of Famer "Pistol" Pete Maravich as the all-time leading scorer—*male or female*—in NCAA Division I basketball history. If that wasn't dazzling enough, she also surpassed Steph Curry's NCAA record for three-pointers in a season. Despite Clark's phenomenal achievements, as the first overall draft pick for the WNBA she will be earning $338,000 over four years. Yet last year's NBA first overall draft pick, Victor Wembanyama, is earning a whopping $55 million for a four-year contract too. Also in 2024, Cole Brauer, a twenty-nine-year-old woman from Long Island, New York, became the first American woman to sail solo around the world. My heart sings each time I see her bright smile on television. It's exhilarating to witness these triumphs.

Yet despite these record-setting accomplishments, I still have male envy. Don't get me wrong. I love being a woman, but today I am still staring at a dinosaur society in politics, corporate America, and too many other professions that are still dominated by men. I look forward to the day when we no longer celebrate women's "firsts."

Yet when I skim the male playbook, I see light. For instance, I always strove for perfection. I don't think many men aim to be perfect. They already believe they are! How liberating to know that nothing can be as perfect as I want it to be.

I answered the one question all of us struggle with: Can we have it all? Men can have it all simultaneously. I succeeded in having it all, although at different stages of my life. First a career, then a baby. It worked spectacularly for me. Surely the topsy-turvy order is not for all.

My closest niece, Nina Chen Langenmayr, who is a decade younger than I, managed to have children while working as a lawyer and partner in a management consulting firm. Working at the same time, she walked in my shoes as an Asian woman in a competitive work environment. Nina helped me analyze why women found climbing the ladder incredibly frustrating. We were doled out only a small sliver of the male-dominated pie. We had to share that small piece, creating unnecessary competition and infighting for the same morsel. It fostered a climate in which women were apt to fail to support one another. Fortunately, today, many women are collegial, but this division of the pie is a syndrome that remains a systemic, ubiquitous problem in the workplace.

Nina credits me for mentoring her as she navigated her long career. Lucky for me, Maury has been my consigliere and guidance counselor. Every woman needs a mentor or a Maury.

Almost twenty years have passed since I had a job reporting the news. To this day, I miss the craft of journalism and working in television news.

Each question I asked was an opportunity to probe for the truth. I knew the viewer would determine if the interviewee was being honest. It was not for me to steer the public in any direction. My job was to elicit the information viewers needed so they could make up their minds themselves.

Along with the work itself, I also believed earning a living was inexorably tied to my self-worth. I paid my own bills and supported my parents all their lives, and then, after marrying Maury, I always split the family finances with him fifty-fifty. Without a salaried job, I felt as if I were not carrying my weight in my household. I deemed myself unproductive without a paycheck to show for my time. Maury never made me feel that way; it was I who took it upon myself to feel the guilt—guilt being my favorite emotion. To make light of it, when people asked me what I was up to, I would say, in a self-deprecating manner, that I was sponging off Maury. I knew quite well that I was lucky to have the choice not to work at a job for pay. That didn't offset my unhappiness over failing to earn money after having done so for so long. I wanted to bring home the bacon and still do.

As I plowed through the morass of my personal archives, I was delighted to uncover some long-ago insights from male news executives who seemed to recognize, even back then, the thorny male response to women's growth in the workplace.

After Barbara Walters was removed as coanchor of the evening news at ABC in 1978, the man who had given her that job, President Roone Arledge, said, "Much of Miss Walters's problems stem from her million-dollar-a-year salary and possible male chauvinism.

Everybody takes shots at her because of it. It makes you wonder if much of Barbara's problem is a male reaction."

And years later, NBC News President Larry Grossman referred to that same toxic climate when he was talking about me. (Larry was the executive who made me ask male producers why they did not want to work with me.) Later, when I was experiencing public floggings, he said, "I always thought of her as a real pro. I think a lot of the [hostility and antagonism] stemmed from the days of male chauvinism." If only Larry had said that while I was at NBC. It certainly would have shut down the naysayers—or at least given them pause.

Arledge and Grossman said out loud what many women and I had been thinking but could not say. Decades ago, we avoided calling out someone's behavior as sexist or even using that word. When I started the coanchor job with Rather, my goal was to establish a precedent for any woman who followed me. "Co" meant "co-and-equal" to me. Equal assignments, equal value, equal consideration.

I assumed my salary was *not* equal to my male coanchor's, but the job description was more important to me. When I was fired from the newscast, I told television critics, "I think that in 1995 it's inappropriate for the only woman on the three major network news programs to have anything less than co- and equal status." Never once did I accuse anyone of sexism. Now women are able to outwardly use the word—even if, at times, some still tend to tread gingerly.

One more quotation stood out. After I lost my dream job, my first network boss, CBS News Bureau Chief Bill Small, called me "the toughest, most aggressive, and one of the best newspeople" he had ever worked with. He added, "It just seems to me that from the word go, she has been exposed to a level of intensive examination that seems a little unfair."

Reading those words now, all these years later, sparked an

epiphany. I realized that the first one through the door is wounded with the heaviest gunfire. And there is always a price to be paid for the benefit gained.

I never knew what the benefit was until a journalist named Connie Wang called. What she told me was manna from heaven that changed my life.

## CHAPTER 31

# Living Legacy

B ack in the eighties, a guy named Guy (Johnson) sent me a birth-day card with the flattering news that he and several California couples (kind of a fan club) had cooked up a reason for a party. They would hold a "ConnieFest" every year on my birthday! If I could remember, I would call them on that most honorable night, and one time I even showed up in Los Angeles. That time I hosted the party, which they called "Connie*Feast*." And another year, I gave each of them a personalized alarm clock with a wake-up call I'd recorded: "Good morning, Guy. This is Connie Chung. Time to get up!"

After being out of the public eye for years, in the fall of 2019, I woke up to two ego-boosting honors.

The International Radio-TV Society anointed me a "Giant of Broadcasting." Still painfully humble, I had always thought of myself as a Lilliputian worker bee, so it was a thrill to be told by a group of media professionals that I would join the rarefied company of other honorees like Walter Cronkite, Johnny Carson, Lucille Ball, Edward R. Murrow, and many more.

Around the same time, I received another heady award. A group called Womankind bestowed upon me its Woman of the Year honor, which had quite a ring to it. I thought to myself, "I must not be chopped liver after all."

Feeling tallish, I walked to the corner nail place for a manicure. It was owned by a Korean woman who employed Korean manicurists—all lovely women I knew by their first names. I was hanging up my coat when a white woman tapped me on the shoulder.

Looking directly at me, she inquired, "I only want a manicure. How long do I have to wait?"

With that simple question, she quickly brought me back to earth. I told the Korean manicurists, and we all had a good laugh.

I told myself, "Fuhgeddaboudit," as James Gandolfini would say in *The Sopranos*.

I am happy to say Gandolfini and I share an honor, along with Whitney Houston, Jon Bon Jovi, and even the legendary Frank Sinatra: we all have rest stops named after us in New Jersey.

How did this happen? For one, my mother (and four sisters) landed in the US by ship at Jersey Pier in 1945. And for years, Maury and I owned a house in New Jersey, and, somehow, that qualified me for induction into the New Jersey Hall of Fame. As if that weren't enough, some of us in the Hall of Fame were honored with a rest stop. Mine is off the Garden State Parkway at milepost 153, between Exit 153A and 151. It is a sight to behold. "CONNIE CHUNG" appears in bold white caps at the top of the entrance. I cannot believe it.

If having a brick-and-mortar structure were not a solid enough affirmation, I learned of an extraordinary honor that is unmatched.

As I mentioned in my first chapter, one spring day in 2019, I received an email out of the blue from a thirty-two-year-old journalist, Connie Wang, the senior features writer for a website called Refinery29. She had uncovered a phenomenon that was surreal.

Born in Jinan, Connie Wang had left Communist China with her parents when her father came to the US to pursue an advanced degree. Connie already had a Chinese name, Xiaokang, but when her parents decided to live in the Midwest permanently, they asked their toddler to choose an American name. Only three years old, she thought about whom she saw on television and came up with two choices: "Connie...or Elmo," she told her parents.

Fortunately for all, her mom and dad chose the human over the Muppet.

Growing up in Minnesota, Connie had always thought having me as her namesake was unique. But when she headed to college at the University of California, Berkeley, joining a student body that was almost 50 percent Asian, she discovered multiple Asian Connies, just like her. Sniffing around, she had already begun to suspect this wasn't a simple coincidence. And as years passed, having grown into a savvy reporter and writer, Connie connected the dots.

She had uncovered a generation of Connies—untold numbers of Asian females whose parents had named their baby daughters Connie, *after me*—a sisterhood of Connies I'd had no idea existed. I gasped at the thought. A living legacy.

I did not absorb the full weight of Connie's email until we followed up on the telephone and she revealed the fruits of her investigation. I was stunned. I asked Maury to pour me a stiff scotch as I soaked in her amazing tale.

A few of them were born in the 1970s, Connie told me, back when I was anchoring local news in Los Angeles. Most were born in the '80s when I was at NBC. And some were born in the '90s when I was at CBS. Their Asian ethnicities ranged from Chinese and Taiwanese to Korean, Japanese, and combinations. Not wanting to forget a word she said, I took copious notes on a pad, just the way I used to do.

Connie's mom, who had been an editor of nonfiction books back in China, had derived comfort from seeing me on television. As Connie wrote in the *New York Times*, "Here was a woman with a face like hers, with great taste in clothes, who wore beautiful makeup and had stylish hair, yet asked aggressive questions of powerful people, most of whom did not seem to treat Ms. Chung any differently because of her appearance."

Then she went on to baffle me with her well-thought-out analysis. Connie declared I had not only shattered glass ceilings for women but bamboo ceilings for Asians. But why, I wondered, would these parents name their babies after me? Connie had an answer at the ready: their lives mirrored mine.

"They have experienced the best and worst that the American Dream has to offer," she surmised, "filled with wild opportunities, humiliating snubs, and lonely challenges that test whether you have the chops and mettle to back up your ambition."

I was stunned by her insight. It was as if she were Tinker Bell, flying alongside me every step of my career, observing my life and now affirming it. I had always perceived my career as rocky. Dare I rethink my life's work was worthy after all? What astounded me was that Connie Wang recognized that the Connie phenomenon is a story about the parents, not about the daughters.

I had told Connie Wang I would work with her in any way she chose to share her sociological study. That set her on a four-year mission. After completing her own memoir, *Oh My Mother!* Connie delivered a beautiful denouement for my book when she wrote a piece published on May 11, 2023, in the Sunday *New York Times* Opinion section, "Generation Connie." Please do google it.

For the article, Opinion section Photo Director Jackie Bates asked her right-hand person, Tenzin Tsagong, to track down as many Asian Connies who had been named after me as possible. Jackie's aim was to take a group photograph of this constellation of Connies with me at the center. Jackie was determined to find a Connie photographer for the shoot. Incredibly, she located Connie Chung Aramaki. With cameras in tow, Connie the photographer flew in from the West Coast just for what was a momentous day for me.

When I walked in the door of the *New York Times* studio, I could not believe what I saw. It was breathtaking. Ten Connies in tiered rows, with an empty spot in the middle for me. Beautiful, happy, smiling Connies.

"Hi, Connie!" I greeted each of them. "Where were you born?" One by one, they filled me in with their personal histories. They hailed from as far west as Palo Alto and Cupertino, in the Midwest from Milwaukee and Saint Paul, and east to Lancaster and Boston.

Unfortunately, writer Connie Wang couldn't come to New York for the shoot, but I met a different Connie Wang, the cofounder of a spice company; Connie Tang, a publicist for a beauty company; and even an autobiographical cartoonist, Connie Sun, whose pen name and nicknames are "Cartoonconnie" and "Conniewonnie." I was her mother's hero, she said, because I was "poised, confident, and successful and spoke perfect, unaccented English." She told me her mom had bought a Connie Chung wig I never knew even existed.

Connie Koh revealed she had named *herself* Connie after college because she had grown up an introvert and was "desperate to be able to stand up for myself, as you had throughout your career." Her eyes filled with tears—I could not hold back as mine started to well up too.

The most emotionally wrenching story came from the photographer, Connie Chung Aramaki. The beginning of her story was one I'd feared. She had been pushed hard to follow in my footsteps, heavily groomed for the camera from the day she could walk and talk—theater, commercials, *The Mickey Mouse Club*. Finally, after attending college at New York University and struggling to get jobs in *front* of the camera, she found her true calling, *behind* the camera.

"I used to get frustrated with my parents telling me that my goal in life was to be the next you," Connie Aramaki told me. She asked herself, "Who is this person and why do I have to be like her?"

Then, in the next breath, she stole my heart when she said, "Then I met you. Immediately, all the years of frustration of carrying the weight and responsibility of your name melted to a feeling of gratitude and a beautiful warm hopefulness."

Connie Aramaki helped me wrap my arms around my legacy. She explained, "I understand now how important it is to have role models who look to you and how that can subconsciously provide you with direction when you need some guidance. The truth is, I might not be who I am now if it were not for the foresight of my dad and mom to name me after someone who paved the way before me."

As we stood together at the shoot, photographer Connie encapsulated it all with three adjectives and adverbs that succinctly described the phenomenon. "What it means is your parents want you to *work hard and be brave and take chances*." That's when I lost it and could not stop crying.

We all pulled ourselves together as Connie Chung Aramaki snapped away, memorializing our gathering. I led my sisterhood to sing the Sister Sledge song: "We are family. I got all my sisters with me." When we couldn't remember the second line of lyrics, we all broke out laughing. And when they told me they were often asked, "How's Maury?" I called Maury on FaceTime so they could say hello.

After the shoot, not wanting to simply bid adieu to these dear sisters, I asked them to join me for dinner around the corner. They were happy for this glorious day to continue. Our group meal was indescribably nourishing, not so much for the food but because I was back in my curious reporter mode, gathering their rich stories.

In the next week, I contacted as many Connies as I could to interview. As children, they were teased, either because they were Asian or because they were named after me. One Connie admitted, "When I was younger, I was embarrassed because every adult laughed at me when I told them my name. As an adult, though, I miss those days."

I was hoping this younger generation might have been spared systemic racism. Sadly, the questions they were often asked were the same I experience to this day: "Where are you from?" "No, where are you really from?" "Do you speak English?" "The girl with the Ch*nk eyes from China."

In her dating life, one Connie noted that she had come across men who were interested in her only because she was Asian. "Fetishism exists," she stated firmly. Another called it "unwanted attention from men who talked about how much they love Asian culture." All these years later, I was extremely disheartened that their lives paralleled mine. Now, with the ugly rise of anti-Asian hate, attitudes have escalated to violence.

Fortunately, another one of us, lawyer Connie Chung Joe, works tirelessly to combat discrimination in her capacity as chief executive officer of Asian Americans Advancing Justice Southern California. It's the nation's largest Asian Pacific Islander civil rights and legal service organization. She has been a brave leader of all of us righting wrongs, as she encourages all of us to speak up and be heard.

I was distressed to find that workplace obstacles that I encountered still exist. One Connie told me, "I'm involved in investments, strongly white-male dominated. I stick out like a sore thumb. I've had to prove myself even more." Another talked about "dismissive attitudes by men and bullying by older white men."

The Connies described the dichotomy of a stereotype that works both for and against us. "We are seen as smart, educated, competent, hardworking." But coupled with that, they are still perceived as "quiet, meek china dolls who are submissive and sexually subservient." All this makes them feel marginalized.

But there was some good news. As one Connie explained, "I have certainly been passed over for deserving promotions. There have been people who have been quick to label me as quiet and amenable because I'm an Asian woman. I've learned to be ever more vocal in advocating for myself because of this."

How proud I was of another Connie who said that in her predominantly male industry, she is "not afraid to speak up and defend myself. I love being Asian and representing my culture. I do not ever let the bigots get me down." This Connie continued, "I think a lot about the hopes and dreams that the name Connie carries for so many Asian American families. It's truly powerful."

Powerful indeed. I never knew how powerful.

As with so many other moments in my life, the timing of the Connie Generation story felt meant to be. Had Connie Wang kept her magical discovery to herself, I might have believed that my journey was for naught and lost to history. Because of her, I have come to realize my career did not go unnoticed, that I did indeed make a difference, not only through the stories I covered but also by fulfilling the dreams of Asian parents, including mine. I always knew my parents were proud of me, but this further underscores the mission my father assigned me—to chisel our name in history. I wish my parents and three eldest sisters were still alive to witness this moment.

I now realize that mine is a story of triumph. Dare I say it? How remarkable that I have never been able to declare myself a success. For those of us who are driven, we perpetually see another mountain to climb and success is ephemeral. But I think I just may be able to—at this stage in my life—shed my reluctance to declare success and embrace it. For that I owe deep gratitude to Connie Wang and to the parents who named their daughters Connie.

For years, Maury encouraged me through my worst moments by telling me, "You are the Jackie Robinson of Asians in television news." I never believed him. Now I do. What I have always known is that I could not have achieved that without him at my side.

And forever at my side as well, my dearest son, Matthew, reminded me of Ralph Waldo Emerson's words, "Do not follow where the path may lead, go instead where there is no path and make a trail." I urge all Connies, now and in the future, to be intellectually curious, speak up, dream big and reach high, learn from mistakes, fear not, and stand up for yourself.

As gratifying as the Connie Generation is, I have one more distinction of superior recognition.

There is a strain of weed named after me. Yes, a strain of marijuana named Connie Chung. I have no clue how it came about. I tried smoking marijuana in college, and unlike Bill Clinton, I *did* inhale. However, still being a straight arrow, I am not a weed smoker, not that there's anything wrong with it.

Nonetheless, if you look up my pot namesake online, you will find my characteristics. I am immensely proud to boast I am easy to grow. I am deeply relaxing and happy; I am helpful under deadline; and I cause dry mouth but very, very little of the scaries. My flavor profile is described as berry, earthy, piney, sweet, and blueberry, with a blast of berry on the exhale. I am best harvested in October. I create a lovely, fragrant flower. And this is a trait that I find the most admirable: I am low maintenance.

I am happy to share my pot namesake with my sisterhood of Connies, along with a message to inhale: remember to have a sense of humor, take your work seriously, don't forget to have a life and—most importantly—stretch your hand to others who are trying to climb on board.

# ACKNOWLEDGMENTS

It's more than a decade or two ago, and I say to Maury I want to write my autobiography and then take my story before an audience the way Billy Crystal and Elaine Stritch did. Yes, I know they are true, experienced professionals and their talents and abilities far exceed my television news history. They are both legendary stars of stage and screen and can dance and sing on the Great White Way. Why can't I try? Doing stand-up onstage has been screaming to get out of me for years. And Lewis Black says he can find a place for me to try out my schtick.

Maury rolls his eyes and shakes his head.

"But, Maury," I counter, "you do crazy things on your show every day!"

"But," he says, "*YOU* have a reputation to uphold."

Then I realize I should pose another question to him. "Are you afraid I might make a fool out of myself?"

His reply is simple: "There is that risk."

"Okay." I sigh and say, "I'll write my memoir" as I mutter to myself, "that could be a risk too...."

At our annual lunch, I tell Lesley Stahl she navigated her career the "right way." No, she says, "I played it safe; you took risks." So I proceed.

A decade passes and I am writing bits and pieces of my tome, cloistered in my garret. Maury comes to me as I stare at my laptop. "Have you gotten your parents out of China yet?" I scoff at his snarky remark. He knows I wasn't born until my parents came to the United States and were living in DC. I know I can write for television news but a book? This is far more difficult. Maury is forced to continue to talk me off the ledge. Sometimes he says, "Want me to write it?" He's a good writer, but it would sound like *him*. My book needs to be in *my* voice. I reply firmly, "No!"

Maury asks his friend Harlan Coben, a novelist who recommends I read *Bird by Bird* by Anne Lamott. Harlan tells me to forge on.

And so it went. Years pass as my son, Matthew, sees me still staring at my laptop. "How's it going?" he says, cheerfully, with a big smile. "Uh, okay," I mumble. His fiancée, Hunter, gives me props for trying to write it myself. My tremendously supportive sister-in-law, Lynn Povich, and her husband, Steve Shepard, who are both writers and editors, gently prod me with words of encouragement.

I hire the best research producer on the planet, John Yuro, who helps me organize my library of digitized tapes, research files, old scripts, and photo archives, and who fact-checks everything. He is my sidekick and guy in the chair (think action movie) assiduously paying intense attention to accuracy.

Three news-business girlfriends, Joanne Chen, Vicki Gordon, and Linda Douglass, assure me the task is not as daunting as I see it and push me forward. Linda introduces me to another news veteran, Robin Sproul, who along with Matt Latimer and Keith Urbahn created Javelin (book agents). Matt works hard to sell my book to the experienced and wonderful Suzanne O'Neill, vice president and executive editor of Hachette Grand Central Publishing.

I write what is commonly called a "shitty first draft." I hire Lisa Napoli, an editor friend of Lynn Povich's, to edit my book. She changes my past tense to past perfect tense, points out mixed metaphors and dangling participles, and asks a lot of questions with the dizzying speed and efficiency of a news pro in the midst of a breaking story.

I call Michael Song, the best IT person in computer land, for help every other day.

Everyone at Hachette circles me with unmatched support and professional advice: Ben Sevier, Colin Dickerman, Jennifer McArdle, Tiffany Porcelli, Lauren Sum, Morgan Spehar, Jacqui Young, Mari C. Okuda, and S. B. Kleinman, plus two men who are exceptional, Jimmy Franco and Albert Tang.

But the key individuals who keep me on track are Maury, Matthew, and his fiancée, Hunter.

I profusely thank all those I named from the bottom of my heart for not allowing me to freak out about this most unusual adventure of writing my memoir.

# ABOUT THE AUTHOR

**Connie Chung**, iconic trailblazer and legendary television journalist, was born in Washington, DC, in 1946, a year after her parents arrived in the US from China with her four older sisters. She was the first Asian to anchor a national network news program in the US, and in 1993 she became the first woman to coanchor the *CBS Evening News*. Connie fulfilled her father's wish that she carry forth the family name and cement it in history. And she was surprised and delighted to learn that a number of Asian parents named their daughters Connie after her. Connie has been married to Maury Povich, the longest-running daytime talk show host in broadcast television history and Lifetime Achievement Emmy winner, since 1984. They have a son, two daughters, and four grandchildren.